WHITE WORK

EMBROIDERY

FRONTISPIECE
Altar cloth, German embroidery,
Altenberg a. d. Lahn. Second half of
thirteenth century. Linen Lenten cloth.
1.5 × 3.75 m (61 × 147½ in.) See page
174. (The Cleveland Museum of
Art, U.S.A. Purchase from the J. H.
Wade Fund)

WHITE WORK

EMBROIDERY

Barbara Dawson

B.T. BATSFORD LTD. LONDON

ISBN 0 7134 3950 5

Typeset by Latimer Trend & Company Ltd, Plymouth
and printed in Great Britain by
R J Acford, Chichester, Sussex

for the publishers
B. T. Batsford Ltd
4 Fitzhardinge Street
London W1H 0AH

Contents

Detail of altar cloth shown in Frontispiece. (The Cleveland Museum of Art, USA. Purchase from the J. H. Wade Fund)

Acknowledgements

I should like to acknowledge the great help given by a number of people towards the completion of this book, and to offer my thanks and appreciation for the loan of examples, some specially worked and others of great historical interest; for the permission to photograph and reproduce them as illustrations; and also permission to reproduce other photographs.

I am grateful for kind co-operation and patient answers to queries from many sources, including the Victoria & Albert Museum, especially the Textile and Conservation Departments; The Museum of London; the Museum, Perth, Western Australia; the Embroiderers' Guild, Hampton Court; the Harrow and Hertfordshire Branches of the Embroiderers' Guild and Joan Carr, Branch Representative. I should also like to thank many students and private collectors, particularly the Marchioness of Salisbury for generously allowing me to visit the Textile Conservation Rooms at Hatfield House and to photograph examples from the beautiful and extensive collection of white work embroidery; Joan Kendall, in charge of the Textile Conservation Rooms, and the voluntary workers there; also Clarice Blakey, Constance Howard and Lise Mossery for their very varied and interesting collections; and the Heads of Departments of Embroidery & Textiles of the following colleges: Glasgow School of Art: figs 132, 133, 135, 141, 231, 232, 297, 300, photographed by their department; Goldsmiths' College School of Art, University of London: figs 87, 88, 126, 131, 155, 159, 268, 270, 271, and those photographed by Mike Sage: figs 37, 38, 39, 318, 319, 320; London College of Fashion: figs 85, 150, 264, 286, 322; Manchester Polytechnic: figs 63, 67, 140, 153, 346, photographed by Terry Waddington; The Education Centre, Tunbridge Wells: figs 42, 47, 92, 93, 181; The Education Centre, Windsor: figs 84, 130, 249, 254, 294; thanks to the Anatole Orient Gallery for the work of Beverley Clark, and to Gina Grant, Irene Ord and Phyllis Ross for their own photographs; also Judith Groves, Sally Freshwater and Cathy Merrowsmith. Sally Freshwater, a Goldsmiths' student, and Lindy Richardson of Glasgow are graduates of the Royal College of Art.

Particular thanks are due to Edward Southey of Beckenham, Kent, for developing and printing countless numbers of photographs, to achieve the best results from my own photography, for all the other illustrations.

I also thank the Cleveland Museum of Art, Ohio, USA, for the photographs of work purchased from the J. H. Wade Fund shown in the frontispiece.

I am indebted to Margaret Swain's book *The Flowerers* (now sadly out of print) for much of the information on Ayrshire embroidery, and to the Shaftesbury Museum's *Notes* on Dorset buttons.

Introduction

Although this book is arranged alphabetically, it is not a real dictionary or encyclopedia. It is, rather, a personal arrangement in order to find a way through the labyrinth of different types of white embroidery, where the same stitches have been in continuous use over the centuries but in different styles of design and technique and in different countries, and often given different names or terms. Buttonhole stitch is practically universal, for instance.

White work is not a restricted subject such as black work, which has one meaning and one place in history and is one accepted technique.

Note: The dates given are approximate throughout the text.

Design

The inventive use of white textures is an inspiration today and techniques such as layering materials, manipulating relief surfaces and modelling into free-standing forms show a lack of the inhibitions which the term 'white work' might imply of historical stitchery.

Design or statements about textile work are well displayed in white as there is no distraction of colour and it makes for clarity in assessing ideas. Strengths and weaknesses are well shown up.

For collectors, design is an indication of date and origin, and to study this subject gives valuable knowledge.

For embroiderers, the emphasis on formal design may wane and give place to experiments, but it will doubtless regain impetus, and efforts to keep informed by lectures and exhibitions are rewarding.

Ground

Information on fibres also creates a new use of backgrounds which is important for developing a continuous interest in white work.

A knowledge of composition of materials, both past and present, provides assistance in choosing backgrounds for embroidery and for the care and presentation of a collection or a few treasured items.

A reminder of the variety and texture of fibres available and obtainable helps to stimulate personal experiments and exploration in materials such as felt, paper or net, and is useful for all types of work.

The wide selection of fibres includes some from the past, such as fine linen, cambric, cotton muslin and silks, and others of today, such as synthetics. Hand or commercial weaving allows the added use of natural fibre or complicated texture.

There are very few books on fibres in relation to embroidery (as distinct from technical information), so an entry has been included to introduce the reader to different characteristics of fibres.

Thread

The variety of threads available has been considerably reduced over the last decade, so that the challenge to invent, make or spin individual threads is one that influences white textures in a new way.

Many past embroidery threads defy imitation, as the conditions of growing the raw material, the use of chemicals and fertilizers, and the process of spinning are all now changed.

Technique

Drawn thread work and pulled work are the earliest processes, as are the stitches buttonhole, satin and punch. Others in continuous use are darning and run stitch, couching, herringbone, overcast and some knot stitches.

Broderie anglaise, cut work and appliqué are later additions and have lace as a trim and machine as an influence.

The imaginative use of these processes makes up nearly all white work embroidery, often with a combination of two or more, such as ladder stitch using back stitch and couching, hollie point using buttonhole and knot, reticella using buttonhole and couching, and Ayrshire using satin stitch and buttonhole. Others have dropped out of general use recently but are found in many old examples such as Italian hemstitch or pointe turque or, like coral stitch, used in a different way, as in hemstitching.

Transferring designs for white work is dealt with under the entry on *Tacking*.

Books

Any omissions, such as details of Tenerife work, the many attractions of white bead embroidery or further explanation of the fine white counted floss embroidery of the Eastern Mediterranean, belong to specialist books. An attempt to cover them all would make a huge, unwieldy volume.

The same applies to any omissions in detailed descriptions of techniques, which are so very fully covered by the many stitch books currently available. Four such books from one publisher alone are on stitches. The use of one of these books avoids unnecessary repetition here, and it is most helpful and valuable to have one to hand. Mrs Christie's *Samplers & Stitches* of 1920 is particularly relevant as the samplers illustrated are in fine technique, excellent design of the time and have very informed explanations of stitchery, all of which make a good stepping-stone between historical work and that of today.

Illustrations

Wherever possible, techniques are illustrated by close-up photographs of working samplers, in the hope that these will show the method of working more clearly than a diagram might do.

The use of pins to display textiles of any sort should be avoided at all times and replaced with tacking. The pins shown in any of the illustrations in this book are temporary or have been in an old notebook for several decades and have not, miraculously, rusted.

Some famous and well loved pieces may not be illustrated. Some historical items may seem fragmentary or of a coarse nature, but the latter represent articles which may be found at local sales, in unconsidered store, or as gifts. They are convenient and easy to recognize and relate, and also have a poignant appeal which leads to the appreciation and understanding of the beautiful and excellent specimens of high quality in musems, which otherwise sometimes seem distant and unobtainable.

The work of today is well published and has a variety of purpose, from the dynamism of new ideas and the enjoyment of technique, to the satisfaction of a wide or personal collection.

Some designs and embroidery by professional artists may be considered static and lifeless, and the undeveloped charm of naive work, or experiment, to have more vitality and attraction. However, a realization of the two standards is a valuable asset and a knowledge of the origins of even humble possessions is an added interest to collectors and, to embroiderers, an excitement to create new techniques to suit new times, materials and purposes, and new thoughts.

A BRIEF HISTORY OF WHITE WORK EMBROIDERY

Early references before the time of Christ mention the linen work of Egyptian, Greek and other civilizations of the Mediterranean; as with silk in China, cotton in India and other natural fibres around the world, it may be a safe speculation that they all used white and also the earliest stitches of run, overcast and buttonhole, which are reflected in their knowledge of basketry.

In AD 679, English records mention gold embroidery and this is referred to again on a white chasuble made by Aethelswitha, King Canute's daughter in the eighth century. Presumably the value of the gold made the work worthy of mention, and it is easy to speculate that white linen embroidery also existed, but was not treasured as it was a local product. The first indication of work in white comes in 1235. The detailed embroid-

ery of the German and Swiss states is recorded at this time, and probably developed from simple earlier work. Boldly stitched details on figures of plain linen show up against a square mesh of drawn or pulled threads. The workmanship is good, but although it may be considered the roots of early Italian reticella work, it is not thought to be as well designed as the contemporary and advanced work of Opus Anglicanum.

Much early work came from professional workrooms, often supported by the custom of rich kings and queens, princesses and the Church.

1503–1599
Samplers are first mentioned in England in this period, presumably as a record of white embroidered patterns in the reticella style with other stitches. These stitches were to decorate the famous Elizabethan stiffened collars, which became ruffs, in white linen. Punto in aria was also used.

Other items of the time include cushions which feature drawn and pulled thread work, satin stitch borders and intricate insertions. Caps were also decorated with hemstitching and quilting. Lacis darning on square-mesh net was worked abundantly in Italy at this time.

1600–1699
Samplers continued as in the previous century, but figures and also letters, names and dates were introduced. The fashion changed from ruffs to collars and cravats of heavy needlemade lace in the Venetian style.

Lacis embroidery from Italy was still popular, as were slashed, paned, braided and stamped white satin.

1700–1799
A great period for white muslin embroidery in England. Cotton muslin embroidery used pulled stitches, satin stitch and counted patterns in amateur work, as well as in professional items, such as aprons. Fichus are typical items in this sort of embroidery.

White quilting appeared on bed covers, caps, petticoats and loose jackets and waistcoats, combined with pulled stitches on linen.

Knotting was used on decorated bed covers, quilts and furnishings.

Stitches on muslin included chain stitch, shadow work, darning and seeding, and also counted patterns and pulled stitches as in Dresden work, which replaced heavy lace in Northern Europe.

Hollie point was used for baby bonnets and insertions, and heavy silk satin christening robes provided a background for embroidery.

Fine lace developed throughout the century, needle-made in France and bobbin in Flanders and Brussels.

1800–1899

Decoration continued from the previous century, along with the popularity of cotton. Net, made by machine, influenced embroidery.

Dress, from the Regency style to crinolines and bustles, and also children's clothes, accessories such as collars and handkerchiefs, bed and table linen, all showed a variety of embroidery on linen and cotton, such as:

Ayrshire embroidery
Broderie anglaise
Cut work
Drawn thread work
Eyelet embroidery
A revival of lacis, known as filet
Hemstitching
Lettering
Mountmellick
Satin stitch

The development of machine embroidery became a great influence. Lace became prolific when worked by machine.

Samplers of embroidery and needlework, often several yards long, were worked as exercises by children.

Societies and schools fostered all types of embroidery, and many were established to provide employment for the poor.

1900–1986

White embroidery continued as before, with greater and more frequent changes in design and fashion as easy communications, materials and laundering improved.

Quilting, as bed covers in traditional patterns, was produced in Wales, Durham and Northumberland to give employment to women.

The twentieth century has been a great period of personal design and expression, developed with an awareness of textures rather than techniques, using simple stitches and popular processes such as:

Appliqué
Collage
Patchwork
Quilting

Experiments are made in all areas, including machine work, and using new materials – synthetics, plastics and natural fibres.

It is sometimes difficult, after the lapse of centuries, to date antique embroidery exactly, and to decide whether it is genuine or a very good imitation but of a later date. The quality of linen, style of design and the manner in which the article handles are clues for the expert. Although many countries produced a great amount of work, embroidery was sometimes carried out abroad for the European market, since it was less expensive and could be bartered for goods by businessmen. India and Turkey are examples, and the influence of the country of origin shows in the finished article.

The great social changes brought about by two world wars made an impact on white embroidery during the second half of the twentieth century. Labour-saving inventions brought about a different way of life, and cheap labour for the commercial production of hand embroidery became a thing of the past.

The introduction of synthetic and drip-dry materials simplified laundering and pressing, and machine embroidery on synthetics does not require the same care as natural fibres.

Today the place of embroidery in previous centuries has become a subject of study, and paintings from the past underline different aspects, such as the weary and exhausted launderesses depicted by Degas. The portraits of Reynolds show the mother of Charles James Fox embroidering a strong design which suggests a very different personality froim the Waldegrave sisters sitting at their tambour work.

The paintings show a variety of materials including elaborate Elizabethan embroidery, and the use of rich white satin and fine white gauze or muslin. Tools and embroidery frames are illustrated as well as heavy pressing irons. The irons used to smooth out creases and others which set off frills were still in use this century, until electricity was installed in most houses and lighter-weight irons reduced the heavy work. Such illustrations have become another area of collection which is appreciated by embroiderers.

The work of the present time continues to reflect current influences such as that of art movements, the use of mixed media and the search for new interpretations.

A

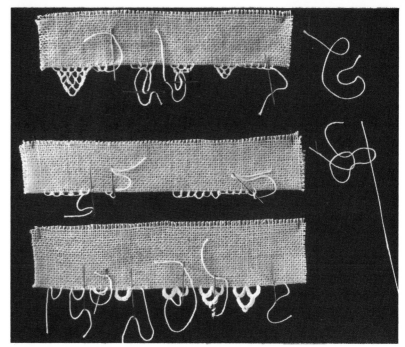

ALGERIAN EYELET

Algerian eyelet, sometimes called square eyelet, to differentiate from eyelet embroidery, is a counted satin stitch with such ideal qualities for white embroidery that variations could form a complete design, simply by changing the texture of the threads and the size of the stitch. An added advantage is that Algerian eyelets are virtually reversible.

The working thread, which makes the eye, or centre hole, is of white silk or shining mercerized cotton and this gives a sparkling tonal contrast to the dark open centre and the ground material.

The background should be evenly and loosely woven to enable the threads to be counted and pulled together.

When working eyelets, a clear sharp definition is made by inserting the needle downwards into the centre and coming up on the edge, so that the stitch is controlled from the right side and any fluff or roughness is taken to the underside. When the needle is brought upwards into the centre, the

stitches previously worked are disturbed.

The number of threads of the background covered for eyelet stitches may vary, but if they are too long they move out of place and the work overall lacks definition. The outer edge may be finished with back stitch.

Algerian eyelets may be worked either in the hand or on a frame. If the centre becomes over-crowded with stitches, a variation may be worked by spacing stitches at regular intervals, to make the centre smooth and even. It will be found that enthusiasts give a name to every variation, so this is an instance of the profusion of terms that occur in stitchery and especially white work and, therefore, a flexible approach needs to be maintained towards nomenclature. Figs 1, 92, 105, 175, 176, 217.

ANTIMACASSAR

Antimacassars or chair-backs were a universal item of household linen from about 1890–1950, and were considered essential to protect the back of upholstered chairs from the macassar oil used by men to dress their hair for a smooth high gloss. This was later replaced by a product called brilliantine or Brylcreem, which was used by the majority of men until about 1960, when free hair styles began to be favoured.

Every type of white embroidery featured as borders on chair-backs,

2 Top: *Armenian edge. Complete point. Work three buttonhole stitches from left to right, two stitches to left, return one stitch to right. Loop thread into edge to return to hem.* Centre left: *Buttonhole edge. Work from left to right.* Centre right: *Antwerp edge. Work from left to right.* Bottom: *loop edge, with picot at top centre.* Right: *weaver's or lace knot.* Right top: *Make a loop in the end of work thread.* Right below: *Pass second loop of thread through first loop. Pass the end of new working thread through second loop. Hold one end of old and new threads in each hand and pull firmly into place.*

Greek lace and reticella being the most prestigious. Net darning and borders of drawn thread were also popular. Fig. 240.

ANTWERP EDGE, ARMENIAN EDGE

A nineteenth-century name given to needle-made edgings in knotted buttonhole stitches, sewn on to the edge of scarves, collars, cuffs, table linen and similar articles. Often seen on headscarves of national or peasant costume. Fig. 2. See *Buttonhole*.

APPLIQUÉ

Appliqué is a French word meaning a piece of one textile applied, or sewn, to another. It is an early and basic type

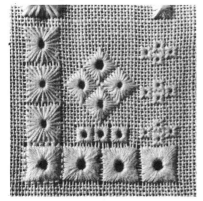

1 *Algerian eyelet in various forms.* Lower left: *back stitching.* Left: *spaced stitching.* Bottom: *close stitching.* Centre: *diamonds.* Right: *groups. Worked by Sheila Joss.*

11

3 Shadow appliqué, showing pin stitching, satin stitch and some cut work. Corner 12 × 12 cm (4¾ × 4¾ in.) (Clarice Blakey).

of embroidery, although very few white examples exist from before the nineteenth century. Figs 3, 4–6, 65, 66, 96, 233, 250, 274–6.

Identification

Appliqué is recognized by the application of a shape, or motif, cut out in material and applied to the ground, so that the design or parts of it are in double thickness. The applied material may be of a contrasting texture to the ground, or the same, and the ground may be semi-transparent to give an opaque quality to the design, when it is known as shadow appliqué. A variety of solid materials may be applied, and the ground may be net to give a further tonal value. Decorative stitchery and punch stitches for textural effects are added in some designs.

History

White appliqué and shadow appliqué derive from the Indian tambour embroidery on muslin imported during the early nineteenth century. The term shadow appliqué denotes a semi-transparent ground with self-appliqué, i.e. the same material. It is a less laborious method than the conventional double back stitch of shadow work or the technique of tambour work.

Later, white muslin, lawn or cambric applied to net developed as an industry in Ireland, particularly at Carrickmacross. Large bertha collars, a metre long (39 in.), are typical examples.

Some peasant embroidery from Hungary is also in the form of a design cut out of one overall piece of muslin or fine cambric and applied to net for use as decorative table mats.

At the present time linen applied to fine linen, used with decorative drawn thread work and stitchery, forms embroidery designs for blouses and handkerchiefs. This is an industry in China with controlled wages, and is for sale to visiting tourists or for export to the West. Other items include table linen which is very popular in American homes. Appliqué carried out in white silk and in cotton materials was used particularly for lingerie in the 1930s.

The use of all types of white textiles for appliqué has developed during the latter part of the twentieth century to interpret designs for panels and hangings designed by artist embroiderers. The huge range of materials both of natural and synthetic fibres, with the use of hand or machine stitchery, is a challenge to exploit texture and to give a new thrill to white work.

Items

Curtains
Collars and cuffs
Children's clothing
Tablecloths and mats
Bed linen
Guest towels
Blouses, dresses
Aprons
Lingerie accessories
Panels and hangings

4 Appliqué on ninon with materials of varied textures, hand and machine stitching. Experiment in use of black thread having the same effect as open cut work or punch stitch. Worked by Lindy Richardson.

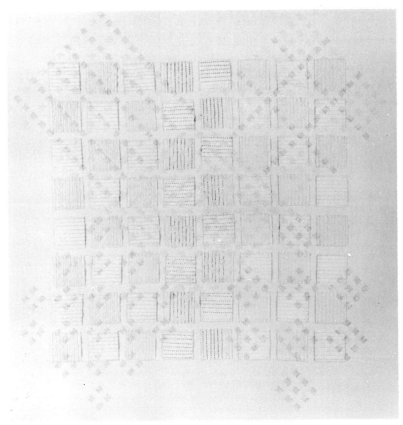

5 *'Hidden Squares'. Spun silk background and lurex thread machine and hand stitched. Worked by Irene Ord.*

6 *Detail of fig. 5. Good example of appliqué attached to the background with decorative stitchery.*

Design

Appliqué is most successful with small, fairly simple, bold shapes, approximately 2.5 cm (1 in.) square, to make cutting out practicable. Large areas attached only at the edges tend to rise in the centre and soon wear out, unless stitchery is added over the double material.

Appliqué in white work was very popular during the 1920s and 1930s and so the design has characteristics of the period, with flowers, butterflies, monograms and nursery motifs as the most usual.

Another area of design interest is that of muslin applied to net, as in Carrickmacross lace where the appliqué is in one continuous piece of muslin, interpreting a lace-like design of the nineteenth century. Hungarian peasant embroidery also used this last method though the designs are bold and simple, often using bird motifs.

Some sophisticated, elegant and luxurious silk lingerie was made during the 1930s and decorated with appliqué lace and net insertions. Hems and edges are finished with applied material and the double thickness makes for strength in otherwise delicate garments. By using openwork embroidery such as a punch stitch to hold the hem in place, an attractive light finish is produced.

White work appliqué is usually considered washable and wearable, and therefore the embroidery and design should answer these requirements. Another most important feature for consideration when designing for appliqué is that the grain of the applied work should match that of the ground, to give a good appearance to the embroidery, otherwise the appliqué will ruck up and appear cobbled.

Grounds and applied materials

Avoid loosely woven materials and those that fray easily. Linen and cotton of all types are suitable, including muslin applied to muslin and linen on linen, making as much play as possible of the different weights to give shadows and textures. Silks such as crêpe de Chine, satin, ninon and gauze do not fray easily. Fine silk, cotton and nets give further contrast.

Organdie is often found in appliqué of the 1930s. It is a very fine and attractive stiffened cotton material, but creases and crushes easily, which permanently marks the surface. It is also harsh on tender skin when worn as dresses and blouses, and is now substituted with a synthetic gauze or organza of nylon or polyester.

All synthetic fibres which have been processed to have similar characteristics to natural fibres are also suitable.

Fine wool crêpe and viyella are very easy to handle. A backing is often a valuable asset. The iron-on type is successful for this purpose, but not for articles that require laundering.

Technique

(*Note*: when cutting the applied shape, the grain of the material should match that of the ground, as this avoids contrary pulling.) Figs 275, 276.

Tools – small, sharp-bladed scissors.

Framing-up – a frame is a useful aid to accurate matching of the grains of the ground and the appliqué and also for adding stitchery, especially trailing and exacting details.

Keep the ground material in the frame slack while tacking, pinning and stitching the applied material in place. Tighten the frame for additional embroidery, as both materials then have the same tension.

Free machine stitching sometimes requires a ring frame, but straight or zig-zag stitching are easily adapted methods on the domestic sewing machine.

Transfer of design – a lightly marked line with a hard pencil or a tacked (basted) line through the design lines marked out on thin paper, such as greaseproof. When tacked, the paper is torn away. Fig. 335.

Needles – crewel for slip hemming the appliqué; chenille for punch stitching.

Threads – fine and strong such as Drima or silk, or a match with the ground fibre.

Join on/off – the usual method of a run or double stitch into design line.

Process – stitch. Punch stitches, slip hemming or decorative stitchery as required.

(*Note*: areas of appliqué ideally should be approximately 5 cm (2 in.) square, as large areas rise from the ground. All applied areas, unless very small, require additional stitchery on the surface to keep a smooth finish.)

1 Mark out design on ground with hard pencil or tacked line.
2 Mark out design on applied material, matching grain.
3 Allow 6 mm ($\frac{1}{4}$ in.) turnings, cut out, tack under turnings to wrong side.
4 Apply to ground and tack in place, matching grain design lines, and laying wrong side of appliqué to right side of ground.
5 Secure with blind hemming or pin stitch.

Alternative:

1 Allowing turnings, cut out shape.
2 Apply to ground without turning under turnings, matching lines as in 4 above.
3 Secure with double punch stitch on design lines and, when complete, cut away surplus material.

ART EMBROIDERY

Art Embroidery or Art Needlework is a term influenced by William Morris and developed in the mid-nineteenth century to differentiate between designs worked or supervised by a trained artist, using embroidery as an art form, and those worked in the home copied from magazines or other sources. By the twentieth century the term was debased by general use in magazines and also commercially. The impetus for design and new thought now comes from trained artists teaching at art schools and on short courses, who also set up professional workshops to work for exhibitions and commissions sponsored by galleries, art societies such as the Fibre Art and Crafts Council, and local authorities. Fig. 305.

AYRSHIRE

Three types of embroidery were produced in the Ayrshire region of Scotland during the late eighteenth and nineteenth centuries. The first type of embroidery, introduced by Ruffini between 1782 and 1801 and known as Dresden embroidery, has a professional but involved design in a rococo manner displaying exceptionally fine open fillings in pulled stitch and with other stitches to set it off. The openwork is sometimes confused with the buttonhole fillings of later work.

The second type, introduced between 1801 and 1820, is influenced

7 *Detail of Dresden work.*
(Embroiderers' Guild).

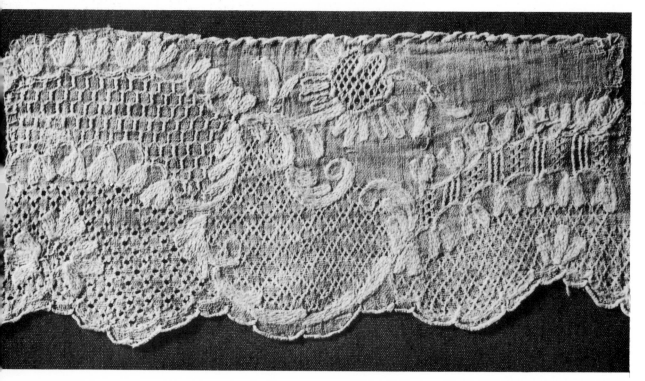

14

by the imported Indian tamboured muslin and shows a simple design of sprigs of flowers worked in chain stitch, stem stitch or couching in a thick thread, with only the borders of the article showing pulled stitches, but in a large variety of fillings.

The third type is influenced by the French needlepoint fillings introduced between 1815 and 1820 in expert designs, with lace fillings set off by satin stitch. It is this type that is known as Ayrshire embroidery today and, as is the case with most embroidery, it came to be worked all over Europe, and was especially fine in France on linen cambric. The embroidery from Ayrshire was exported extensively, to markets including America, France and Russia.

Although most techniques revive and recur through history, the use of buttonhole fillings in designs has not, except with the studious embroiderer and also in the Genoese type of cutwork. Fragments of Ayrshire work may be found assembled to form individual garments in 1980s styles. Figs 8–17, 24–8, 56–8, 204–6.

Identification

Ayrshire embroidery is identified by the delicate buttonhole or loop stitch fillings worked in fine lace thread to form part or the whole of a flower shape. This element of the work is best seen and appreciated by using a magnifying glass to distinguish it from fine pulled stitch fillings of similar work carried out in Ayrshire. The fine white cotton muslin ground is cut away behind the buttonhole stitches to give the flower the light airy look of a cobweb laden with dew. The leaves and flower petals surrounding the open centre or open areas are worked in satin stitch using unmercerized cotton. Other stitches used include back stitch, chain stitch, seeding, stem, French knots and punch stitch, eyelets and buttonhole edging. Figs 8–12.

The fillings of Ayrshire embroidery are similar to French and Italian loop or buttonhole lace stitches, of which there are an immense number. In the best Ayrshire designs no two

8 Buttonhole filling in flower centre, 1.5 × 1 cm ($\frac{1}{3} \times \frac{1}{4}$ in.). Compare with fig. 9. Typical late Ayrshire.

9 Early pulled stitch filling worked on fine muslin, 1 × 0.5 cm ($\frac{1}{2} \times \frac{1}{3}$ in.), probably embroidered in Ayrshire, possibly Indian.

10 Ayrshire buttonhole fillings in flower centre, 4 mm diameter, petals in divided satin stitch and surrounded with rows of back stitch, eyelets, overcasting and trailing.

15

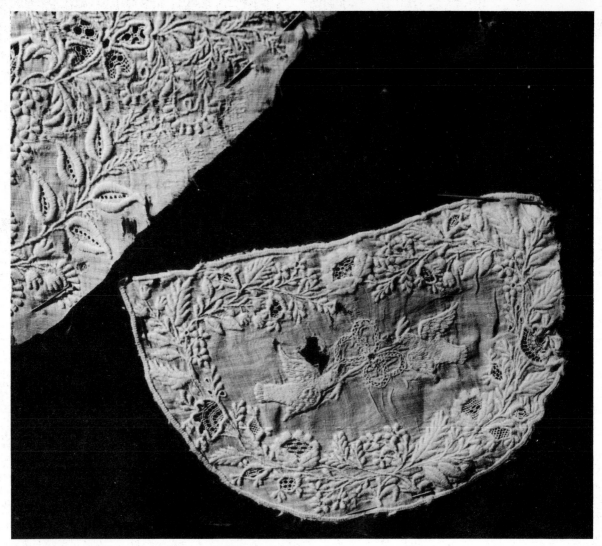

11 *A variety of fillings in buttonhole,*
with a punch stitched ribbon and open
back stitch (ladder stitch) in leaves of
satin stitch, on a pocket. 10 × 7 cm
(4 × 2¾ in.).

fillings are alike and this is a tribute to
the inventiveness of the workers, especially as such a huge amount of
work was produced. Later, one filling
was used throughout a design. A
recognizable and typical feature of an
Ayrshire christening robe, or child's
garment, is the triangular section at
the front bodice. The point is at the
approximate waistline and the opposite flat edge at the neck. The front
panel of the skirt of the robe is often
edged with a separately attached and
embroidered gathered border or frill,
which frames the beautiful texture
and fine workmanship of the front
panel embroidery. Figs 13–17.

Collectors' items

Christening robes are today much
sought after as collectors' items.
Equally so the babies' bonnets and
caps which had embroidery on the
circular section at the back to make
the crown.

Sprigged muslin was decorated
with isolated motifs, and was fashionable during the Regency of the 1800s.

Other items to search for when
collecting this intriguing embroidery
are:

Muslin collars
Dresses
Edging
Frilled caps
Lappets
Chemisettes
Frock bodies
Children's dresses and baby dresses
Pelerines
Morning caps

Crowns, bonnets
Robes
Insertion, trimmings
Habit shirts
Cuffs
Flouncing

History

At first, in the early 1700s, the new
wonder-fibre and fashion cloth, cotton muslin, was imported as a spun
yarn into England from India and
woven into cloth, by the usual system
of the time, cottage industry. Later,

12 *Bonnet. Superb variety of*
buttonhole fillings and tones of white.
Note double row of flower centres. 8 cm
(3⅛ in.) diameter. (Embroiderers'
Guild).

16

13 Detail of a design for an Ayrshire robe. The repetition of one filling and slightly heavier muslin or lawn indicate later work, c. 1860. (Constance Howard).

from 1779 onwards, the raw cotton was imported and spun into yarn and woven into cloth by the newly invented English machines of Arkwright and Crompton.

Mill owners set up mills on the west coast of Scotland where there were many suitable sites for mill streams, as water was the power used to drive the mechanical spinning and weaving machines. In this way Ayrshire became a centre for the manufacture of muslin, with steam power being developed later.

The cotton arrived in Lancashire from India and was transported from Manchester to Ayr, taking three days over rough unmade roads up and down mountains, a frightening and dangerous journey in the days before the mail coach.

By 1780 the fashion craze for white muslin worn with rich silk dresses was well established, but after the French Revolution the simplicity of the white cotton for complete dresses expressed a renewed purity and honesty. The classical embroidery designs of the

early 1800s bordered full-length dresses with high waists of the Regency style, and also designs with the all-pervading Indian influence which showed in fashions of every kind, from dress to architecture such as the Brighton Pavilion.

Ayr was one of the districts that prospered with the production of cotton muslin and its embroidery, by satisfying the demands of the fashion rage all over Europe. Although work was provided for a very large number of people, particularly women and children for embroidery, the conditions and hours were usually hard and long, especially in the mills. The prosperity, however, made comfortable conditions for many other people who indulged in the fashion both for business and display.

Two personalities became closely involved with Ayrshire embroidery, one an artist-designer and the other a fashionable aristocrat, and they seem typical of the element that chance plays in the success of new ideas. The first was Luigi Ruffini, an Italian textile or embroidery designer who arrived in Edinburgh in 1789. He brought some exquisite examples of Dresden embroidered lace on fine linen, known also as Danish, Flemish or Saxony work, to show to the Board of Trustees in the hope of obtaining a grant or loan to set up a workroom. He was successful in this and his workrooms had young chil-

dren of eight to twelve years as apprentices to learn the pulled stitches of Dresden work. He became famed for good design and for introducing the embroidered muslin trade to Scotland. Fig. 18.

Ruffini continued developing his trade, in spite of many of the usual difficulties contingent on employing children, such as infectious illness and the length of time required to learn speed and technique, but he did not make a business fortune. In 1801, towards the end of his career, a fund was established to help him financially by the grateful cotton merchants of Glasgow, who acknowledged their great debt to him for having introduced the flourishing embroidered muslin trade and an awareness of the value of good design. Perhaps Ruffini preferred the reward of the design creativity he saw and the impact he made on the artistic life of the community, when applying to the Drawing Academy for his apprentices to learn drawing and design in order to keep a high standard in his workrooms. This made the Academy

14 Christening robe showing pointed bodice, french knots on casing and flat frill or robing, edging centre panel. Pulled stitch rather than buttonhole fillings, ladder and satin stitch and eyelets are included in the embroidery. (Embroiderers' Guild).

15 *Detail of hem of christening robe, with embroidery on side frills and centre.*

16 *Detail of centre in fig. 15, with pulled stitch fillings.*

Committee restate their principles of teaching design for industry, as well as for the personal expression of the students. The students had to be over thirteen years of age and to show some talent in the first six months before continuing for two years of study.

The embroidered muslin industry was enriched by a technique introduced by Lady Mary Montgomerie, who was the second personality involved in the work. She was brought up in Ayr and was presumably familiar with the powerful cotton industry. In 1812 she married Lord Montgomerie, an army officer, and followed her husband to Sicily for battle in the Napoleonic War. She was able to employ a Frenchwoman for sewing who, it may be assumed, had been taught needlepoint lace stitches as part of her education. When Lady Mary gave birth to a son while abroad, a christening robe was made using the white muslin embroidery from Scotland as well as the needlemade fillings familiar to her French needlewoman. Unfortunately Lady Mary was widowed in 1814 and returned home with her baby son and the christening robe. The robe was shown to Mrs Jamieson, one of the influential organizers of the distribution and working of the muslin embroidery at Ayr. She taught needlepoint or buttonhole filling stitches to the embroiderers and so the new technique was generally accepted in the workrooms on the west coast, spreading to Edinburgh and also to Ireland in order to satisfy the intense demand. The workers were known as 'flowerers' and the work as flowering or floo'ering, as well as tambouring on webs or on webs of muslin. Linen was occasionally used in an effort to prevent a decline in its production. In Ireland 'sprigging' described the work of embroidered muslin. It became a vast business organization, and some

17 *Design for the centre bodice panel of an Ayrshire robe. One pattern of buttonhole filling and many eyelets indicate later work and broderie anglaise influence. (Constance Howard).*

19

18 *Three examples of Dresden work.*
(Embroiderers' Guild).

of the terms and procedures were as follows:

Spinning yarn
Warping
Weaving – in the weft
Reeling – for embroidery threads
Design – drawing and transferring design
Despatch to 400 or 500 agents in Scotland or Ireland
Distribution to the embroiderers – first to specialists in satin stitch etc., then to those specializing in openwork

Collection of finished embroidery
Return to agents
Examination of work
Bleaching – many other stages, e.g. final pressing and finishing
Return to warehouses
Making up – pressing
Folding and ticketing
Sorting – quality and price
Boxing, with fancy paper
Packing
Despatch to home and foreign markets

The wages of early embroiderers are of interest, for about 1790, girls of nine to twelve years of age were apprenticed for four years as daily workers, at first earning two shillings a week, gradually increasing to three

shillings, or with a yearly premium. Tambourers were paid sixpence a day or four shillings a week.

Girls in groups of thirty to several hundred were employed from towns and villages to do dotting and tambouring, and some at eight years old for sixpence a day.

Later, about 1840, flowerers earned six shillings to ten shillings a week, while weavers earned about six shillings for a sixty-nine-hour week. Designers were considered an élite and earned about forty shillings a week, but were unnamed.

Food costs were of course also different from today, as chickens were fourpence each, beef and mutton fourpence a pound, and cod fish one penny for two pounds.

In 1829, however, Joshua Heilmann of Mulhouse, Switzerland, invented a working embroidery machine, and with the introduction of successful sewing machines in 1846, which over the next twenty years were improved and were able to imitate intricate embroidery, Ayrshire work became threatened. The machine-made embroideries were known as Hamburgs and were very much cheaper than the hand versions. In 1856 a young American drapery representative, Mr Gibbs, bought all the machine embroidery that could be produced in Switzerland at St Gall to sell in America instead of Ayrshire handwork. In Glasgow the Swiss then set up an office near to that of the Ayrshire agent and showed samples of the excellent but different machine work, and within another ten years (by about 1870) Ayrshire work was obsolete.

Gradually more and more of the cheaper machine-made goods were sold. The Ayrshire workers went on to other techniques such as broderie anglaise and eyelet embroidery, and these too soon met with the same fate. Many young workers were then employed on farms or in domestic service, at about £10 a year, food and heat included, for those who had become prosperous from industry.

Some linen and cotton firms, such as Knox linen thread, survived until the 1950s, but Clarks and also Coats are ongoing businesses today.

Design
The well-thought-out professional design of Ayrshire embroidery is a great contributory factor to the suc-

cess of the exquisite lace fillings. The design has a classical influence but is also charmingly floral, with graceful trailing borders, rich corners, panels and insertions to give an air of freshness and deceptive simplicity.

The flowers, which are approximately 13–38 mm ($\frac{1}{2}$–1$\frac{1}{2}$ in.) overall, are fantastic in a minor scale and do not represent natural forms. Small ovate leaves of approximately 6–13 mm ($\frac{1}{4}$–$\frac{1}{2}$ in.) surround the stems and flowers. The open areas are seldom larger than 13–25 mm ($\frac{1}{2}$–1 in.).

The three tones of white, the very white solid satin stitch, the dark cutout areas and opaque muslin ground, give an inspired play of textures accentuated with the use of surface stitches.

Ground

Cotton muslin was the fashionable ground material, imported at first from India, later, about 1830, from America, and after 1860 from India again. Occasionally it may be found that very fine linen or cambric from Ireland or France has been used.

In later work, including christening robes, the ground was more solid for practical reasons and this gave a more even texture.

Technique

Precise historical methods of work are not recorded, for an air of mystery seems to have been usual in professional workrooms, especially when employing apprentices, and also to preserve the secrets and high standards from visitors; this avoided pirating by business competitors. The design was considered of the highest importance.

Tools – stiletto. Fig. 23.

Framing-up – optional, but probably used in professional workrooms and in later productions where several workers sat at one piece of work.

Transfer of design – the design, drawn out in ink on to strong white paper, was laid under the muslin and fixed securely with tacking (basting) or pins, matching centre lines of the design with the grain of the material. The lines of the design seen through the muslin were traced out with a faint blue paint, or hard pencil, line. Fig. 335.

Later, rollers with border edges and patterns were carved out of wood, dipped in paint and rolled out on to

the cloth. The muslin was also lithographed with the design and with the price to be paid to the embroiderer for the completed work. Fig. 42.

Needles – crewel 8–12. A round eye was probably used at the time.

Thread – unmercerized cotton, i.e. a matt surface of thread now usually found at sales. The shiny mercerized threads of today look completely artificial, false and flashy.

Join on/off – run stitch in on paint line, or into back on previous work.

Process – stitch. The embroidery of satin, ladder, back, stem stitches, eyelets, trailing and overcasting is completed before the cutwork.

The open area is cut at right angles as in broderie anglaise, close to the edge of satin stitch previously worked. Figs 34, 278–80.

Buttonhole fillings are worked from one side of the open space to the other, or from the outer edge of a circular shape to the centre.

B

BACKING

A material tacked to the back of another is known as a backing, and is used in making up, but also for strength to support closely worked embroidery. Net darning and patchwork require a stiff backing of firm material or drawing paper. Quilting requires a soft backing such as mull to enclose the padding and, in another context, a completed embroidery is mounted on to a good backing material for display.

There is a considerable art in selecting a suitable backing for embroidery and for making up, as although it needs to be strong it should not destroy the delicate and pliable quality of the material it is supporting. Conversely it should not be too flimsy to serve its purpose of giving strength to a lightweight or loosely woven ground that has a considerable amount of embroidery, such as padded satin stitch. Cambric and lawns

(either linen or cotton) provide various weights and are usually ideal. Calico often has too coarse a grain, and bonded and iron-on bonded backings are frequently unsympathetic and lack flexibility. Surplus backing should be cut away at seams and corners and where double thickness gives a bulky finish in making up, or close to the completed embroidery if it is an isolated motif. Figs 74, 84, 154, 162, 174, 334. See *Book muslin, Fibres.*

BACK STITCH

A basic stitch for fine, clearly defined lines and outlines, and also for a solid filling when worked in close rows. Back stitch may be interlaced with an additional thread or used for fine details such as facial features. Back stitch is useful where it is not practical to use a machine stitch, as in detailed designs of quilting and where the interest in stitchery is minimal but form paramount. Figs 1, 6, 10, 19, 181, 306.

19 *Design outlined in back stitch, plain and whipped. A cross formed of simple hem stitch and drawn thread work; circles are outlined in buttonhole stitch with the loops on the inside and wheels attached with twisted or interlaced bars. 10 cm (4 in.) square. (Nora Jones).*

BAR OR BRIDE

A bar, or the French term bride, is worked free from the ground material and connects opposite sides of an open area, as in cut work, or in lace when motifs of design are joined together with bars.

Coxcombs, open cross bar, pearls, legs, and ties are all terms for types or

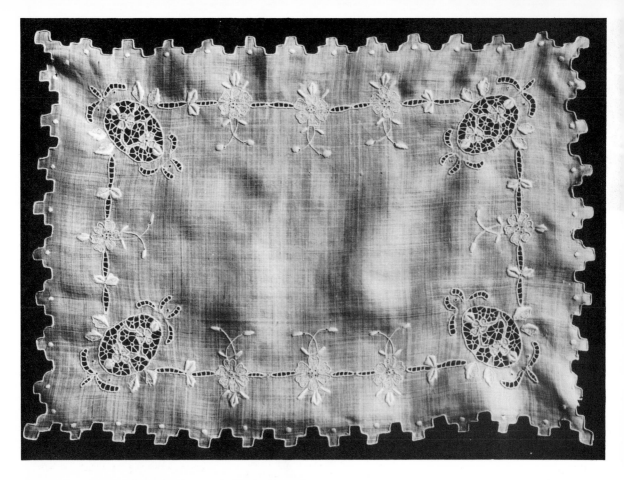

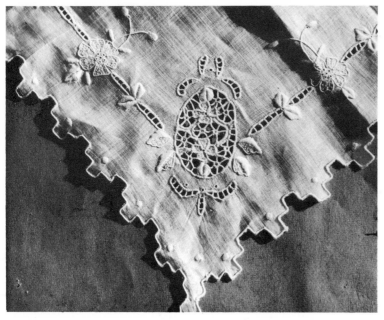

21 *Detail of fig. 20, showing cross bars and wheels, also divided satin stitch, seeding, trailing and eyelets.*

20 *Example of cut work, suggesting a pineapple, probably on a pina cloth, using bars of buttonhole stitch, and designed round a centre wheel.*
15 × 36 cm (6 × 14 in.). (Clarice Blakey).

arrangements of bars to connect various solid areas and even seams. The threads forming the bar are sometimes wrapped, entwined or covered with buttonhole stitch, and may be made in many forms, such as circular wheels or star-shaped, square or triangular, and arranged to enhance the main design.

The length of a bar should not be longer than 1 cm ($\frac{3}{8}$ in.) and usually shorter, because if longer they tend to catch on objects, and in the iron when laundering, and so eventually break. Bars may be decorated with picots. A button-hole bar worked across the end of a buttonhole helps to prevent tearing. Figs 20–22, 52, 83, 86–8, 99, 105, 189, 209, 217. See *Broderie anglaise, Cut work.*

BATISTE

A familiar term (until very recently) for cotton muslins, having a fair amount of dressing and used for sum-

22 Detail showing arrangement of bars in Carrickmacross, designed to fit the shape.

mer dresses, interlinings or linings until the mid-twentieth century. Batiste fell from popularity because of a tendency to shrink, and with improved processes of production more reliable cottons became available to give a more uniform standard of shrink and crease resistance. Batiste was used for mounting lace or shadow work as sachets and cushions, and was replaced rather than laundered.

Batiste is also a French term for cambric or fine linen, named after the inventor Baptista, a linen weaver of the thirteenth century from Cambrai in France. This fine baptismal linen was used for towels at christenings, and this may be another derivation for the term. See *Fibres*.

BATTLEMENTED EMBROIDERY

A form of Holbein counted work in white on white. The stitches are all the same size, that is, over and under four threads and worked as a row of run stitch, to form the indented pattern. The spaces are filled on the return row to make a continuous battlemented or castellated line. Sometimes referred to as Russian work because the squared line relates to the squared outline of Russian ground designs. Figs 41, 304. See *Crenelle*.

BEADING

Collective term referring to a simple edging and insertion, and for a needle-worked or buttonhole edge, or a single line of French knots. Also a general term referring to bead embroidery, which when worked in a variety of white beads can be very distinctive. Figs 14, 56, 60–62, 167.

BEADS

White beads sewn on net or used as a hair decoration are a recurring fashion as in Regency styles, and are mentioned by Jane Austen. They are also used as repeating all-over patterns or motifs, worked either by hand tambour or machine and sold by the yard.

23 Tools connected with white work embroidery. Top left: chenille needle with chenille thread, smaller size chenille needle. Top right: buttonhole scissors with gauge below blades to keep all cuts the same size, and prevent blades slipping and cutting stitchery. Bottom right: two stilettos, two steel bodkins, one flat bone bodkin, possibly for elastic, one tatting shuttle.

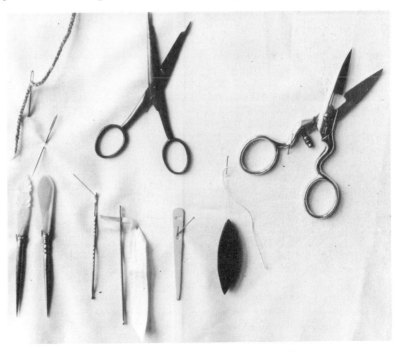

Fine and impressive designs for dress occur throughout the twentieth century. Figs 150–52, 184, 350.

BLANKET STITCH

A variation of buttonhole known as embroidery buttonhole, it is worked widely spaced and used over the hem of a blanket. There are many variations, such as crossed and vandyke, and it is revived from time to time as a dress decoration. This stitch, like embroidery buttonhole, is worked without the extra knot, or twist, used in making a buttonhole for garments. It is also found worked by machine as a variation of chain stitch, when one pull of a broken thread may undo several stitches. Figs 145, 197, 201, 278 (Y–Z). See *Buttonhole stitch*.

BOBBIN, PILLOW or BONE LACE

Terms which refer to the bobbins made of bone in bobbin lace and to the pillow on which it is made. Bobbin lace is mounted sometimes on a hand-made but usually on a machine-made net as in Honiton, Duchesse or Flanders lace. A bobbin is another term for a reel, spool or cop on which to wind thread for sewing, embroidery or weaving. Figs 212–13, 245.

BODKIN

A large needle with a long eye and a

blunt point. The shaft may be flat or round and if round sometimes has a knob to prevent the bodkin piercing the cloth as it threads a tape or ribbon through a fold or casing of material, or when slotted through eyelets of lace or embroidered trimming. Securing clothes with tie tapes was the usual method until hooks and eyes, elastic and, later, zip fasteners appeared. Bodkins are a particularly English tool, first mentioned in 1368. They served as stilettos before the appearance of the continental tool. There are at least four references to bodkins in Shakespeare. Figs 23, 316.

BONNETS

In the past, white bonnets tended to accentuate femininity, from the simple frill of the mob cap encircling the face, to the poke bonnet trimmed with ruching and lined with rows of frills in lace and embroidery. The elegant, casual swathe of a Limerick net embroidered stole was also considered a fascinator.

In the nineteenth century it was thought correct for widows to wear bonnets or caps at home and indoors, as well as when travelling or visiting, and these developed into flattering mixtures of lace and embroidery which were often finished with lappets falling either side of the face.

Bonnets for presentation to, or for the christening of, a baby are affectionate showpieces of embroidery and tokens of love and esteem, illustrating some of the finest white work embroidery. Ayrshire, hollie point and Dresden crowns or circles for the backs of bonnets for infants, and worked in the most breathtaking way, are probably the most renowned, though there are examples of quilting, net, lace, broderie anglaise, satin and punch stitches all having exquisite workmanship. In the twentieth century bonnets were out of favour with the medical profession as being restrictive to growth.

Bonnets worn by adults and children may be seen in paintings and photographs which show the charm, or eccentricity, of past fashions. Figs 27, 28.

Other forms of headgear were worn for practical purposes, such as cleanliness and warmth; for example, quilted linen caps covered the heads of

24 Bonnet with Ayrshire fillings at the crown, satin and punch stitches, and front band trimmed with Bucks lace. (Embroiderers' Guild).

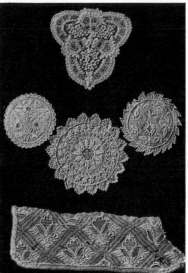

25 A sample of prepared Ayrshire bonnet crowns, for making up by the customer. Note variety of scalloped edges. (Embroiderers' Guild).

26 Bonnet crown with coarser fillings. (Embroiderers' Guild).

men and women when wigs were removed, and also informally at home.

Many men and women wore night caps, as an asset for warmth before the days of centrally heated homes.

Sun bonnets were worn as a protection from the sun for women working in the fields, as milkmaids, or at haymaking in the eighteenth and nineteenth centuries. A deep frill at the front and across the back protected the face and the back of the neck. The bonnets, of lightweight

27 *Bonnet showing satin stitch and hemstitching in borders, with fine wrapped threads.* (Constance Howard).

28 *Bonnet from fig. 27, showing sprigged motif at centre back. Satin stitch circles and dots, with punch stitch.*

linen or cotton, and ruched or gathered in rows around a crown at the back, were also worn by country children generally for school. Copies of these sun bonnets were made in the first part of the twentieth century and were worn by children when playing on the beach by the sea. Fig. 29.

In the first quarter of the twentieth century boudoir caps were worn by women to keep the fashionably short-cut and carefully waved hair in place. Boudoir caps were often made in bands or rows of elaborate mixtures using satin ribbon, net, embroidery and lace faggoted together, all light-weight and all trimmed with frills, flowers and ribbon rosettes. The caps were usually made in a straight strip and gathered at the top, and tied under the chin with a ribbon bow.

The religious influence of previous centuries favoured head coverings, and especially for women. The styles reflect the fashion and spirit of the times, such as the heart-shaped cap formed by a dipping peak at centre front and edged with pearls, so often associated with Mary Queen of Scots, or the very plain white linen bonnets of the Puritans, both contrasting with

29 *Sun bonnet with ruching and frills. In traditional style but probably c. 1920.* (Margaret Hall).

30 Cotton cap worked in rows of running stitch to form a pattern on double material. The cap is cut on the bias for ease in fitting, and given a folded edge as a finish. Nigerian. (Eirian Short).

31 A cap worked with borders of satin stitch triangles. (Constance Howard).

the elaborate flamboyance of the Restoration period.

Another example of a religious influence is the white cap worn by men of the Muslim faith, which ranges over a wide geographical area. Many of the caps are beautifully decorated with a hard-wearing and practical type of embroidery, such as run stitching to form patterns. This helps, with the shaping, to fit the cap to the head, as the thread is more closely drawn up towards the crown. The material is usually a firm cotton, often used double and folded on the bias grain (indicated by the diagonal seams), which makes a simple but ingenious method of fitting. The caps are sometimes finished with a tassel at the top, or with a flat crown. Other techniques are used to make the caps, such as counted satin and punch stitches. Figs 30, 31.

Many bonnets and headdresses complete a national or regional costume, and a well known example is

the tall and imposing headdress of Breton women. It is made of stiffened cotton and has streamers trimmed with torchon lace to flutter in the breeze. Dutch bonnets, by contrast, are very simple, but have appealing upturned sides.

Headscarves are a peasant head covering from Norway to the Mediterranean. Decoration ranges from embroidery in neat counted patterns from Scandinavia to the rich drawn thread work borders of Italy, France, Spain and Cyprus, or sometimes simply trimmed with the local lace or needlework edging, such as Antwerp or Armenian edge. Fig. 2.

BOOK MUSLIN

Book muslin, a stiffened cotton, was originally an early Swiss production before the English cotton trade. It was used for working in a frame in the seventeenth century to support or back embroidery, such as punto in aria, during the working process. See *Fibres.*

BRAID

Braids and cords developed from the cut ends of threads of a woven cloth, which were plaited or twisted to give strength. Gradually the braids were made separately to strengthen the edges of other articles or garments,

32 Hand-sewn braids, on net with faggoting. (Constance Howard).

33 Detail of fig. 32, showing border with faggoting and interlaced braid.

and this activity is thought to be the basis from which bobbin lace developed.

A design tacked (basted) out on a garment or article of white material or net, and sewn over in white braids, is often used as decorative edging for a fastening (known as frogs), as well as for bold designs on dress. Figs 32, 33, 69, 74–6, 214.

BRETON LACE or BRITTANY LACE

Breton lace is a popular and coarse type of torchon lace made for the tourist trade in Brittany. It is also a floral design on net, in outline only, and in run stitch, but which is sometimes filled in with stem or satin stitch (allied to embroidery on net) and used for edgings. Similar work was carried out on the Isle of Wight in the nineteenth century. Fig. 332.

BRICK STITCH

A type of couched filling, usually

worked in metal thread, but may also be worked in laid threads of contrasting white texture to the tying-down stitches. The stitches are spaced alternately to form a pattern of bricks over close rows of couching for a filling. Fig. 201 (H).

BRIDAL LACE

An early Italian lace like reticella or drawn thread, frequently with the mottoes and coats of arms of families being united by marriage, and used at festive occasions. The intricate work is indicative of the time spent by women at needlework, and of their high status and condition, and also of a competitive spirit amongst rich families. Also known as carnival lace, similar to the letters in fig. 217 and the edging in 219.

BRIDE

See *Bar*

BRODER and BRODERIE

French terms for 'to embroider' and 'embroidery'.

BRODERIE ANGLAISE

Identification

Broderie anglaise is at first glance composed entirely of eyelets, either circular, rounded, square or oval, and blocked geometrically in varying sizes or graded to indicate a spike of flowers. Ladder work, introduced later, is also typical. Fig. 78.

Satin stitch and stem stitch are added to the design, and a buttonholed edge to the border or frill in the form of scallops or vandyke points. A fascinating aspect of the study and collection of broderie anglaise is in discovering examples made by hand and machine. Fig. 35.

The machine work imitated hand work so closely in all aspects, such as the oversewing round eyelets, satin stitch, fern stitch and in a type of buttonhole, that the only clue is to turn to the back of the work to see how the threads pass from one part of the design to another. In machine work it is always at the same point with unremitting regularity, but in hand embroidery this regularity is not achieved, even with regularly cut lengths of thread. In hand work the

34   Sampler of broderie anglaise. Note decorative edges, and ladder work at centre. 13 cm (5 in.) square.

35   Detail of satin stitch and eyelets, added to a buttonhole edge. Note padding under buttonhole stitch. (Constance Howard).

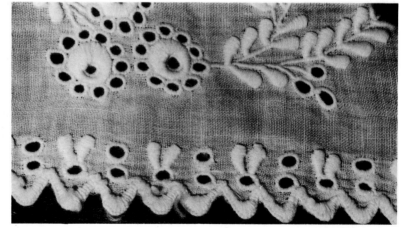

thread may also be secured invisibly into the back of the embroidery already completed. Fig. 36.

A reminder to note is that cut work forms the design, while, conversely, in cut work the background is cut away and the solid areas form the design. See also figs 37–43.

History

Broderie anglaise rivalled Ayrshire embroidery in popularity. It is worked on a heavier cotton than the softly falling fine cotton and muslin, which may be considered limp. Eye-lets took over from the needlework fillings and though some satin stitch remained this eventually decreased.

The design became repetitive and is seen mainly as borders for dress deco-ration. The repetitive quality is ideal for exploitation by embroidery machines, which became extremely efficient and productive from 1870 onwards. At this time fashion changed to bustles, and though a glimpse of white embroidery on underwear was still seen, the embroi-dered borders of enormously full

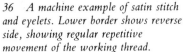

36 A machine example of satin stitch and eyelets. Lower border shows reverse side, showing regular repetitive movement of the working thread.

known, is often worked on a light-weight cotton and sometimes in a pale blue embroidery thread.

Design

Eyelets, which are the distinctive feature of the designs, are composed into scalloped borders in circular, oval and crescent shapes, and ordered into a floral type of design. Trailing lines of graded eyelets are typical. All echo scalloped and buttonholed edges. Ladder work, narrow ribbon-like open shapes, forms part of the designs, and is held in place with whipped or wrapped or overcast bars, which appear as the rungs of a ladder. Figs 37–41.

Ground

Firm lightweight cotton, produced from the immense English cotton trade of Manchester and Lancashire. Linen was also used, but is not typical.

Technique

Tools – stiletto, pointed scissors.

Framing-up – worked successfully in the hand, possibly framed-up for pro-

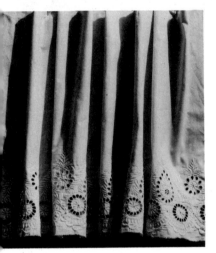

skirts and petticoats were not.

Broderie anglaise in fashion today is usually machine-made and has the same enduring appeal as hand work especially for wedding dresses and decorative women's and children's clothing, and also for table and bed linen.

Although there are many examples of eyelet embroidery from Switzerland similar to broderie anglaise, the greatest quantity was produced in England and Scotland both by hand and machine, and so became known as broderie anglaise.

Broderie anglaise or eyelet embroidery was one of the industries set up by English women to give employment and create business in Madeira, where the local wine industry had failed. Madeira work, as this important embroidery export became

37 Flounce of broderie anglaise before edge is cut, hand-worked by the yard.

38 Detail of fig. 37.

39 Detail of fig. 37, showing reverse side.

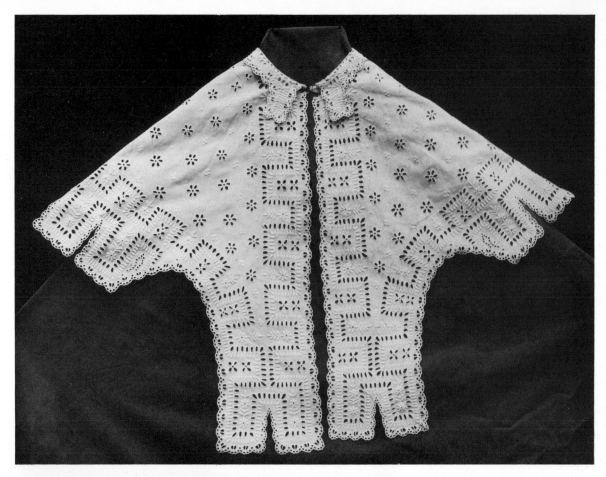

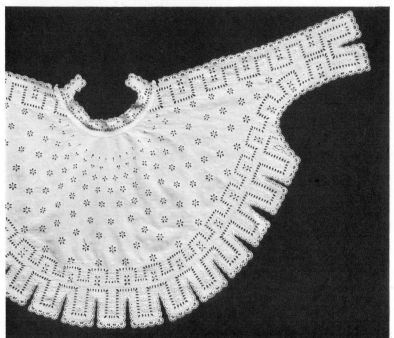

40 *Pelisse for a child, showing gradation of satin stitch groups from the neck to horizontal at hem. The left-hand side has been pressed; note difference in length, approximately 40 cm (16 in.), at centre front. 1860. (Clarice Blakey).*

fessional purposes, so that more than one worker may sit at a piece.

Transfer of design – with light blue paint line. Some practice is advised to get the paint dry so that it does not run into the material, but wet enough to make a continuous line. Carved rollers may be used. Fig. 42.

Needles – crewel 8, approximately.

Threads – stranded cotton, coton à broder, or similar.

Join on/off – a run stitch on the paint line.

Process – stitch. Satin stitch, overcast.

41 *Detail of pelisse in fig. 40. Note well-thought-out design from neck to hem. The small oval eyelets develop through two petals to four, five and six, and are graded in size. Satin stitch petals at the crenellated hem echo the eyelets.*

42 *A roller for marking out scalloped edges, with alternative barrels. The small roll of material held and controlled the flow of blue paint, further supplies of paint being added to the roll as required. (Tunbridge Wells Centre).*

Small eyelets

Back stitch on outline – do not cut thread. Pierce centre with stiletto. Continue with the same thread to oversew round hole covering back stitching. Figs 34, 35.

Large eyelet hole

Take running stitches round outline – do not cut thread. Cut centre vertically and horizontally. Fold under one quarter of material and continue with same thread to oversew on fold over running stitches. Fold under subsequent quarter. Turn to reverse side and trim turnings.

Petal shape

Run stitch round outline, leave thread hanging. Cut centre vertically and horizontally. Fold under one quarter of material. Oversew on fold over running stitches. Continue all round shape, taking extra long stitch to accentuate point. Turn to reverse side and trim turned back pieces.

Leaf shape

Take running stitches round outline. Work several more rows of running stitch round curved end. Cut and fold back as for petal shape. Take oversewing stitches over all rows of running stitches, starting at widest point and graduating stitches towards point, taking extra long stitch at point. Trim reverse side.

Ladder work
Overcast bars

Take running stitches down the right-hand side until the position of the first bar is reached. Pick up small stitch on left side, then on right-hand side, then back to the left side, forming three long threads on line of bar. Oversew over these strands (do not catch material) back to the right-hand side. Take running stitches to next bar and repeat. Continue until all bars are worked and running stitch on outline is complete. Cut vertically at centre and diagonally into each corner. Fig. 278. Fold back the edges under run-

43 *Chemisette in broderie anglaise, embroidered by hand with machine-made casing for a ribbon at the waist. 1860.*

ning stitches. Oversew all round, taking a double stitch each side of every bar (for strength) and a longer stitch into corners or points. Neaten back of work. Fig. 34.

Stems or lines

Overcast stitch over three strands of thread, or stem stitch. Fig. 43.

BRODERIE DE NANCY

Similar to Dresden point, which is a form of fine pulled stitch work, sometimes with a mixture of cut and drawn out threads for a mesh, but not hemstitched.

BULLION KNOT

Bullion knot is a good stitch to use in

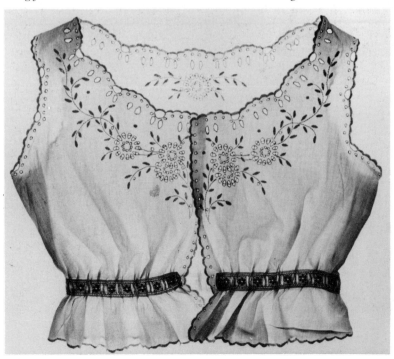

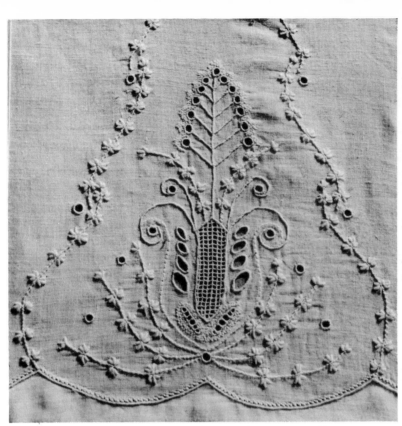

44 *Detail of embroidery showing bullion knots as flower buds.*
18 × 15 cm (7 × 6 in.). (Nora Jones).
See also 234, 235, 350.

white work for texture, as it is raised and firmly made. In some respects it is similar to a french knot, but longer, and the working thread has a greater number of twists round the needle. It resembles the coiled shape of gold bullion or purl. Use a small 8 crewel needle and one or two threads. Practise the stitch on a larger scale for best results. Figs. 44, 45, 103, 234, 236, 344. See *Spines.*

BUTTONHOLE STITCH

One of the most important stitches in white work, buttonhole stitch is constantly recurring and is extensively used for edges, either plain or scalloped; for fillings in Ayrshire work and reticella; for bars for the many forms of cut work; and for all forms

45 *Detail of a head, with features moulded by bullion knots in white and some colours. 1985. Worked by Mary Cozens-Walker.*

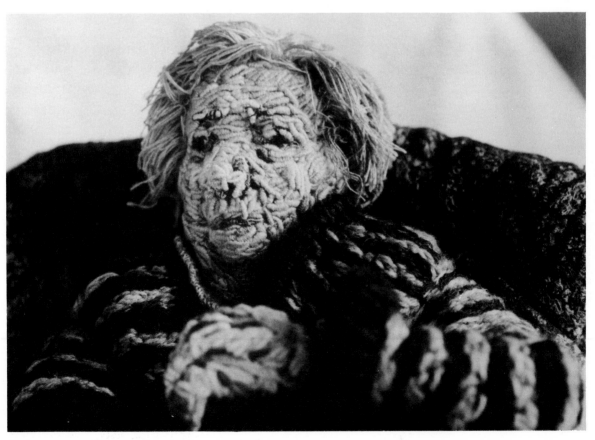

of needle-made lace. The variety of the stitch is almost unending, and many affectionate or geographical names have been given to simple arrangements, such as feston or Sorrento point for triangles and blocks. Loop stitch is also a designation. Frontispiece, figs 189, 193, 194, 197 (F), 201 (B), 237, 278 (Y–Z).

Fillings

When used as a solid filling the stitch is seen in Venetian laces at its heaviest in gros point, and its lightest in pointe de neige. Many open patterns are also worked, and all named in vast variety.

Grounds

Buttonhole stitch worked as an open filling also forms grounds of a net, or réseau, with a mesh formed of hexagons (see *Lace*). (*Note*: in the twentieth century buttonhole fillings in decorative patterns from lace lingered on as embroidered fillings worked into solid linen backgrounds, but are not now generally worked. Great care is needed for the stitches to fit easily into the ground without being squeezed together or too widely spaced.)

Bars

An important use for buttonhole; see *Bar*, *Cut work*.

Edges

Buttonhole stitch may be used to finish the edge of a garment or article instead of a plain hem, and the decoration may take the form of scallops, vandyke points, or a crenellated edge. It is also used as gussets in garments, for example shirt tails. Figs. 2, 35, 37, 197.

Buttonholes

In dressmaking or needlework, a worked or buttonhole-stitched buttonhole is distinct from a bound or machine-made buttonhole, and also from a tailor's buttonhole, where the stitch has an extra twist for strength on heavier garments.

Ornamental buttonholes – a recurring novelty, with a design of embroidery camouflaging the hole. The design is often in rococo style.

False buttonhole – a decoration using bullion knots or cord to outline a buttonhole shape and with a button sewn on one end.

Tailor's buttonhole – there are two

46 Example of stump work, showing small figures. 1985. Worked by Barbara Hirst.

uses for this stitch, one for buttonholes and the other for inserting the thumb into gloves in glovemaking, as, when several rows are worked, it gives more elasticity.

Stump work

A padded buttonhole technique which is of great interest today and usually worked in colour, but is suitable for white work as the stitchery shows to advantage.

1 Frame up as for gold work, i.e. a firm backing tightly stretched in a frame, so that the padding is raised on the top surface and the back is flat.
2 Mark out the area to be worked on the backing and pad as for gold work, with layers of felt and a smooth top surface.
3 Work buttonhole filling over the padding and avoid stitching into the padded surface. Fig. 46.

Separate free or individual pieces for application may be made by working without padding, but with a secure outline or cordonnet to work on. (*Note*: the skill is in making the direction of the stitches follow the form of the design, and in the division of the form into workable shapes and sizes.)

BUTTONS

Many embroiderers enjoy experimenting with button making today. In the past, material and threads of linen and silk were used to cover button moulds or form the button from a needle-made buttonhole wheel.

Buttons became a fashion but were not generally used until the eighteenth century, when they were made on a base of a twist of linen or coarse cotton material which was worked over with whipped bars of back stitch or buttonhole stitch and sometimes stiffened for strength. Buttons became decorative at this time, as garments were usually held together with ties of cords, tapes or decorative plaits, and fastened with pins or brooches. Figs. 47, 316.

47 A group of embroidered buttons. Each: 2 cm ($\frac{3}{4}$ in.) diameter. (Tunbridge Wells Centre).

48 *Examples of Dorset buttons. Those on the left-hand side are cartwheels, approximately 0.7 cm ($\frac{1}{5}$ in.) diameter. (Embroiderers' Guild).*

49 *Stages in making a Dorset type button. Top left: cover a plastic ring (or curtain ring) with spaced buttonhole stitch. Leave a very long thread (50 cm or 20 in.) at the start, and join loops by working the last stitch into the first. Top right: slicking. Turn loops of buttonhole into the centre. Ensure that the space of one thread is left between each stitch. Centre left: with the long thread, wrap over the ring, fitting the thread between each stitch. Lower left: when complete, secure top wrapped stitches with a coral stitch, knot and run in end. (It should be noted that the pin is a display property only.)*

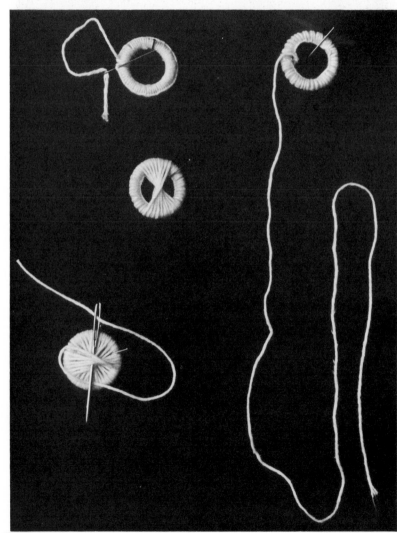

like a sequin or spangle, and this miniature disc had a hole in the centre. It was covered with a piece of linen and worked over with needle and thread, as a back stitch wheel on a buttonhole-stitched edge. Alternatively, a conical cloth foundation was entirely covered with buttonhole stitch in the form of a miniature cap. The process made buttons called High Tops which were worked for embroidered waistcoats, and chiefly as a decoration. The buttons were treasured possessions and a set lasted a lifetime.

About 1700 a button called the Knob was made, and it was a little flatter than a High Top, followed by a Bird's Eye, a smaller button used for children's clothes.

Button making became a cottage industry in Dorset and spread to surrounding towns and villages including Blandford. In 1793 four thousand women were employed in Shaftesbury and were paid 3/6d ($32\frac{1}{2}$ p) for a gross of top quality, and it was possible to make a gross a day. Women walked from their cottages to deliver their work to the various depots, often covering 12 miles each way.

Later, metal rings were used which did not rust, as they were made of a special alloy invented by Peter Case, a grandson of Abraham.

In 1851 an invention by Ashton of a button making machine was exhibited at the Great Exhibition, and from that date the Dorset button industry began to die.

Dorset buttons

In 1688 Abraham Case founded a button industry in Shaftesbury, Dorset, employing local men, women and children. He became very prosperous, eventually exporting large quantities to America.

The buttons were hand-made on a base of finely cut sheep's or ram's horn. The base was flat and shaped

In Shaftesbury 350 families were out of work, as there was no other employment, and the only alternative to starvation or begging and theft was a government passage, or deportation, to Canada or Australia. Figs. 48, 49.

High Tops

High Top buttons, like a few other techniques of the past, seem to defy present-day workmanship to make an exact copy. One reason may be the difference in thread and the type of spinning.

Terms in the making of a simple button are:

Casting – tie one end of the thread to the ring and cover the ring closely with buttonhole stitch, including the loose end of the knot for a few stitches. Ensure the ring does not show through.

Slicking – turn the looped edge of the buttonhole inwards, so that the outer edge of the ring is smooth.

Laying – continue with the same thread, and make spokes by passing between the buttonhole on the ring. Fasten at the centre with a knot stitch such as coral stitch, run in end and knot.

Rounding – from the centre work a back stitch wheel, that is, back over one spoke, forward under two, and repeat.

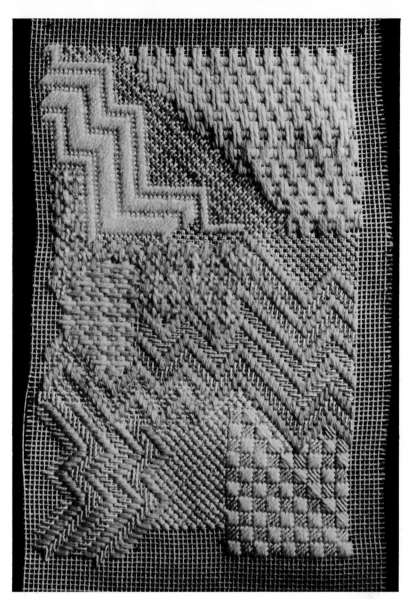

CALIFORNIAN EMBROIDERY

A type of early American Indian embroidery in natural or bleached colour, using fine cords cut from whale skin in place of thread.

CAMBRIC

Originally a fine linen material. Later of cotton in similar weight, but cheaper. See *Fibres*.

CANVAS

Canvas stitches are well displayed when worked in white threads, as the shadows cast by the stitches show up the form. Heavy thick threads such as wool contrast well with finer stitches in silk.

Cross stitch, tent, leviathan, double cross, gobelin or satin stitch are all simple stitches with a number of alternatives, as is tufting, also in the form of Turkey knot stitch or Surrey stitch. Figs. 50, 201 (A), 348.

CAPS

See *Bonnets*.

CARRICKMACROSS

Carrickmacross embroidery evolved

50 Canvas work showing a variety of stitches and threads for textures in white; also tufting (see also figs. 201 (A) and 348). 20 × 14 cm (8 × 5½ in.). Worked by Clarice Blakey.

in the early 1800s and with the introduction of machine net it became popular during the 1850s as one of the many types of needlework, embroidery, lace, knitting and crochet encouraged in Ireland by Englishwomen and nuns to provide training and employment after the failure of the potato crop of 1846. The products, made in schools, convents and workrooms, were purchased in England and abroad to support this deserving cause and to decorate the home as well as

51 *Carrickmacross bertha collar with appliqué in muslin on net and counted patterns worked on the net. The collar is in two layers, the top one having a vandyke edge. 200 × 20 cm (78½ × 7⅘ in.).*

dresses, parasols and other fashionable extravagances. Figs. 51, 52, 73, 74–6, 335.

Carrickmacross stoles and collars are typical examples of this embroidery and include large bertha styles and also lappets. This work is difficult to launder and press, but may be pinned out as for lace. Fig. 164.

Process

An intricate lace-like design of flowers is traced out on muslin. The muslin is then tacked to an equal-sized piece of net, using upright tacking, making the two materials as one.

Couching covers the outlines of the design. In some instances the design is first run stitched on the outline for extra strength.

When the couching is complete the muslin of the background is cut away close to the couched edge of the design and taking great care to avoid cutting the net background. A pair of scissors with a guard or knob and fine sharp blades is useful for this process.

Alternative method

1 Couch over the lines of the design without working through the paper, which is previously tacked under muslin.
2 As the work proceeds make bars where required to connect the open areas of the design. The bars may be further decorated with small loops or picots.
3 An important part of design is to consider and incorporate bars into the design, as they hold the work together. If picots are used they should face one way or form an ordered arrangement throughout the work.

52 Detail of collar in fig. 51, showing looped picots on the outer edge and buttonhole picots on bars in the openwork. The outer edge of the muslin is couched with a fine cord. Note the eyelets worked on net in fine buttonhole.

4 When the couching is completed, remove paper backing. Cut away the surplus background close to the couching to leave the design as a continuous piece of muslin. (*Note*: a frame may be used for large pieces of work.) See *Irish embroidery, Limerick lace.*

CASTELGUIDI

An obscure type of heavy linen embroidery, including raised stitchery such as raised stem stitch and padded buttonhole filling as in stump work.

CHAIN STITCH

Chain stitch is familiar in hand embroidery, and shows an interesting fall of light on curved lines and shaped filling.

Every stitch is the same size and tension, with the reverse forming a back stitch, to give a close, neat raised appearance for the definition of symbols and letters.

It is a strong stitch and so washes well, and as it is also reversible it is suitable for church linen as well as for dress and household decoration. Frontispiece, figs 53, 190, 197, 201 (G).

53 Crosses suitable for fair linen. Top left: machine satin stitch cross with chain stitch by hand. Lower right: satin stitched cross embroidered by hand with machine whipped stitch. (Nora Jones).

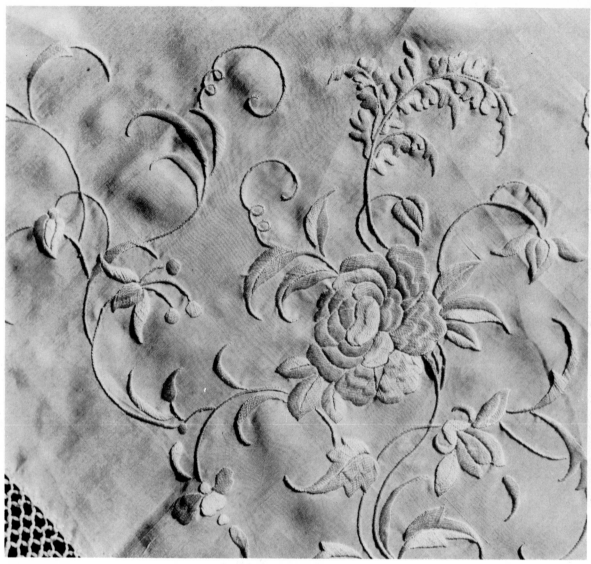

There are many types of chain stitch, including rope stitch and detached chain, as well as threading, interlacing and whipping the basic form.

The appearance is similar to tambour work and to the work produced by the Cornely chain stitch machine; both types run freely when undone, whilst hand chain stitch does not. See *Hedebo, Tambour work.*

CHARITY BAZAARS

Charity and church bazaars were the highlight of social life in many homes during the late nineteenth and early twentieth centuries. Work was prepared for months to sell in a deserving cause. Many pieces and fragments of perfectly good white embroidery and lace were cut up and sewn together to

54 Detail of satin stitch in silk, showing voiding in leaves and buds. Note the changes in the fall of light, the tightly twisted thread, and the encroaching satin stitch of the centre flower raised by a padding of stem or chain stitch. The outer petals are worked first. Chinese, c. 1900.

make small saleable items such as pin cushions and sachets, which varied greatly in charm and success. Many other magnificent embroideries, fallen from fashionable favour, were cut up to be re-used in some way that was thought more suitable.

Boudoir caps made of rows of lace and ribbon gathered at the top for shape, and dickies (or modesty vests or false fronts), to sew into the very deep V-necked dresses of the 1920s, are often found at sales.

Charity work was also produced by the English and other European communities abroad, especially in the East, and here the styles were even more mixed by the skilled work of local embroiderers and establishments such as convents and schools.

CHENILLE

A tufted thread used in embroidery and also in an eighteenth-century coarse French lace with fine chenille outline. Chenille is the name of a needle originally used for this work. It has a large eye to take the tufted thread without crushing it, and a sharp point to pierce and separate, without splitting or damaging, the threads of the silk background in order to receive the thick shaft of the needle. The thick shaft makes a suffi-

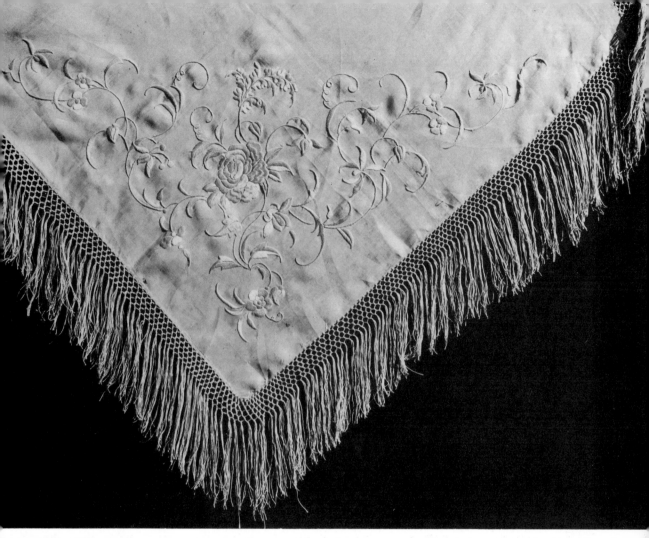

55 Fringed shawl with satin stitch embroidery, showing complete design. 50 cm (19½ in.) across; fringe 12 cm (4¾ in.).

ciently large hole for the chenille thread to be drawn through the background without damage. Fig. 23.

CHIKAN

The term refers to a district of India where white cotton embroidery was carried out, showing a strong influence of Ayrshire embroidery, which was introduced by Europeans. The difference is quite noticeable when the two styles of embroidery are compared, for the Chikan openwork is nearly always cut out as triangles and filled very lightly with a few single threads, worked as wheels, or crossed bars which are twisted or woven together at the centre. The

supporting embroidery of stem stitch and satin stitch is also sketched in compared with the detail of Ayrshire. It was worked mainly for export and is an interesting item for collection as it shows the spread of, and the great demand for, white work.

CHINESE EMBROIDERY

As mentioned in the entry on appliqué, there is a great export industry in embroidery from China to the West which includes silk blouses with satin stitch in floral designs.

A typical style of the late nineteenth century and early twentieth century is the embroidery from the Canton district in white silk thread on a ground of white silk with flowing floral designs, which are worked in satin stitch, including encroaching and voided, and with both sides alike. The sheen of the silk is displayed beautifully as shawls or presentation handkerchiefs, and both are heavily

fringed in silk. In the first half of the twentieth century Chinese embroidery in white cotton thread interpreted large designs in western techniques for export and incorporated the symbolic dragon. Later, the more practical embroidery of appliqué and hemstitching decorated table linen, blouses and handkerchiefs. Figs 54, 55, 272, 332.

CHRISTENING ROBES

The christening ceremony stimulates and inspires embroiderers to produce a showpiece to the best of their ability to match the joyful occasion of family display. The most prestigious christening robes are those decorated with Ayrshire embroidery.

A typical example of an Ayrshire robe has a triangular centre front panel to the bodice, charming layered sleeves and a long skirt with a design rising from the hem of a centre front panel, which is characteristically

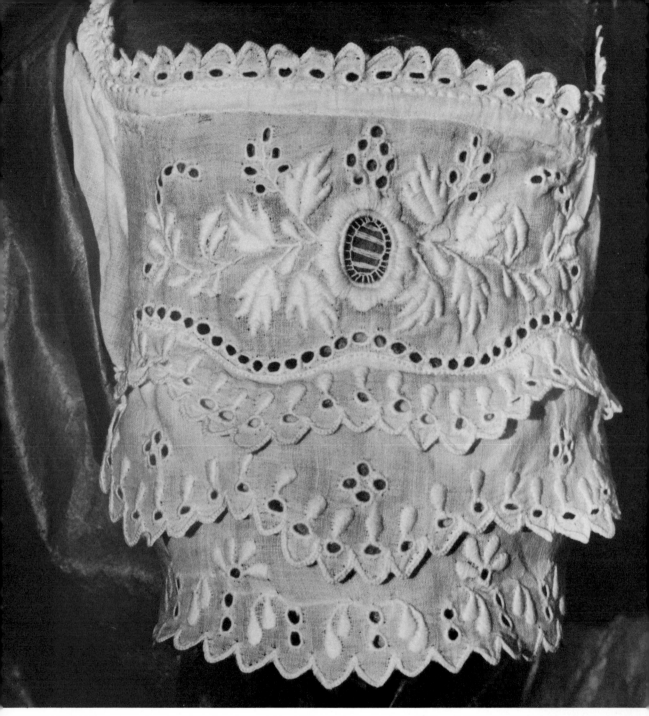

56 *Layered sleeve of a late Ayrshire christening robe. The pieces for the robe were embroidered as a set and then sold to be made up by the customer, as the machine stitching indicates. Note design of lower frill, well organized from the centre, and the beading of french knots at neckline.* (Constance Howard).

edged with a frill. All have appropriate embroidered motifs which relate to the main design of the centre embroidered panel, and details of the design are worth a study. The cotton material of the later robes is stronger and more solid than the early muslin examples. Many robes are very elaborate, commanding great admiration, but occasionally overpower the infant.

In most robes the point of the bodice finishes at the gathers of the waistline, which are covered by a casing decorated with French knots. Later examples affected an embroidered point which falls over the waistline for a boy, and has a slot in the waist seam for the point to be tucked into, for a girl. Moreover some later examples were assembled at home by purchasing the sections with the embroidery already completed. The workmanship of the making up in these garments is variable and does not always live up to the embroidery,

which is highly professional and
exact, but with most of the fillings in
the same pattern, resulting in less
interest.

Other examples include a Georgian
royal robe of white satin, which
makes the rich material seem symbolic of the official destiny of a royal

59 *Christening robe showing machine-embroidered frilling.*

baby. The robe has a pattern of scrolling and scalloped lines, using a delicate fly braid which is sewn down on the material before making up. It was a popular process of the eighteenth century and one which is often seen on constume.

Some peculiar quilted garments suggest a harness in store for the vulnerable occupant, while the goss-amer silk net of Honiton lace has a fragility not always in keeping with a loudly protesting baby.

Many, many robes exist, carrying every type of embroidery, but they are frequently over-decorated with too large a scale of work, using quantities of broderie anglaise, eyelet and drawn thread borders, insets of lace, or made entirely of lace, weighed down with frills, or made up of parts of adult clothes such as skirts.

A post-First World War example (fig. 59), somewhat modest in decoration, with simple restrained machine-embroidered insertions, has a charm associated with the serious side of the proceedings and with the materials freely and inexpensively available which are assembled together as a *tour de force* of light texture, neatness, accuracy and skill, suitable to the times of frugality. Figs 59–62.

The material has the very slight shine of a lightweight mercerized cotton and the bodice of the yoke has fourteen seams joining insertions of hand-tucking and embroidery, with strips of minute open insertion or

60 *Detail of bodice showing fourteen seams, decoratively made.*

beading 1 mm ($\frac{1}{25}$ in.) wide. Bordered with plain cotton edges for use as a tiny rolled or whipped seam, the two pieces of material for the seam are rolled together and lightly overcast to make a minuscule yet strong neatened seam. The sleeve is attached to one edge of the beading, and the yoke to the other, by oversewing to make a decorative and virtually invisible seam.

The gathers of the skirt show the stroking method of joining it to the bodice, and the finishing with the beading shows true craftsmanship. Nowadays most raw edges of the skirt are set into a double yoke with at least five thicknesses of material at the seams. The frills at the hem show how tucks and embroidery hold out the fullness.

Many of the historic and early robes are clumsily put together with thick seams and bulky gathering at the yoke or waist, and are frequently concocted from other garments, which detracts from their value both monetarily and artistically, but shows a sense of economy and the love and devotion attached to the ceremony and occasion.

The traditional sources are an inspiration for the present-day robes of synthetic material and soft machine embroidery, making them easily washable, fresh, light, strong and inexpensive. Fig. 63.

CHURCH EMBROIDERY

White is the colour of purity and sacrifice and is used for white linen, or 'fair linen', such as altar cloths which cover the top of the altar and hang down the sides. The cloth is bordered with embroidery, but the top surface is not embroidered and should be smooth so that the chalice and other vessels may rest steadily.

Fair linen also includes palls, corporals and purificators used to cover and clean the communion cup. White vestments made in linen and sometimes cotton include albs, cottas and rochets.

Almost any white work technique may be used to decorate fair linen, including drawn thread work, satin stitch and line stitches.

Designs are usually symbolic and include monograms such as IHS, standing for the name of Jesus, and PAX, peace.

White is also the liturgical colour for vestments used at church festivals such as Easter, Christmas and weddings. A rich silk is usually used and decorated with gold embroidery. A

62 Wrong side of bodice in fig. 60, showing neatening.

63 Detail of design for christening robe by Carol Hutchinson, 1985.

64 A cross for fair linen in blocks of satin stitch, worked by Nora Jones.

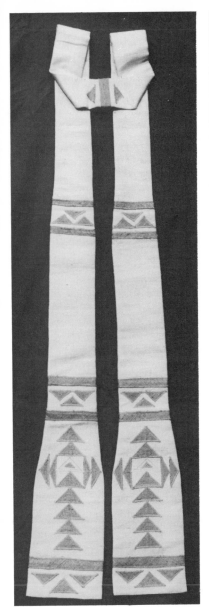

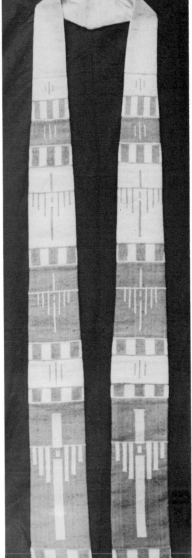

67   Detail of altar cloth with a variety of machine embroidery techniques, worked by Christine Hall.

68   Cut work fillings from the cloth in fig. 67.

65   A stole in white silk with gold silk appliqué, showing machine satin stitch edges. Worked by Barbara Dawson.

66   A stole in appliqué and machine satin stitch, worked by Barbara Dawson.

complete set of vestments includes a cope, mitre, chasuble, stole, burse, veil, dalmatic, tunicle and altar frontal.

A nineteenth-century square net embroidery was known as 'church lace', as so much was used to decorate vestments. Figs 19, 53, 64–8.

CLOTH STITCH

A darning stitch on net where the horizontal threads interweave with the vertical threads, similar to the main stitch in bobbin lace. Fig. 238. See also *Darning, Net*.

CONSERVATION

See *Fibres*

CORAL STITCH

Coral stitch is a knotted stitch making a textured line similar to knotting a thread. For white work it is also used to tie groups of threads together in drawn thread work, to secure the centre threads or spokes of a wheel or corner medallion. Figs 99, 201 (D).

CORD

A cord usually consists of several threads twisted together to form a raised and rounded outline for a decorative finish. The twisted threads may be wrapped or buttonholed over. Other methods of cord making include knotting and plaiting and machine methods.

A practical use for cords was as drawstrings for clothing in the past and at present for decorative blouses.

Cord has many possibilities for experiment in embroidery, as well as being used in the normal way for outlines and as the sole method of

70 *Detail of pelisse in fig. 69.*

69 A pelisse of lightweight cotton twill decorated with a continuous scrolling design carried out in soutache braid, or flat cord, is edged with a cotton fringe, as is the small collar. The point at centre back of the hem is echoed at the back of the collar. 1840–60. (Western Australian Museum).

into which buttonhole fillings are worked for lace and hollie point. Figs 286, 287.

CORONET

Embroidered coronets are a fascinating find on white linen, as they are an indication of the owner, and are sometimes accompanied by a family heraldic device. Coronets are found all over Europe and are very difficult to identify exactly. Fig. 72.

A coronet has less status than a crown and was first used by Edward III. Nowadays used on state occasions,

- the coronet of a Duke bears eight strawberry leaves;
- the coronet of a Marquis bears four strawberry leaves and four pearls on short points;
- the coronet of an Earl bears eight high points, each with a pearl alternating with eight strawberry leaves;
- the coronet of a Viscount bears sixteen pearls on the rim of the coronet.

COUCHING

To 'couch' is an old term meaning to lie down or rest. Couching is a basic stitch used for decoration and construction and, in working it, the thread rests or is laid on the outline on the background. It is sewn in place with a separate thread known as the couching thread, and this is usually

71 A first vest, with a drawn thread edge to the casing for a ribbon or cord, to join the garment at the neck edge. Note the button. (Western Australian Museum).

72 Detail of an embroidered coronet for an earl, with eight points and eight strawberry leaves. Tacks rather than pins should be used for display. 2.3 cm ($\frac{9}{10}$ in.) high; 2.5–3.5 cm (1–1$\frac{1}{3}$ in.) wide.

decoration, as in braids. Figs 52, 69–71, 162, 296, 316.

Cord stitch and cording are similar to trailing or closely overcast couching, where the couching stitches are so

close that they form a smooth satin-like raised line, and should be worked in a frame for best results.

Cordonnet is an outline used in lace and consists of a laid thread couched in place, which may also be buttonholed over to give a raised edge as in Alençon. It is an outline of a design

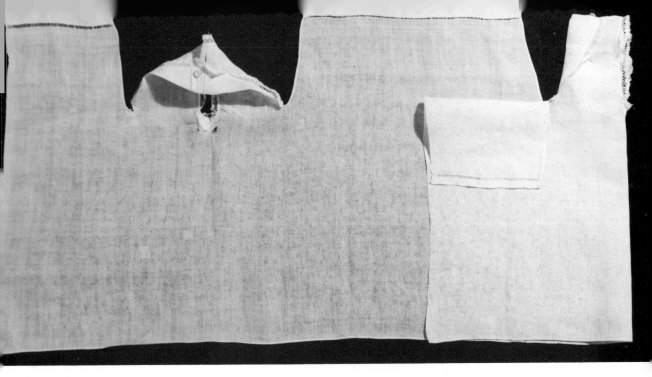

73 Two crochet collars with raised petals at the flower centres. (Hatfield House Textile Conservation Rooms).

much finer than the laid or couched thread. The process is called couching.

This method is used for attaching cordonnet to outline lace, and in Carrickmacross embroidery to edge the applied muslin, so forming part of the construction. Couching is also the base for punto in aria and other lace, as it outlines the design on a firm ground.

Couching in embroidery has almost unlimited variations for decorative outlines and fillings, as the couching-down stitches may be shaped diagonally to form a cross or triangle, or grouped in a pattern, and may also be of a contrasting texture, such as silk on cotton or wool. Figs 52, 121, 201 (H), 277, 284, 335.

CRENELLE

A strip of material with one edge battlemented or of square-shaped scallops, used for a decorative border or trimming, often in place of a frill.

Examples are mainly early nineteenth century, when white was fashionable during the Regency. Figs 41, 304.

CREVA DRAWN WORK

An obscure embroidery made in Brazil as a nineteenth-century copy

48

of Italian drawn thread work or cut work, and introduced by nuns and mission workers; it is an example of the spread of white work.

CROCHET

Crochet is worked with a hook, similar to a tambour hook, and in designs that imitate torchon lace, and filet in embroidery, with which crochet is sometimes confused. It also takes the names of embroideries to describe the patterns, such as Carrickmacross, where the crochet showed a flower design with separate petals. It reached a very high standard and was used for insertions for blouses and chemises; it is much admired today.

Enormous quantities of crochet were produced all over Europe in the late nineteenth and early twentieth centuries, as it was easily portable for working in the home and on holiday, as well as professionally. Dress, bed

and table linen and church vestments were decorated with huge borders. Sometimes referred to as needlework. Figs 73, 107, 215–16, 243. See *Irish embroidery*.

CROWNS

A crown is used in decorating ceremonial linen or other articles belonging to or commemorating a king or queen, such as the muslin apron for a royal christening. A 'crown' is also a decorative type of picot to the cordonnet in needle-made lace. Figs 24–6, 204. See *Bonnets, Coronet, Picot*.

CUCUMBER BRAID or TAPE

An example of a plaiting or a shaped machine-made braid or tape of the nineteenth century, used in tape lace. This type of patterned braid or tape may be found in jumble sales and old work boxes. Figs 74, 76.

74 *Sampler showing the use of cucumber braid. Note the net tacked over the design, which is drawn out in ink on paper. On the right is a card of the braid. (Embroiderers' Guild).*

CUT WORK

Identification

The term often used to describe all white work embroidery with open areas, but it is a specific term for a type of embroidery which has the background cut out and the design in solid ground. It is in contrast to broderie anglaise, where the design is cut out of the background. Both types may require bars. Figs 20, 21, 77–88.

Cut work today includes five different types; four refer to designs of small cut-out ground shapes which are edged or reinforced with buttonhole stitch and are known as:

75 *Detail showing braid outlines to net counted patterns, and leaves composed of sections of the braid. Probably Irish work.*

76 *A sampler of the use of cucumber braid held together with bars, some with looped picots.*

77 *Part of a tea cloth in cut work showing the ground cut away to display the design and the use of plain bars. Compare with fig. 78. (Lise Mossery).*

78 *Design for a basket of flowers cut out as in broderie anglaise, with ladder work. (Lise Mossery).*

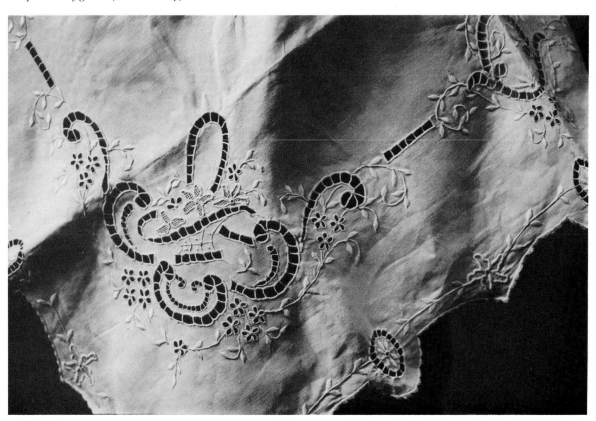

79 Elaborate openwork for a hand towel is shown both as the design in the basket and as a background to the handle and the flowers. Unexpectedly worked on huckaback, probably from the 1920s. (Clarice Blakey).

1 Simple cut work, small cut-out areas of background with no bars.
2 Renaissance cut work, where the cut-out shapes become larger and require the support of worked bars.
3 Richelieu cut work, similar to Renaissance, but the bars are decorated with picots and worked wheels. Guipure Richelieu or Richelieu guipure, impressive terms beloved by Victorian needlewomen, refer to large scale and coarse work, for furnishings.
4 Venetian or padded cut work, with a padding of threads under the buttonhole-stitched edge. It may also have padded satin stitch and larger open areas filled with lace stitches of buttonhole filling in the design. Genoese is also padded, using a cord, picots and sometimes eyelets, and some lace fillings in buttonhole stitch. Fig. 80.

The fifth type is known historically as:

5 Italian cut work, and refers to a form of drawn thread work developed in the seventeenth century (where only threads of the background are removed) and now known as reticella and punto in aria. Figs 102–6.

History

The first four types of cut work are a development of the scalloped buttonhole edges of Ayrshire and broderie anglaise, and also of the influence of John Ruskin's love of the past integrity of craftsmanship as opposed to the anonymous machine work. This led to a study of old embroidery and the term 'Richelieu' was adopted for work inspired by the Italian 'cut workes' of former centuries.

Cut work relates to the early work of open areas around the solid design, the difference being that the solid areas in early work are made of buttonhole fillings in geometric design, while in the nineteenth century the solid areas are of the background material in floral design. The effect of the workers' skill in keeping rows of buttonhole stitch evenly spaced in width and thickness is highly admired, although the hours spent at the work are rarely appreciated either

by students or collectors, as indeed is the case with most white work.

Cut work is used for church linen and in the home. It had a considerable vogue until 1940 as decoration on collars and cuffs, which were worn with dark-coloured frocks and dresses and considered very suitable for secretaries and clerks, as well as being part of the uniform of maids and waitresses. It may be noticed that, like many other forms of white embroidery, many of the heroines of films in the 1920s and 1930s wear this work as the fashion of the time.

Many commercial-style kits were produced for this work, either for transferring to personal materials or already prepared. Fig. 82.

80 A bodice and fashion garment of about 1920, probably for flattening the bosom, though a casing for boning may be seen. The shoulder straps are faggoted. (Maria Wittenveen).

81 Detail of fig. 80, showing cut work embroidery. The buttonhole filling at the hem and in the leaves is typical of the Genoese style of cut work, but is not professional work.

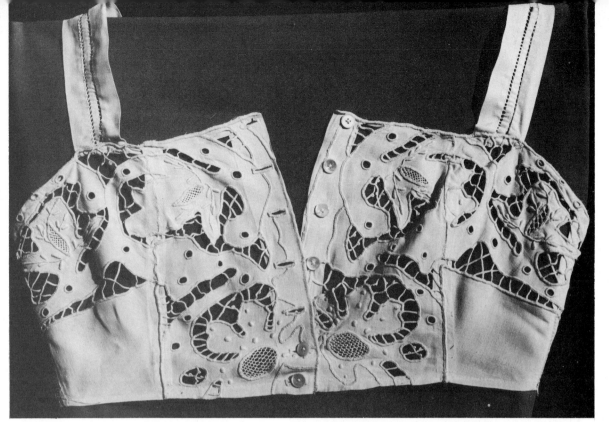

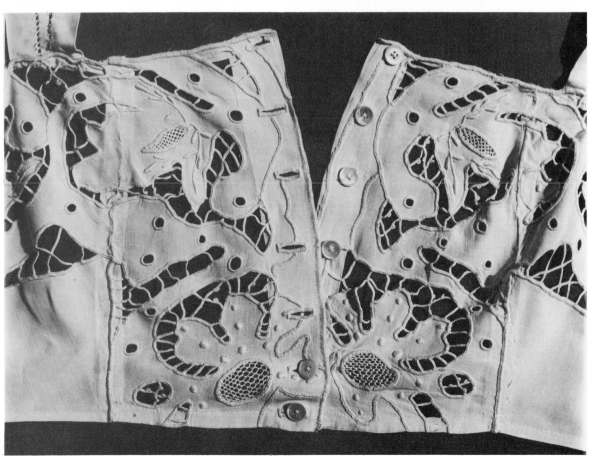

Within the image:
Given Away with the September 1938 Number of Go...

Use PERI-LUSTA Stranded (Boilf...

82 *Commercially prepared designs.*
Left: *design on linen.* Right: *a prepared transfer for ironing on to linen.* Below: *border for use as detached chain stitch (lazy daisy).*

Cut work is another area taken over by machine embroidery and is now produced extremely inexpensively. It bears little resemblance to the original details of the technique, although some characteristics of the earlier design are retained. It is sometimes known under the all-purpose term of guipure, and is worked on the Schiffli machine.

Design

Floral designs with leaves and arabesques are arranged in varying widths to give a hard-wearing, practical and decorative finish to white dress accessories, as well as to household linen.

The outer edge of the article is buttonholed in scallops and may have the additional decoration of picots.

As the cut-out areas of the design increase in size they are then held in place by bars, worked from one side of an open area to the other, and covered with buttonhole stitch. The bars often have picots added, and the

large open spaces are sometimes filled with open wheels or spiders.

The additional decoration of bars and picots, which derive from coarse early lace, give a bold richness to a simple form of embroidery which is found in many articles from dress accessories to huge mantel covers. It is often mounted over rich-coloured silk satins and velvets.

Many attractive and personal interpretations of this technique are made today. Fig. 84.

Ground

Firm strong linen with a close weave,

83 *Sampler of cut work. Buttonhole edges to the design and bars with picots, wheels and cross bars. Note decorative edges. 13 cm (5 in.) square.*

so that the edge does not fray easily when cut.

Cotton and other fibres may be used, provided the scale of embroidery is adapted, together with the design and thread, all suiting each other.

Technique

Tools – small scissors, sharp-pointed with sharp blades, which may also be made with a gauge.

Frame – usually worked in the hand. Large professional pieces may be framed for several workers to embroider at the same time.

Transfer of design – by light blue paint or print line, or hard 2H pencil.

Needles – crewel, around size 8.

Thread – stranded cotton, coton à broder. Personal choice and experiment is necessary, as specialized threads are not always available, and also if the background is individually chosen and needs a related thread.

Join on/off – run in by paint line where it will be worked over.

Process

1 Run stitch on lines of design for strength and as a padding to set off buttonhole stitch.
2 Work buttonhole stitch with the loops against the cutting edge. Fig. 88.

At this stage it is necessary to calculate and plan where the cut edges occur, as any large open areas will need a bar to hold the ground together and to avoid tears and damage during wear.

The bars and wheels and picots are incorporated into the buttonhole outline as the work proceeds, but of course these lie on the surface and do not go through the ground material.

When the stitchery is complete, the open areas are formed by cutting away the ground material close to the looped edges of the buttonhole stitch, using fine sharp-pointed scissors.

It may be helpful to wash the completed embroidery, to settle the stitchery into the ground and to remove any discoloration in working threads, before cutting out the open areas.

84 Cut work. A design of a church window displays buttonhole stitch, picots and woven picots (worked over pins) to form the leaves at the base. Mounted over hand-tinted silk. 20 × 16 cm (7$\frac{4}{5}$ × 6 in.). Worked by Elena Pike.

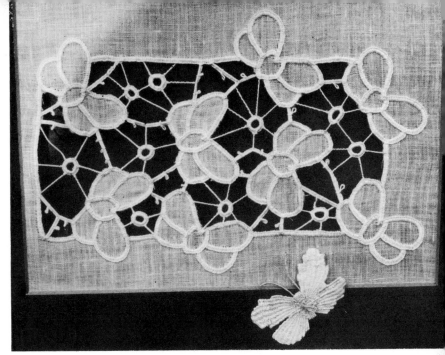

85 Sampler of cut work, with a design of bees and a butterfly in Tenerife work, by Sue Herbert.

86 Detail of sampler in fig. 85, showing bars, buttonhole rings, twisted or entwined bars, and looped picots.

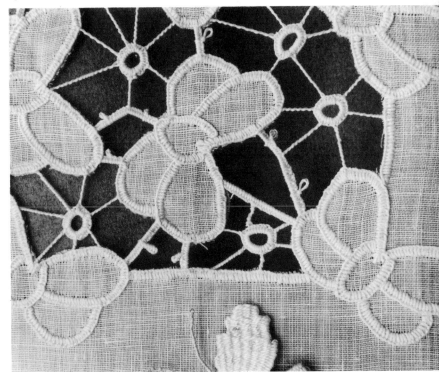

To work a buttonholed wheel

Work small running stitches around outline. Pierce hole in centre with a stiletto. Work buttonhole stitch by putting needle into centre hole for every stitch, carefully radiating stitches on outside of circle.

To work a detached ring

Wind a single thread six times round a pencil, slip off carefully and work buttonhole stitch over these threads. When reaching the first stitch, pass the needle through the first loop to make a continuous ring. Thread the needle through the back of several stitches to finish off. Cut off thread. Pin or tack ring into position. Work buttonhole stitch on design lines and make bars to attach the ring to the work. Cut material away behind bars and ring with great care. A picot can be worked as a decoration in the centre of a bar. Fig. 88.

To work a picot

Work buttonhole stitch to centre of bar. Insert needle downwards into last stitch made and wind the thread three times round the needle. Pull the needle

87 *Sampler showing stages of cut work.* Top row: 1 *forming a bar;* 2 *buttonholing bar;* 3 *completed edge. Lower row:* 1 *run-stitched outlines. The first row of stitches for a two-sided bar;* 2 *completed two-sided bar and the development of a cross bar below it;* 3 *completed shape.*

through. Insert needle upwards into last buttonhole stitch and pull through. A small circular knot or picot is thus made. Complete bar.

Buttonhole stitch edge

Draw a double line in scallop shape near edge of fabric. Work small running stitches on both lines. Pad between these lines using rows of chain stitch, stem stitch, split stitch or long running stitch. Loose threads laid in place can also be used. Buttonhole stitch is worked over both outlines, over the padding. Stitches can be straight, or they can radiate round the curve. Cut close to looped edge. (*Note*: work small running stitches on all outlines. Work buttonhole stitch (close blanket stitch/loop stitch) over running stitch. Keep stitches at right angles to outline. Radiate stitches on curved lines. Take a longer stitch at points to keep a good shape and for strength. Work loops of buttonhole stitch on edge to be cut.)

To work a bar

Complete buttonhole stitch to second

end of bar position, then insert needle upwards into buttonhole stitch at opposite end of bar. Insert needle upwards into last buttonhole stitch worked, then go back to stitch at opposite end of bar. Buttonhole stitch back over these three strands. Do not catch material. At end of bar, insert needle upwards into last buttonhole stitch worked on outline and continue with buttonhole stitch.

To work a narrow bar that is to be cut on both edges

Work running stitch on both edges. Cover both running stitch rows with buttonhole stitch but leave a space the width of one stitch between each stitch. At end of strip, reverse work and take buttonhole stitches over both rows of running stitches between first row of buttonhole stitches, but the looped edge on opposite edge.

To work a double bar or cross

1 Complete buttonhole stitch to fourth spoke of a cross. Take thread across to opposite side making

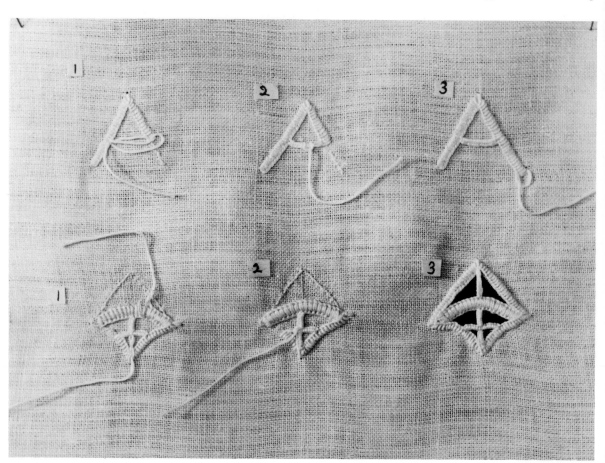

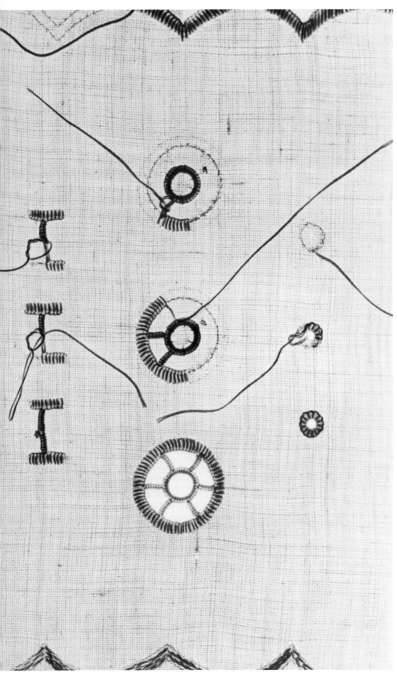

88 Sampler. Centre top: circles show at the top a separately made ring tacked in place. Centre middle: buttonhole outlining circle and bars in process of work. Centre below: completed open shape. Left: method of making a picot bar. Right: buttonholed eyelet. Worked by Barbara Hicks (Goldsmiths' College Collection).

three strands and work buttonhole stitch to centre using method as for bar.

2 Complete remaining three spokes in rotation and continue with outline.

When all stitching is complete, dampen work and using small, very sharp scissors cut close to the looped edges of the buttonhole stitches on the wrong side. Take great care not to cut bars. See *Broderie anglaise, Buttonhole, Drawn thread work.*

DARNING
Identification
Darning in embroidery is a decorative, regularly worked run stitch which gives a texture of pattern or direction to the background of designs in, for example, satin stitch or appliqué, both of which are rather static techniques. The background of a design may be simply darned leaving the design unworked, or the design darned and the ground unworked, when an evenweave material is usually chosen.

Darning worked on a square mesh net is known as lacis or filet and on a dress net or tulle as Limerick lace, when it includes counted satin stitch patterns. A single line of run stitch in and out of net, to form a design in outline only, is another form of darning. Fig. 240.

Darning appears in other work such as drawn thread work, pulled stitch and huckaback linen, and it is, of course, a well-known repair stitch. The back of darning is an important clue for identification, as the wrong side forms a reverse or negative pattern of the right side and in this way it is closely integrated with the ground.

Pattern darning on linen and patterns of counted satin stitch on linen may at first glance appear to be identical, but the working process is different. In darning each row is completed by working in and out of the background in rows to build up the pattern. In counted satin stitch, patterns are completed by a form of oversewing, so that the wrong side may show a regular pattern of working which is not a reverse or negative of the right side.

Although darning is sometimes given other names such as woven bars or needleweaving, when used in drawn thread work, or as tapestry weaving when referring to Coptic borders of the early centuries AD, it is the same process of passing the working thread over and under alternate threads of the background or warp. See figs 89, 90, 91, 99, 105, 110, 115, 161, 217, 291, 299, 303, 304.

gauze imitated complicated weaves and are known as damask darning.

Morris darning is an English decorative darning with a regular surface pattern used in white linen embroidery.

In the twentieth century darning recurs from time to time and in the 1930s panels worked by artists showed the technique used freely. Fig. 96.

It seems to be an overlooked technique but well suited to the present time for restrained, subtle and thoughtful work.

Design

Texture is an important consideration for design, and the geometric patterns formed by counting the threads of the ground give great variety and include diamonds, squares, chevrons and stripes. Free darning gives life to present-day embroidery.

Darning is often used to set off a design of flowers, figures or letters, frequently in the form of borders, with the background darned in patterns and the design of plain unworked ground.

Variations in size of working thread give textures from a mere subtle shadow, using a fine thread, to a heavy richness, using a thick thread.

Darning on net forms designs of various styles and weight, covering a gamut of geometrics, to fill areas of conventional and realistic designs, symbolic emblems and letters for church embroidery. The design is usually darned, though occasionally it is left as open net and the background is in solid darning; this is known as *réservé*. Figs 90–93, 96.

Grounds

Evenweave linen or huckaback linen and similar grounds. Square nets – made by hand or by machine and bought by the yard from specialists. Machine-made dress nets, cotton, silk or man-made, available by the yard. Mesh made by drawn-out threads or pulled stitches.

Experiment is advisable for present-day materials and those of the past, such as Java canvas and nets,

89 *Darning, showing:* Right (top pattern): *diamond darning in dark and light thread;* (second pattern) *reverse side;* (third pattern) *satin stitch in diamond pattern;* (fourth pattern) *reverse side of satin stitch. Note the slanting stitch, and also the difference between the wrong side of darning and satin stitch.* Left: *various textures of darning:* (top pattern) *plain run darning;* (below) *damask darning. Worked by Sheila Joss.*

History

Decorative darning may originate from the eastern Mediterranean, worked in silk to form interlacing and diaper patterns, that is, a pattern of diamonds. In appearance the patterns are almost identical to those in medieval manuscripts of the eleventh and twelfth centuries. Turkey and France are famous for a high standard of silk darning at this time, and there are also early examples of bold decorative linen darning from German states and Switzerland.

In the seventeenth century influences from trade with India and the Oriental East brought intricate patterns to Europe, and in the eighteenth century simple white darning, similar to a run stitch, was used as a background to make a delightful foil for a design of flowers.

Later and into the early nineteenth century darning samplers on fine silk

90 & 91 *Darning experiments, 1985. Worked by Judith Groves.*

92 A design of a tree using darning stitches and pulled stitch, with the stem in Algerian eyelets. 1980. (Tunbridge Wells Centre).

93 Reverse side of design in fig. 92.

when found at jumble sales or charity shops.

Technique

Framing-up – optional.

Transfer of design – tack line or as required.

Needles – tapestry.

Thread – same size as threads of background, or thicker for greater emphasis, or finer for shadows.

Join on/off – run stitch into ground in area to be covered by embroidery.

Process – stitch.

Darning

The stitches pass over and under the threads of the ground alternately, either vertically or horizontally. Figs 89, 96.

Plain run darning

Run stitches of even size and space are worked in rows with a stitch and spaces alternating, and may be curved or diagonal. Fig. 89.

Pattern darning

Run stitches of different sizes, as well as even size, are worked in rows to build up a pattern. Fig. 89.

There are many variations such as:

Damask darning

Stitches are worked in one direction first vertically, and then horizontally, fitting spaces left on the first row. Figs 89, 299.

Morris darning

A form of counted satin stitch; the term refers not to May Morris, who used darning, but probably to a Moorish origin. Figs 303, 304.

Close darning

Rows of darning worked close together in net. Figs 94, 99, 110.

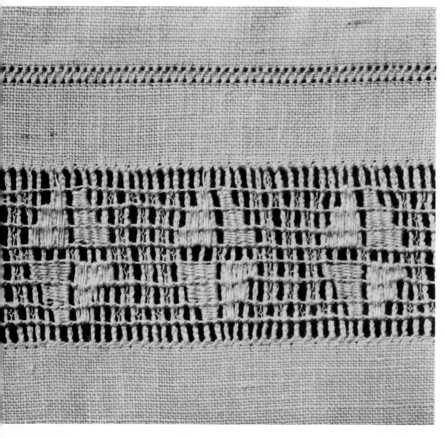

94 Close darning, horizontal and vertical. Note bands of coral stitch with loop stitch filling and hemstitched edges. Italian hemstitch at hemmed edge.

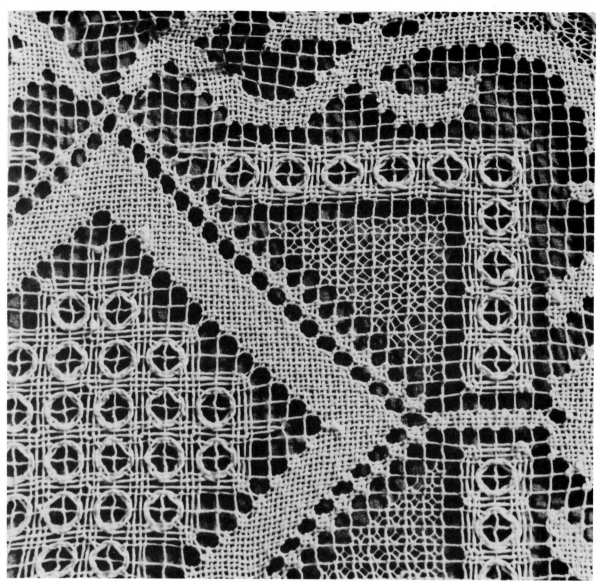

95 *Darning in cloth stitch on square net. Note also use of loop stitch.*

Cloth stitch
Rows of darning spaced out so that another row may be fitted in between in the opposite direction. Figs 95, 238.

Net darning
The patterns in net darning may be either counted or satin stitch or darned, as in Limerick. Figs 202 (D), 252, 296.

Lacis/Filet
Darning on a square net, knotted, interwoven or machine-made. Fig. 238.

Darned lace
This refers to darning on square net. Alternative names are filet brodé (net embroidery), guipure d'art, dessin réservé (background worked, design plain) and filet reprisé (net darning). Fig. 238.

Darned muslin
Now known as shadow work, and worked in herringbone stitch on fine muslin or organdie using a thicker thread than that of the ground. Figs 317, 318.

Needlerun net
A term for embroidery on net worked by the Schiffli machine. Fig. 223.

Swiss darning
This is a form of invisible repair on knitted textiles, usually hand knitted. See *Irish embroidery, Net.*

DENTELLE
French word for lace.

DETACHED CHAIN
Forms a delightful powdering, or seeding, but it is a stitch often debased as badly formed stitches representing flower petals – 'lazy daisy'. The stitch should be roundly formed and only a very little longer than it is wide. Figs 82, 97.

DORSET BUTTONS
See *Buttons*

DOUBLE BACK STITCH
See *Herringbone*

63

96 (Opposite page) A progressive white hand embroidery by Rebecca Crompton, 1930s. The shapes to the left and lower right of the face are in darning, outlined in chain. The eye on the left is cut and oversewn to show a shining white material inlaid, and this material also passes under the nose, mouth and neck to give a raised and rounded form to the face, and to cast the right side into shadow. The radiating lines and the leaves surrounding the face are in a free overcasting herringbone in fine black thread, giving an effect of openwork. (Victoria & Albert Museum).

97 (Above) Border of detached chain stitch in freely formed flowers. On the left the embroidery has been dampened and stretched, and on the right it has been pressed where it appears flattened. (Nora Jones).

98 Sampler of drawn thread work 37.5 × 32cm (14¾ × 12½ in.). Note the open squares at the corners of the border and drawn mesh for flower centres. 60 threads = 2.5cm (1 in.).

99 Detail of corners, showing needlewoven or darned bars to work into. Note on the left rows of coral stitch as a scaffold for a decorative border into which the pattern is darned or woven. On the right, a border in close darning between rows of coral stitch.

DRAWN THREAD WORK

Identification

Drawn thread work refers to embroidery in which individual threads of the background are cut and withdrawn to give open areas in the form of borders. The decoration ranges from hems, where only one or two threads are drawn out, to elaborate borders several inches wide.

Threads may be cut from either the

examples and, if necessary, a careful and judicious decision to unpick some of the stitches may have to be made. Figs 98–114, 217, 283, 291, 298.

History

Drawn thread work has early origins and is a type of decoration almost world-wide, wherever woven cloth is produced. Drawn thread work borders are extremely varied and the earliest come from countries bordering the Mediterranean, later spreading to the rest of Europe as civilization developed peacefully, enabling such pursuits as crafts to prosper. Fragments of linen, Coptic or Egyptian work of the first century AD, are early existing examples of needleweaving. Arabic borders on fine linen also include needleweaving, but in silk, as do elaborate borders of Italian and Spanish embroidery of the sixteenth century. Spanish work was similar to Italian but had a Moorish influence.

Drawn thread work of this fine

100   A darned corner worked on spokes; note decorative border at the top.

warp, the weft or from both to form an all-over geometric design. The spaces at the corners of borders are filled with loop stitch or woven wheels, spiders or fans, and the remaining threads are grouped together with hemstitching. The groups are further decorated, sometimes tied together with coral stitch, wrapping (or whipping), buttonhole, darning or needleweaving.

A mesh, like net, may also be formed from drawn thread work, for example by cutting and withdrawing four threads and leaving two threads alternately from the warp and weft of the ground. The remaining threads are whipped for sharper definition.

A very similar mesh may be formed on a loosely woven ground by pulling the threads together with overcasting and not cutting any threads out. This technique is known as pulled stitch work and care is needed to distinguish it from drawn thread work.

A magnifying glass helps to examine these details when used on a fine scale. The problem is, however, occasionally unresolved in historical

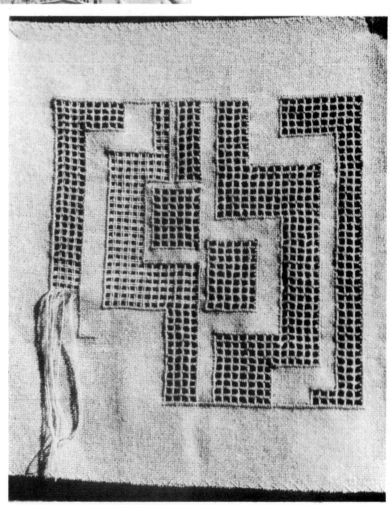

101   Sampler of drawn thread work mesh.

type decorated the spectacular ruffs shown in Elizabethan portraits and certainly appears to have had the crispness of frost. White linen vestments for the church also displayed the work.

The samplers of the period record variations of stitches, patterns and designs. They are unmatched in technical detail and are a collection of the workers' personal favourite patterns which were passed from one embroiderer to another. There were few pattern books or prints, and a sampler was the best method of learning the intricacies of buttonhole stitch, darning and counted patterns.

Linen cushions which also displayed the patterns were a new luxury and carried a status of wealth and civilized awareness, for they were used not to sit on but to present or support and carry gifts of books, gloves and other precious articles.

102 Drawn thread work on linen of Elizabethan times. Cushion made up of three borders and four reticella borders, possibly as a bird shape. Punto in aria lace edges the cushion. Note the use of counted satin stitch, needleweaving, punch stitches, trailing, overcasting, and Italian hemstitching. 38 × 33 cm (15 × 13 in.). (Hatfield House Textile Conservation Rooms).

103 Detail showing reticella centres in borders of sumptuous and intricate embroidery, probably Italian. The work is typical of that shown on white work samplers. (Hatfield House Textile Conservation Rooms).

were joined together to make cushions with embroidery all over the top surface. Although the work is early, they are not made up in period fashion, but this may well have preserved the embroidery. Figs 102–6.

Other interesting work looks like drawn thread work but is on the diagonal (or true bias) of the ground. It is cut work within a basic diagonal shape of punch or pulled stitches. The cut out shape is then worked with bars, picots and added stitchery including bullion knots. The edges of the drawn thread are also strengthened with a stitch known as Italian hemstitching, somewhat like three-sided stitch but not the hemstitching used so prolifically in the nineteenth century. Punch stitch, counted satin stitch, trailing, buttonhole stitch with picots set off the open work; all are worked on an extremely fine and detailed scale. A magnifying glass is useful to classify different stitches.

Another unusual form of cut and drawn thread work shows an even number of warp and weft threads cut

The finely embroidered cushion covers were made to show involved borders and insets of drawn thread work. The centre of the cushion is plain linen, with the borders and sides embroidered. Many early fragments found in the late nineteenth century

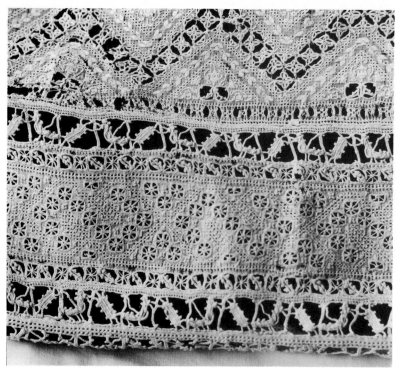

104 *Detail showing needleweaving with Italian hemstitched edges.* Top: *satin stitch and trailing.* Bottom: *border with diagonal pulled stitch pattern surrounds cut work. Border 0.5 cm ($\frac{1}{5}$ in.).* (Hatfield House Textile Conservation Rooms).

away to form an open mesh and then buttonholed (or pulled together) to make either square or honeycomb mesh which surrounds a design of plain ground, similar to early German and Swiss work.

In the early eighteenth century the introduction of cotton muslin led to the mania for embroidered muslin as fashionable wear and drawn thread work is sometimes to be found on this flimsy material.

Drawn thread work examples of about 1200 from Germany and Switzerland are in museums there and in the USA, and incorporate an open mesh background with figures of plain ground material which have details such as faces, drapery and surrounding pattern in stitches such as stem and chain. The work has an intricacy of craftsmanship which surpasses all linen work of the time and it illustrates stories of saints, birds and animals. Other work included simple bold borders in counted satin stitch and cross stitch, and designs with the figures in buttonhole filling and foliage in chain and stem. They may appear unrefined. Flax grown in Germany provided the linen ground for the embroidery to thrive, particularly at Lüneburg.

It was once thought that, during the centuries up to the fifteenth, drawn thread work embroidery was

105 *Border showing diagonal lines of punch stitch and cut work with woven bars, flanking a bird motif in reticella, and a fine needlewoven border at either side. The whole border is used as the side of a cushion, and shows satin stitch, trailing, picots, darned or woven bars and eyelets. Cushion 38 × 30 cm (15 × 12 in.). Insertion border 4 cm (1½ in.).* (Hatfield House Textile Conservation Rooms).

106 *Complete cushion with authentic plain centre which has embroidered borders to decorative insertion. 48 × 30 cm (19 × 12 in.) approx. Insertion 5 cm (2 in.).* (Hatfield House Textile Conservation Rooms).

embroidery for secular and domestic purposes. What was known as the 'forbidden stitch' and used only for vestments came to be called frostworke, and used for dress, but this is mere speculation.

Convent work may achieve high standards, but is often considered very uneven. It is the professional workshops with a good standard that are recorded fact, and high standing civilians, convents and monasteries were customers throughout the centuries.

The embroidery of the sixteenth century had such a large number of threads cut and withdrawn from the warp and weft that they were strengthened and decorated with darning and needleweaving, and with threads added diagonally and in curves which were held in place with bars. Larger open areas were filled with close buttonhole stitches to form techniques known as reticella and punto in aria. Latin and French terms were used, as they were universal languages of the time, much as English is today.

In the later nineteenth and early twentieth centuries an enormous quantity of drawn thread work was produced on linen and cotton to decorate bed linen; sheets, pillowcases, bolster cases, huge bedspreads and tablecloths were bordered with drawn thread work. Trailing designs of stem stitch, satin stitch and crochet borders added to a rich impression.

Brides-to-be and families had immense collections of decorated linen, further embellished with initials and floral designs in satin stitch.

Drawn thread work is another embroidery technique, like broderie anglaise, which was introduced to Madeira to help hard conditions. Heavily embroidered bedspreads are a typical item, but are frequently worked on cotton material. Ireland also became famous for drawn thread work and in fact many countries produced examples to give their name to particular methods:

108 Detail, showing threads without a hemstitched edge but with close overcasting, and with the use of loop stitch filling in the open spaces. French knots texture the plain material.

worked in the seclusion of convents, acquiring a mystique, as there was no other embroidery of such intricacy, and that about the fourteenth century noble ladies wished to learn the embroidery. They were taught by the nuns, which led to the use of this fine

109 Two examples of early twentieth-century drawn thread work. Lower left: *a small display tablecloth of fine linen, richly decorated with a variety of techniques. 130 cm (51 in.)* square. 6 threads to 1 mm ($\frac{1}{25}$ in.). Right: *a large double bedspread in cotton showing eyelets, satin stitch as in a coarse broderie anglaise, and typical of Madeira work. 250 cm (98$\frac{1}{2}$ in.) square;* 5 threads to 2 mm ($\frac{2}{25}$ in.).

110 *Details of drawn thread work, woven corners, darning, needleweaving.*

111 *A yoke of Russian drawn ground. The threads have been cut and withdrawn to form the mesh for the pattern to be darned into. (Margaret Potts).*

112 *Detail of fig. 111. Right side.*

Russian

Borders with several rows of hemstitching and needleweaving spaced to form a pattern. A mesh background with a solid design is also often considered typically Russian. Figs 111–14.

Greek

Wide borders with a skeleton of threads, and regular repeating open areas closely stitched in buttonhole with bars and picots, woven wheels and quartered corners, in a coarse copy of reticella. Like Ruskin work, it is a name given to a revival in the last century.

Mexican

This showed the Spanish influence of a large all-over pattern worked diagonally, in openwork with woven bars.

English

Ruskin work in the late nineteenth and early twentieth centuries was a revival of reticella, worked in the Lake District under the influence of John Ruskin, and also William Morris, who advocated a return to designs of integrity and antiquity, and the use of hand work. Hand-woven linen was

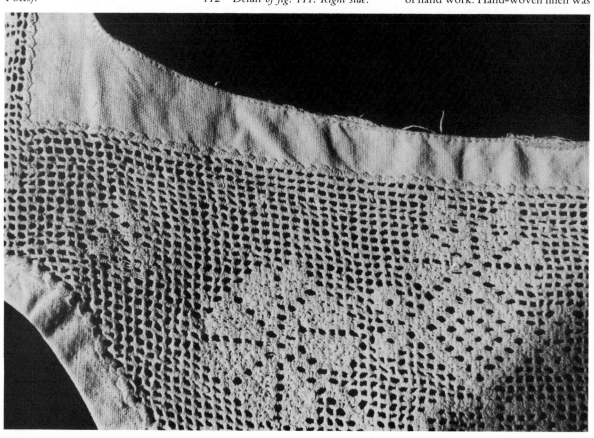

113 Detail of fig. 111. Wrong side.

114 Russian drawn ground, with solid plain material for the pattern, which usually indicates that the ground threads are not cut but worked as a pulled ground. (Margaret Potts).

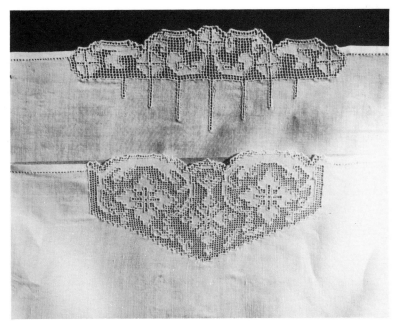

produced in the traditional galleries of the Lake District cottages, and locally grown flax was spun for the linen. The industry prospered when Americans visited Europe looking for art treasures, much as the English had visited Italy in the previous century.

It seems worth while to clarify the difference between the cut work of the sixteenth and seventeenth centuries and that of the nineteenth century. Drawn thread work of the sixteenth and seventeenth centuries in the reticella and punto in aria form is described historically as Italian cut work, and that of the nineteenth-century revival as Ruskin work or Greek lace. By the nineteenth century the term cut work referred to embroidery with the background cut away from a design edged in buttonhole stitch. See also *Cut Work* (history). Drawn thread work has only threads removed, but cut work has small areas of the background cut away.

At the present time, hemstitching and drawn thread are used experimentally and for technical interest.

Design

Designs are controlled by the threads of the ground so that a geometric style is always to be found, sometimes softened by trailing designs of stem and satin stitch in more recent times. Figs 107–10, 115.

Ground

Linen, especially hand-woven for Ruskin work. Cambric, cotton, silk, and some synthetic fibres of the twentieth century treated to look like linen, are also suitable.

Technique

(*Note*: it is advisable to work a test piece.)

73

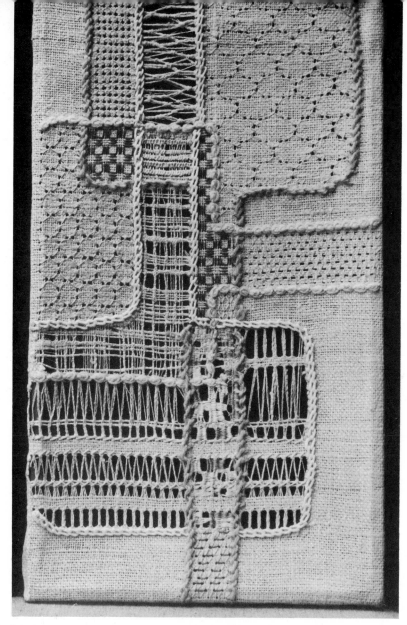

secution working in the area and producing high quality articles, by the nineteenth century the lace had become a coarse type of torchon.

E

ÉCRU

The very pale colour of natural linen before bleaching and a French name for the colour of raw silk, linen and cotton.

EDGE

The edges of lace are identified by the straight edge, known as a footing or *engralure*, to be sewn to an article. The other edge, often fancy or scalloped, is called a heading. Fig. 2.

EDGINGS

A term for narrow strips of machine embroidery or lace made of cambric, muslin or net as frills or insertions, sold by the yard for use as trimming. Before the advent of the machine, produced by hand in workroom or cottages. Figs 2, 216.

EYELET

The word 'eyelet' derived from the French for eye, *oeil*, and is a small opening in any material, either for decoration or to receive a threaded tape or ribbon.

A simple eyelet is worked by:

1 Using a stiletto to make the hole.
2 Oversewing by inserting the needle down into the centre of the hole.
3 Re-marking the hole with the stiletto as the oversewing proceeds.
4 Making a run stitch round the hole before oversewing to add strength.

Shaped eyelets, such as oval, are explained under *Broderie anglaise*.

Tools – scissors with sharp and pointed blades.

Framing-up – optional; used for large pieces and professional work and slightly slack in the frame.

Transfer of design – by tacking out a plan for borders measured from a paper design, and by counting threads.

Needle – tapestry with rounded blunt point.

Thread – similar in thickness to background or finer.

Join on/off – into hem when available, or run into previous work.

Process – stitches: hemstitching, needleweaving, darning, loop stitch. See figs 99, 108, 287 (F1–2, Y-2).

DRESDEN WORK

This is a historically interesting form of pulled stitches on fine linen or muslin and became a substitute for lace in Germany and Denmark during the eighteenth century. The embroidery is of the highest standard in design and technique and includes fine satin stitch, and double back stitch in the floral design. Dresden embroidery was the forerunner of Ayrshire work. Figs 18, 71, 255–8. See also *Ayrshire, Pulled stitches*.

Dresden point also refers to an early industry of lace founded by Barbara Uttman (1514–75) to help relieve poverty in that district. In spite of many refugees from religious per-

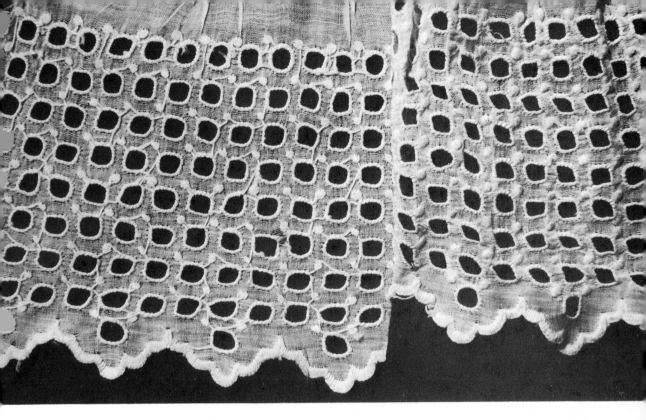

116 *Machine-made eyelets. On the left, the wrong side, showing the repetitive working thread. On the right, the right side with satin stitch blocks, and although the edge looks like a hand buttonhole stitch, it is in fact a machine stitch.* (Constance Howard).

Although a hand embroidery technique, eyelets were soon imitated by machine and became a feature of this work.

Eyelet embroidery is often classed as broderie anglaise, and the two types certainly overlap; the latter often includes ladder work, satin, stem and other stitches, while eyelet embroidery is generally considered to consist of eyelets only with, perhaps, the smallest and most unobtrusive amount of additional stitchery.

Eyelets form a simple spotted, but also a dark and glinting, pattern on all white materials from silk, cotton and linen to synthetics, and are frequently incorporated in white work of all periods, particularly in the cotton muslin embroidery of the eighteenth century when they are often outlined in graded satin stitch. Another extensive use of eyelets on cotton are the many examples where they are the

117 *Group of false sleeves showing eyelet embroidery. Average length 25 cm (9⅘ in.).* (Constance Howard, Lise Mossery).

only embroidery technique used to interpret a design, either for dress decoration, children's clothes or light-

weight furnishings, such as cushions, curtains and table linen.

False sleeves or sleeve ends worn under the three-quarter-length sleeves of a bodice, in silk, wool or heavy cotton, were a fashion of 1840–60 and worn by Florence Nightingale, as seen on the current ten pound note sterling. The embroidered sleeve ends are gathered into an embroidered wristband or cuff, with the sleeve

118   The raw edge of a sleeve, rolled, gathered and attached to cuff.

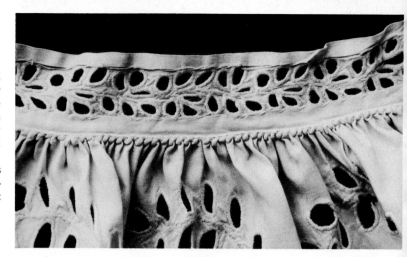

seam often permanently unmade and only lightly stitched together for wear and unstitched for laundering. The sleeve and the embroidery are thus much easier to iron as the sleeve may be laid out flat. (This fashion recurred in Edwardian times.)

Huge and bold embroidery designs made large hands seem, by comparison, attractively small, while light

119   Unseamed sleeve.

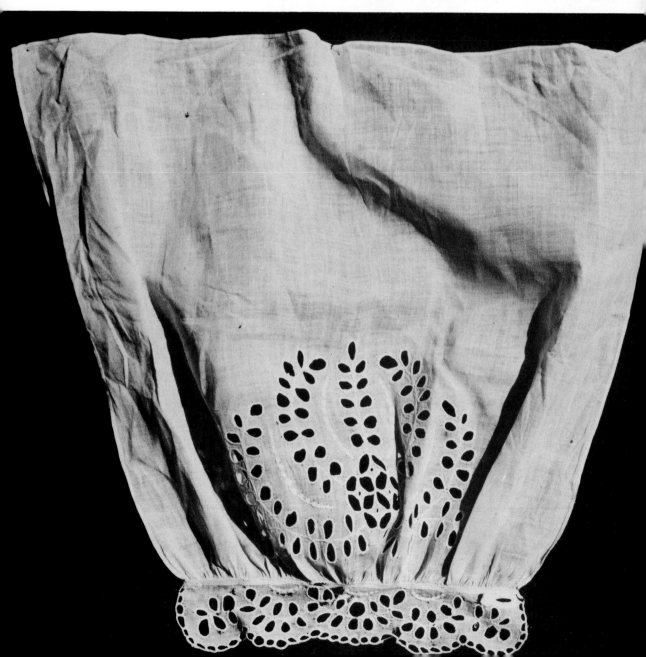

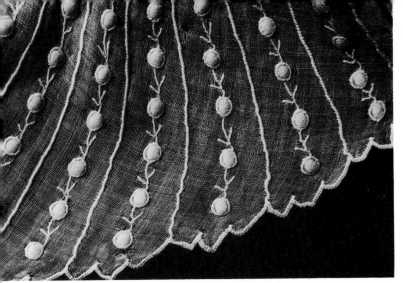

embroidery enhanced the only part of the body left unclothed at a time when fashion decreed that collars should be close fitting, dresses have long skirts and ankles be covered with boots.

Eyelets also serve an important and practical purpose in historical garments as an opening or hole to insert tapes or ribbons, through folded edges or casings. These may then be drawn up to secure fullness at the waist, neck, wrist and knee of all types of garments. Fig. 43.

120 *Detail of ruffle, with satin stitch on muslin. The design follows the movement of the wrist.*

121 *Detail of cuff, showing spaced rows of Bokhara couching to texture the background of the eyelet design. The edge is hand-buttonholed. The work has a typical appearance of the early 1900s.*

F

FAGGOTING

Identification

Faggoting is an openwork method for joining two pieces of material together, as for seams and for decorative insertions in dress or articles of household linen such as sachets, cushions and tea-cosies. The use of insertion and interlacing stitchery for joins is termed faggoting. Figs 33, 80, 122, 142.

History

Faggoting or insertion stitches have a long history and an elementary form is found in articles belonging to primitive communities, where leaves, skins or simple woven textiles are loosely lashed together.

Jackets, shirts, shifts and other articles, from nearly all centuries, all countries and all standards of living, from peasant and ethnic to aristocratic, have been adorned with open decorative seams to give individuality. Plain unobtrusive seams for construction belong mainly to the nineteenth century. In previous centuries many parts of garments were pinned in place, such as sleeves and stomachers, and took the form of interchangeable 'separates'.

The shirt in which Charles I is thought to have been executed is an example of a garment with decorated seams. There are peasant blouses, as well as fashion blouses, tea-gowns and négligés, which exhibit great variety.

In the late nineteenth and twentieth centuries the popularity of added rouleau gave great decorative scope. Rouleau is a strip of material cut on the true bias; the raw edges are folded together for a seam and the strip is then placed on paper and tacked in rows which are stitched together with faggoting to make an important decorative seam.

Rouleau is occasionally used to form an entire article or garment such

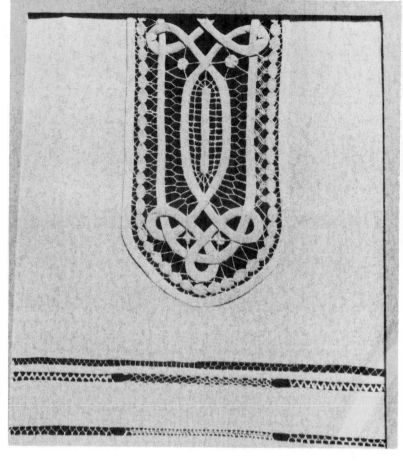

as a blouse or gilet (waistcoat) by working a scrolling design over the pattern shape of the garment.

This work is extremely well displayed in white materials, being dramatic and impressive.

Design

The design follows the seams of a garment or may be a decorative insertion and developed into scrolling lines as well as curves, coils, waves and straight lines to form yokes, collars and cuffs.

Ground

All types of material show seams in this work. For insertions and scrolling designs, the material should be soft and pliable in order to be manipulated into curves. Silk crêpe de Chine, satin, thin cotton crêpe, muslin and dress cotton are ideal.

Technique

Framing-up – not required, but a base of firm paper is needed to tack out the folded edge of material to the ink lines

122 *Faggoting sampler, showing rouleau worked into a design including shell rouleau. At the base, various insertion stitches. Rouleau insertion* $12 \times 7\,cm$ *($4\frac{3}{4} \times 2\frac{3}{4}$ in.).*

of the design. Leave a space of approximately 3 mm ($\frac{1}{8}$ in.) between each folded edge.

Needles – crewel, size to suit scale of work.

Threads – varied to suit work, and related to work.

Join on/off – use a double stitch and end into fold of seam.

Process – stitch. Faggotting stitches are variations of herringbone and button-hole.

FAIR LINEN

See *Church Embroidery*

FENDU

Cut or slashed material, often seen in

Elizabethan portraits, such as one of a lady in a white dress at Rangers House, Blackheath, London.

FENT

Cut end of calico, now known as a remnant.

FESTON

A term derived from small triangular flags, and used to describe buttonhole fillings either in the shape of or composed of triangles forming a pattern or edging. Cones or pyramids are alternative names. Fig. 237.

FIBRES

(including Conservation)
The study of white work accentuates the textures which different fibres give to the background and the stitchery, so that a short survey of fibres seems fundamental. There is today great emphasis and interest in making an individually constructed background other than by spinning and weaving, for instance by a natural ground such as stitched fleece, wrapped threads, felt or paper, or stitches such as a net of buttonhole or machine-worked threads, or wrapping, plaiting or twisting. In this way, with personally selected fibres from fleece to synthetics, the ground becomes part of an integrated embroidery. Figs 123–59.

A return to the basic fibres of early civilization may be a refreshing inspiration when it seems that white work needs new life, and that the relevance is lost of working the same techniques in formal designs, either of the past, however charming and successful, or of the present day, however new.

In this context the real challenge for embroidery lies in a new use of techniques such as:

- darning, fig. 141
- wrapping, figs 123, 139, 158
- netting, figs 137, 146, 148
- buttonhole, figs 143, 342
- needleweaving, fig. 126
- twining, figs 128, 143
- loopstitch, fig. 146
- plaiting, fig. 140
- layering, figs 56, 147, 150

The use of grasses, leaves, feathers and leather, or cutting and manipulating conventionally woven cloth, felt and

123 Detail showing right: *papyrus grass split in half and then wrapped in different threads;* left: *top, or right side of wrapping. Worked by Gwenda Fairbairn.*

124 Detail showing texture and use of small beads.

paper relates to today's concern for the natural world.

Introduction to fibre characteristics

Natural fibre, like human tissue, is made up of microscopic cells and has a life cycle. The cells, in time, or with rough treatment (especially incorrect washing, as they hold water when immersed, or wringing), break down or felt together and eventually decay to dust. The shrinkages of wool and the perishable nature of silk are two examples.

Synthetic fibres are composed of chemicals and under a microscope

125 *Wrapped threads over papyrus grass, to form a hanging with added tassels. Worked by Gwenda Fairbairn.*

appear by comparison with natural fibres to be solid, with no cell formation, resembling a rod of plastic. The tiny flexible rods form the raw material of yarn for weaving. In washing, the fibres do not absorb water and therefore cannot shrink.

The water is held only between the threads of the weave, and most of it may be shaken off to give drip-dry or quick-drying qualities. Some synthetic fibres melt under heat.

Blends are yarns spun of two different fibres, for example synthetic fibre and wool.

Mixtures are a weave of two or more different yarns, such as nylon warp with cotton weft.

Origin of fibres

Animal
● wool, from the fleece of sheep, goat, camel, llama;
● silk, from the cocoon spun by a worm;
● leather or skin, cat gut;
● fur and feather, quills.

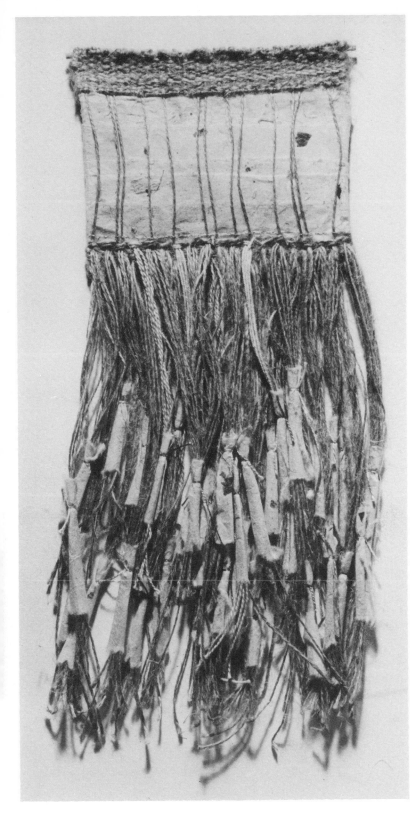

126 *Details of needleweaving and hand-made paper with stitchery. Worked by Judith Groves.*

grass, hemp, jute, bark, aloe, leaf fibre and many brushwoods and palms that give a brittle fibre. These are of interest, but not hard-wearing. Paper and wood shavings or chips, and rushes, dried and plaited, form a coarse foundation, for mats in typical use in the tropics.

Mineral

metal, gold, silver, copper, glass, mica, asbestos.

Organic

synthetic fibres from coal (phenol), petroleum, nitrogen, oxygen, chemicals, and cellulose from wood and cotton linters (waste).

Basic fibres

Linen and cotton fibres are the most frequently used in white embroidery, but there are various other interesting natural fibres in white or bleached neutral tones, and their use can add a richness which is sometimes overlooked. They come from brushwood, scrub, leaves, twigs, skins and beaten or shredded bark in an amazing selection of twining, plaiting and felting, and all offer inspiration. The famous bark cloths are the earliest approach to a textile, for if the bark is suitable for shredding, this forms a staple fibre, but if suitable for beating forms a felt, for which it can be mistaken.

The hot dry climates of such places as Africa, Polynesia and some areas of Central and South America produce certain trees with a bark which converts into a pliable felt-like cloth. The Chinese use the bark of the paper mulberry, the bread fruit tree. Bark cloth is made in Ponape in the Caroline Islands but is usually woven from pandanus leaves; spun banana and hibiscus fibre are also used.

The inner bark is softened by soaking in water, and after stripping away the fibrous portion it is then hammered with fluted beaters into varying degrees of fineness. The fibres are matted together to form a type of felt, and the beaters give a texture to the cloth similar to present-day repp (a horizontal rib).

Bark cloth is sometimes dyed and decorated by printing from wood blocks which have raised patterns cut on to the wood. The patterns are often derived from basketry, weaving and embroidery. The cloth is used for the same purposes as skins and woven

Vegetable

cotton, from the flower of a plant;
linen, the stalks of flax plants

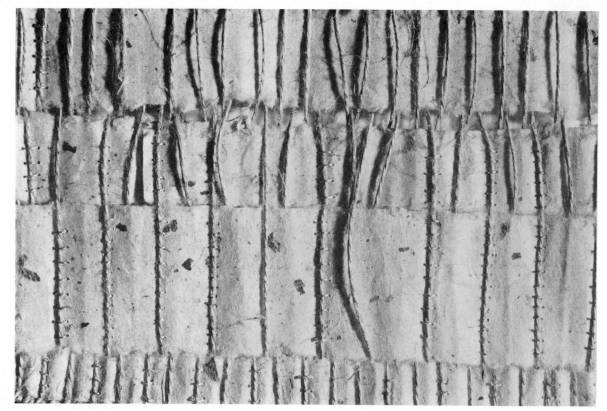

cloths in other civilizations, namely dress, wraps, carrying cloths, sleeping covers and mats. Some bark cloths are over a mile long and are made as a status symbol or display article.

Bark used for weaving purposes requires fibres lying parallel to the growth of the tree, such as the raffia palm, the cottonwood, willow cedar and also spun hibiscus and banana fibre, which when heckled or softened can be shredded very finely. Some of the best woven bark cloths have the appearance of silk, and the threads are also used for net making which is so fine it may be mistaken for silk. There are many examples of this in public collections, such as the Museum of Mankind (London), the Anthropological Museum at Cambridge, and Kew.

Thread made from the fibre of aloes became a novelty during the nineteenth century. It was similar to silk in appearance and a pale straw colour; the thread was used for satin stitch.

Raffia

The advance of fibre thread is shown in the rare Bushonga raffia-embroidered cloths which have buttonhole,

127 Borders of hand-made paper with stitchery. Worked by Judith Groves.

drawn thread and other stitches on fine cloth.

Some of these materials may be intertwined without the aid of a loom, particularly in the earliest examples. The fibre mats found in the pre-dynastic graves in Egypt were probably of this construction. Examples of tapestry weaving also exist, and a fine example of weaving without a shuttle is the ceremonial blanket, thought to be of bark with a symbolic pattern intertwined with wool from the mountain goat, worn by the Chilkat Indians of Alaska.

The strands of fibre are set up in a frame for a warp and the wool forming the pattern is intertwined with the fingers and beaten down over the warp fibre to cover it like tapestry. This is a common form of decorative weaving in North America.

The Polynesians used strands of bark from the hibiscus and using their fingers could produce a piece of fabric almost 3 m long and over 1 m wide (9 ft by 4 ft). In Africa and Mexico expert handwork made the fine products. The Maon mantle with its

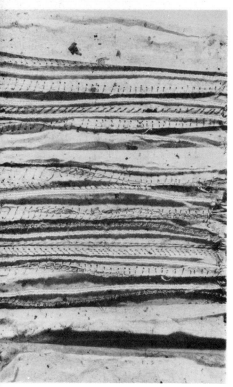

128 Hand-made paper in strips oversewn with natural fibres. Worked by Judith Groves.

129   Hand-made paper tucked and stitched. Worked by Judith Groves.

beautifully patterned border appears to be made of twined stitches with a needle. Figs 123–9, 150, 341.

Grass

Grass cloths may be made on a loom, as in Africa, the Caroline Islands and elsewhere. Grass skirts are made of pandanus leaves and fibre, and mats of leaf fibre have a spun thread warp, but the weft is not spun. Figs 123–9, 150, 341.

Brushwood

Early North American yarn or cordage is formed from twisted sage, brush and cedar bark, native hemp, flax and yucca leaves, twined or looped to make sandals, nets, bags and belts. These have been found in dry cave sites of old desert cultures from near California and surrounding areas, and date from remote history. Robes made of fibre cords wrapped with strings of rabbit fur or soft feathers twined together were made in early times. Various basts, threads, twining and plaiting have been found to be composed of rabbit and buffalo hair, mulberry bark, basswood, wild hemp and palmetto leaves, corn husk fibre and twined rush.

Shawls were made from the bark of trees with white and grey feathers, the inner bark being softened to become like flax. Figs 123–9, 341.

Skin/Fur

Mantles from mulberry bark thread are white and neat, and many other fibres bleach to a white or neutral colour to be used as twisted cords of hemp, cedar bark, and sage brush with bird skins and fur strips. Fur, feather and twined leaves of yucca have also been used in the past. Fig. 341.

For the modern embroiderer, personally made threads from basic fibre can add variety to the diminishing number of commercial threads available today. Figs 341, 347.

Feather/Fur/Hair

Around the South American area of the Colombia River, duck down and fireweed fibres have been spun into yarn. Fine mountain goat and fleecy dog's hair fibres are mixed with those of lynx, bear and others.

An early use of the fibres of slippery elm, basswood and occasionally nettle, was with false embroidery. Moose or caribou hair and feathers wrapped round the warp or weft to form a decorative textile may also be found. Fig. 341.

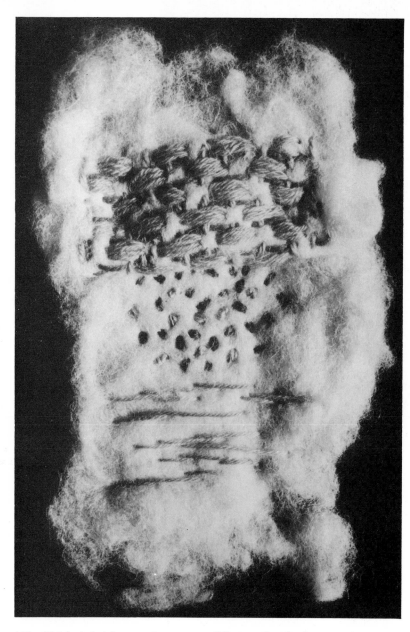

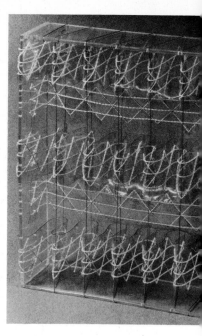

as others have proved too brittle, friable and short-lived for daily wear and tear, although they have an appeal of their own.

Terms in composition of woven cloth or textile

The basis of a true textile is that it should be woven from a spun thread.

Staple

Fibres are composed of staple, which varies in length from approximately 2.5 cm (1 in.) to 10 or 12 cm (4 or 5 in.); this is spun into a yarn. Longer staple gives a better quality yarn.

Filament

A continuous filament is produced in silk and in some synthetic fibres. It is usually cut into short lengths to be used as a staple fibre. Sometimes several filaments are bonded together to make a yarn, as in the finest silk crêpe de Chine.

Spun yarn

Fibre was originally spun by the use of a distaff and spindle, with the raw material held aloft on the distaff and eased out, weighted down and twisted into a yarn by the spindle on which the yarn is then wound. Later

130 Hand-stitched fleece used as an experimental ground of natural fibre. 1985. Worked by Mavis Gordon.

Quills/Leather

American Indians used porcupine quills which, being smooth and hollow, become flexible when wet and may be flattened and dyed. They are applied to skin or leather by wrapping or folding in various ways around a single sinew thread or darned between two. Other decoration on skin or fibre cloth consists of beads, seeds, shells and ribbons of available materials. The Eskimos use finely shredded sinew to make a thread for sewing or spinning. Figs 46, 150, 341.

Pineapple cloth

Pineapple cloth was produced in India and the Philippines during the eighteenth century as an experimental substitute for cotton. Figs 20, 21.

Flax

Flax (from which linen is produced), grown in India, America, western Asia, Africa and Egypt, has especially early records, as it was known in Greece before 1500 BC, when there was a well-established trade between Mycenae (Greece) and Troy (Turkey).

Cotton, flax, silk and wool are the most hard-wearing of natural fibres,

132 *Fabric texture with machine embroidery and paint. The material has singed edges and is mounted on to silk gauze. 1985. Worked by Caroline Robinson.*

the spinning wheel developed and was eventually replaced by a spinning engine or 'jenny'.

Loom

The yarn is woven into a textile on a loom, using one of many types, from the simple strap back loom of primitive nomadic tribes to the electrically powered and sophisticated looms of enormous factories.

Weaving

All looms have warp threads which run vertically from a bar at the top to a beam at the bottom.

Weft threads are passed or woven in and out of the warp by throwing a shuttle between the warp threads. The shuttle contains the weft thread wound on a reel, and a simple weave is made by passing it over and under the threads of the warp alternately.

From this method develops a huge range of patterns known as weave, such as:

Basket weave – similar to evenweave, but usually double threads. Also a patterned weave.

Crêpe – the warp and weft are tightly spun and woven so that when released they very slightly twist back (or contract) to form a softly elastic and textured textile. Fig. 149.

Damask – a pattern is woven into the textile in self colour, as in linen. It is also used in silk and often in two colours, as in shot silk. The pattern is in a satin weave.

Denim – heavy cotton twill.

Dupion – similar to slubbed. Usually refers to silk where two cocoons have merged together and reeling is uneven (from the French meaning double). Imitated in man-made fibres. Fig. 149.

Embossed – a pattern stamped on to a textile by hot irons during manufacture.

133 *An interlacing design in hand-made paper with torn out shapes and paint. 1985. Worked by Caroline Robinson.*

Evenweave – the warp and weft are of equal size. Figs 109, 149, 260.

Jean – a heavy cotton, now thought of as trousers. In nineteenth century a heavy white cotton satin for embroidery on household goods. Fig. 236.

Piqué – a vertically ribbed white cotton for dress. Very popular in 1930s for tennis wear. Fig. 149.

Satin – a smooth glassy weave used traditionally for silk but also in linen, cotton and silk damasks. Fig. 350.

Shot silk, shot taffeta – 'shot' is a term indicating that the warp is of one colour, for example white, and the weft is another, such as gold. In some lights this appears as white shot with gold, and in others gold with white.

Slubbed – an unevenly spun yarn with thick areas in the thread.

Spun silk – made from the cut and short lengths of filament from a broken cocoon. Fig. 5.

Taffeta, nylon taffeta – taffeta is usually thought of as a stiff, crackling type of woven silk. The type of weave is often used in synthetic textiles such as paper taffeta and nylon taffeta.

Twill – a diagonal weave, usually, for embroidery, top left to bottom right. Fig. 149.

Velvet – a pile or tufted surface, which is usually cut, but may be left uncut. Fig. 146.

Cotton

A natural vegetable fibre from a shrub, gossypium; it is the easiest of all fibres to process.

Gossypium barbadense – the finest, with the longest staple. From Egypt and American Sea Island, and some Caribbean islands.

134 Experiment with a thread mesh, paper, polystyrene and pearl buttons. 1985.

Gossypium herbaceum – shorter staples. American uplands.

Gossypium hersutum – Indian, African, Chinese and Asiatic.

Gossypium peruvianum, Gossypium arboreum – Indian, South and Central America.

Cotton is a natural vegetable fibre from the seed pods of mature flowers bursting open into three or five segments to show the lint or fleecy centre. This produces a short-length staple for spinning. The longest staple, of about five inches, comes from Egypt and southern America states. Figs 135, 138, 149, 159.

Characteristics and properties

Cotton is a good conductor of heat, so that when it is worn the heat of the body passes through and escapes, allowing fresh air to enter. Cotton does not, therefore, insulate, but is non-static and does not cling to the body. It is comfortable to wear,

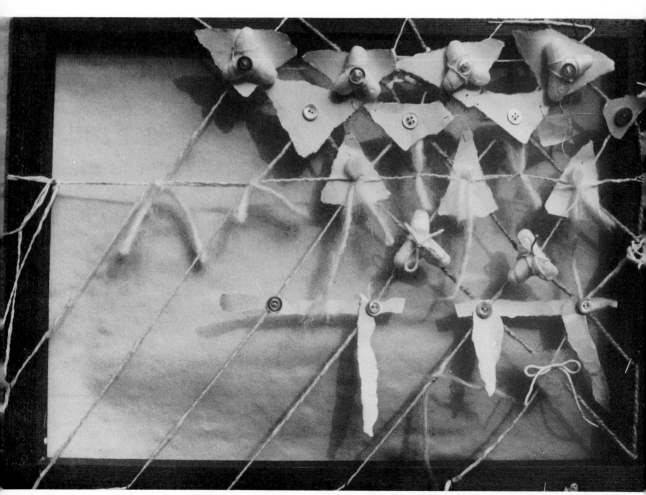

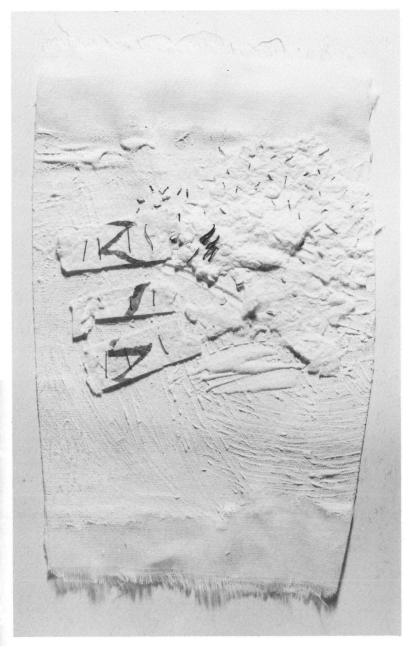

*136   Free patchwork and lines of
stitchery made by machine and hand.
1985. Worked by Lynda Graham.*

*135   The use of muslin and applied
material with paint and stitchery. 1985.
Worked by Lynda Graham.*

absorbent, hard-wearing and moth-proof, but if stored in damp conditions it tends to mildew. It is easy to launder, accepting hot water, soap or detergent, and a hot iron to remove creases. A damp cloth is also useful for pressing.

It tends to shrink but may be treated with resistants and also with shower-, water- and stain-repellents during manufacture.

Cotton bleaches well and accepts dyes, and is particularly versatile in production finishes, from lightweight muslins to heavy duck and denim. It is greatly used in blends and mixtures such as viyella, and also with synthetics, for many types of weaves such as crêpe and satin, and for prints. It is also frequently mercerized, as in poplin and embroidery threads, when its naturally matt surface is given a shiny silky finish.

Mercerizing

Mercerizing was invented in 1850 by John Mercer, a calico printer of north-east Lancashire. The process gives cotton yarn and cloth the appearance of silk and also reduces shrinkage, makes the fibres more receptive to dyes and increases strength. The cotton is specially prepared with many processes and steeped in a solution of caustic soda for a minute or two, washed and soaked in dilute sulphuric acid for a short time and later finished.

Embroidery threads

Before 1850 all cotton was matt, including embroidery thread. With the shiny silk finish of mercerizing many cotton embroidery threads came to be called silks.

Embroidered cotton probably constitutes the largest area of white work available today. An account of some of the details of its development therefore claims greater interest than other fibres, particularly from the British point of view, as the bulk of cotton textiles are mechanically produced. The machines were of British invention and made Britain the first industrialized nation in the world and the leading exporter.

History

Cotton has a long history in India and its places of origin, but it was brought to England from the Mediterranean, via Turkey and India, in the Tudor

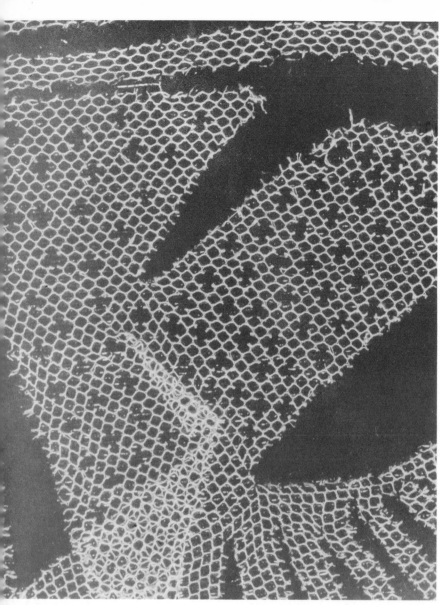

More and more cotton was required to meet the demand all over the world, and the export trade in Europe was becoming fiercely competitive, with Britain at this time a leader. It is difficult to realize how much exchange of goods and ideas was carried out in what we now consider primitive conditions of travel. However, this was a challenge with a thrill of danger to brave men and there was money as a reward. Many regions and climates were prospected, including the Caribbean and the new lands of the Virginian coast of America, both proving very successful in producing a long-staple fibre for fine cotton equal to that of Egypt. Later Brazil was also a producer.

The real home of cotton was India, but supplies declined because of the collapse of the Mogul Empire, war and the lack of proper organization. Thus supplies from America and the West Indies increased, as did the appalling slave trade to supply workers.

During the mid-eighteenth century in England, important mechanical inventions became successful for textile manufacture (dates are approximate):

1741 – Paul invented a mechanical spinning device but it was not developed.

1753 – Kay invented a flying shuttle for weaving.

1761 – Hargreaves invented a spinning machine or engine, the jinny or jenny, turned by hand and working at least eight spindles to make a fine thread.

1769 – Arkwright used water power for a big millwheel to turn the spinning machines, or jennys, to make a coarse thread. He set up his famous mill at Cromford, Derbyshire, by water and in the countryside, away from angry spinners who saw their livelihood threatened. All processes, including carding, were carried out on the machine.

1779 – Crompton invented the spin-

137 Experiment of cut work on net. 1985. Worked by Irene Ord.

period, when it was generally a coarse stiff textile like calico. English traders and merchants explored the world for expansion and development, more so than other European countries which had greater natural resources and were not so dependent on trade for survival. In the seventeenth century, through the East India Trading Company, more cotton was imported and it became more refined, so that by 1701 there are records of a fine semi-transparent cotton known as muslin in use as overskirts to silk dresses and as decorative aprons. The improved

cotton muslin was soft, pliable, light and strong, easy to keep clean and very inexpensive; it quickly proved so popular that it amounted to an obsession.

Ships with cotton from India arrived at Liverpool and Manchester, sailing up the west coast of England. A cottage industry was well established with agents distributing the cotton imports, either as raw cotton for spinning or as yarn for weaving, and then collecting the finished work and distributing it for sale all over the country and for export.

The muslin imported from India was so fine and delicate it was romantically known as Evening Dew and Flowing Water. It was spun by the most primitive distaff and spindle and

138 Experiment with cotton net darning. 1985. Worked by Irene Ord.

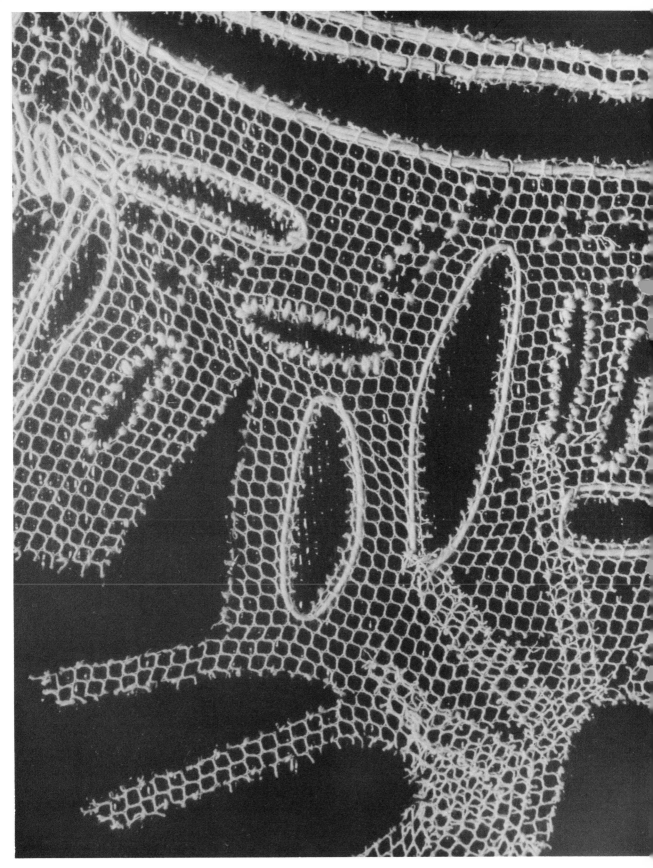

139 *Experiment with machine embroidery and wrapped threads. 1985. Worked by Maria Wittenveen.*

ning mule, a hybrid combining the spinning machine and water power to produce a fine thread. It was a time of violent riots and the production was delayed, but later successful searches for mill streams by all manufacturers continued, and his mule ousted the inventions of Hargreaves and Arkwright.

1778 – Watt invented steam power.

1786 – Cartwright, a professor of poetry at Oxford, invented a steam-powered loom.

1787 – Many mills, huge buildings by streams or rivers, were established for weaving and spinning.

An astounding change had occurred during twenty years, for in 1770 every process was carried out by hand at home by skilled workers, but by 1790 machines with one worker did

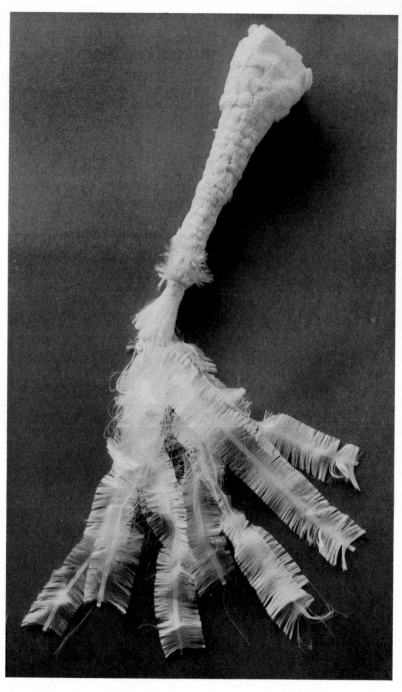

140 *A free form of plaited nylon and synthetic materials. 1985. Worked by Simon Nelson.*

the work of two or three hundred men, whereby the raw cotton was

● opened – to remove dead seeds;
● cleaned;
● spread;
● carded – staples and fibres combed parallel;
● drawn – into lengths;
● roved – made into long, soft, continuous loose round lengths;
● spun – twisted into strong yarn;
● on to spools or bobbin;
● warped – on to the loom, long threads running the whole length and wound round the beam at the front of the loom;
● dressed;
● woven.

Workers from derelict farms flocked

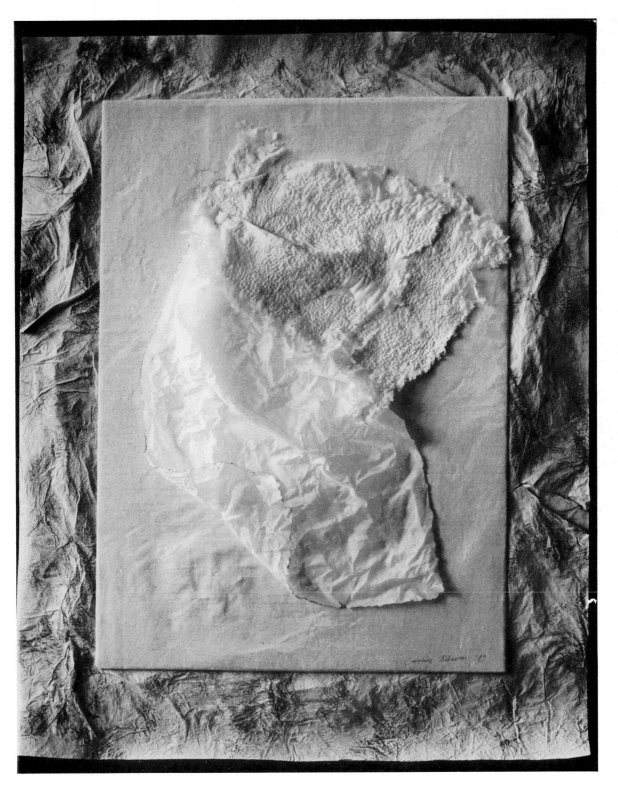

141 Darning on stiffened silk mounted on hand-worked paper. 1985. Worked by Caroline Robinson.

to the mills for employment, with hand weavers in great demand. The poor conditions of the mills were preferred to near-starvation and degradation in the rural communities, where common land which had been cultivated by freemen, yeomen, labourers and peasants was claimed by landowners and enclosed to give greater productivity. The labourers were left without any means of subsistence, other than begging, apart from

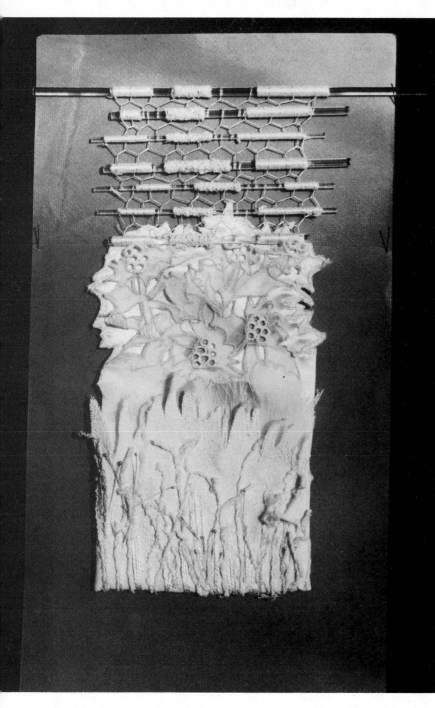

of working conditions, such as at Cromford. There were many famous reformers, such as Lord Shaftesbury, who were sincerely appalled by the conditions.

By 1864 Britain's trade with America had collapsed because of the Civil War, and trade with India was now successfully reopened and revived, so that the industry in the cotton mills in the north of England was maintained, with notorious employment conditions, including the use of child labour.

Cotton continued to be the king of textiles for another hundred years and formed the basis of white work embroideries, both hand- and machine-made, well into the twentieth century.

In 1945, after two world wars, conditions in the mills were revolutionized but, after the advent of synthetic fibres, the huge cotton mills of the nineteenth century stood empty by the canals which had been built to transport the products. Some are now preserved as of interest to the tourist and historian.

Synthetic fibres took over in popularity, being easy to care for, quick to dry, crease-resistant and very cheap to produce. Later the clamminess of synthetics in wear proved to be a disadvantage, but this has been overcome by mixing and blending with natural fibres, particularly cotton, to form an ideal textile.

By 1980, cost considerations reduced the production of the wide variety of cottons, so that specialist backgrounds for embroidery are limited and embroiderers tend to adapt techniques to available supplies.

Names associated with cotton

Cotton lawn, cotton cambric – lawn and cambric were orginally linen, but cottons were produced with the appearance and qualities of linen in order to extend cotton's use, purpose and sale.

Calico – known as calicut, about 1712. Fents are the ends of calicoes, cheap types formerly being dressed with lime and china clay and unbleached. Best quality calico has an even weave, warp and weft, without knots, and a good selvedge.

Mull muslin – a thin, soft type of muslin. Swiss mull is dressed and stiffened. Mull muslin is pure white, finer than nainsook.

142 *Machine-embroidered hanging, using silk satin, organdie, thick cotton and textured threads with plastic rods and faggoting. 30 × 13 cm (11¾ × 5 in.). 1985. Worked by Peggy Field.*

a few who could earn a shilling a day. In the mills a labourer earned ten shillings a week, and with his family made £2 a week, so that he was able to rent a stone- or brick-built dwelling at two shillings a week instead of a decaying, damp, unrepaired cottage.

Men, women and children worked long hours in stifling, damp, hot and poorly ventilated mills, and were housed in what became overcrowded and deprived living conditions. Emigration was the only alternative. Many of the mill owners and landowners were men of compassion such as Strutt, a former partner of Arkwright, and Owen in Scotland, who set up a comparatively high standard

143 An experiment with varied layers of white bonded Terylene, to hang in an environment designed for the partially sighted and blind by John Penton, ARIBA. The hanging may be read by touch and the background seen tonally. 1 × 1.5 m (39 × 59 in.). Worked by Barbara Dawson.

Muslin – a name derived from Mosul or Moosul, a town in Turkey, for a thin, nearly transparent cotton from the East. There are many types of muslin and many were developed and then rendered obsolete as demands and purposes changed. Buke or book muslin was for stiffening, clear and soft for interlining or stiff for millinery.

Sprigged and figured muslins and cambric were all popular during the Regency period of the nineteenth century, and were mentioned in Jane Austen's novels. Leno was a type of stiffened gauze.

These are a few evocative names, some already obsolete but many used until the last thirty years. Indian muslin was introduced about 1670, and later manufactured at Paisley and Glasgow from 1700.

Scotch cambric – a nineteenth-century term for a cotton produced in Scotland for handkerchiefs.

Scrim – a loosely woven fine canvas or coarse mull. Suitable for present-day experiments of pulled stitches, where the working of the stitch is easily displayed.

Swiss muslin – muslin manufactured at St Gall and Zurich in the early eighteenth century, long before production in England. See *Figured muslin, Swiss cambric*.

Linen

A natural vegetable fibre from the flax plant, *Lineum usitatissimum* of the Linacae family, which is an annual plant native to Europe. Particularly fine linen comes from Chambray, in France, and is prolific in south German states, Ireland and England.

The stems are processed into a soft flexible state and produce a long staple

144 Hand-made paper and net, with machine embroidery and twined threads forming a mesh. 38 × 28 cm (15 × 11 in.). 1985. Worked by Peggy Field.

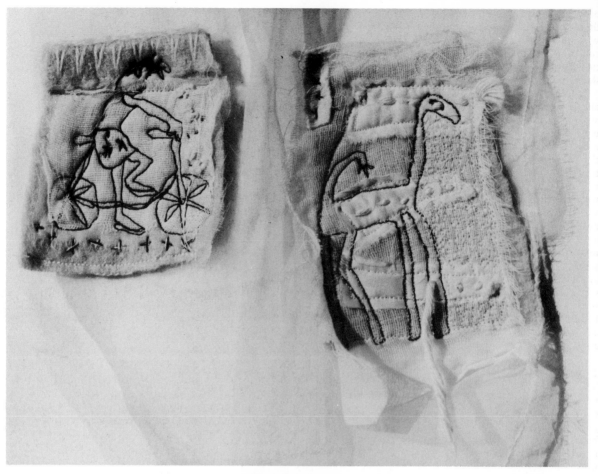

145 *Experiment on blanket cloth with muslin and stitchery. 1985. Worked by Lindy Richardson.*

fibre for spinning and weaving. Figs 53, 102, 109, 149, 217, 228, 298, 310.

Characteristics

Linen like cotton, is a good conductor of heat. In wear it allows heat to pass through so that the body is kept cool by the fresh air entering and maintaining an even temperature.

Linen does not insulate and is therefore very comfortable to wear. It is particularly absorbent and has a lustrous soft sheen when expertly spun and woven, and a slight but attractive slub which is displayed by pressing on the wrong side with a damp cloth.

Linen is stronger when wet and dries slightly crisp and stiffened. As it

146 *Freely made net with cotton velvet appliqué, seeding and silk buttonhole, mounted on synthetic brocade with ink drawing on cotton. 1985. Worked by Lindy Richardson.*

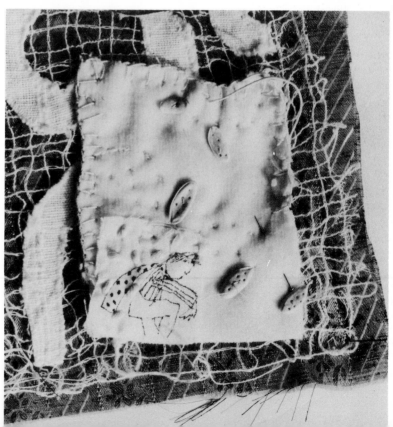

is hard-wearing, it is good for articles that need frequent washing, which with its absorbent qualities explains its continued use for tea towels and particularly for lace, as it maintains its shape whereas cotton flops.

Linen does not get statically charged and so does not attract dust and dirt; it also launders well, accepting hot water, soap and detergents. It requires damp pressing to deal with the tendency to crease and shrink. A further precaution against shrinkage is to plunge linen into hot water and then press before beginning a piece of work requiring accurate measurement. Linen was used as a backing for embroidery in the past, but now a mix with synthetic fibres generally serves this purpose since pure linen is as expensive as silk; sometimes more so. It is impossible to tear linen; it is wrenched apart leaving frayed edges. It does not accept chemicals as easily as cotton, and dyes have a muted appearance.

History

Throughout the centuries and in many countries linen has a long history of use for embroidery, and has great ceremonial associations. It has been used for all forms of dress, from ritual robes for priests to basic garments for peasants. A comprehensive survey would be a specialized subject, but some details show its development from early civilizations.

Early centuries BC – linen of very fine quality was made at Memphis, Egypt.

1200 BC – linen was produced at Pylos, Greece, at the time of Homer. Workers imported from Troy (in present-day Turkey) retted flax by the River Linaria at Pylos.

AD 100 – linen was used in burial grounds in Britain.

1000–1100 – weavers from the Flemish Netherlands (now Belgium and Holland) came to England.

1368 – a company of weavers was founded. Women and girls at this time provided linen for household purposes by growing, spinning and weaving flax. On marriage they provided a woven length or 'web' for setting up a home. Some linen weavers were known as 'websters'.

1600–1700 – English, Scottish and Irish linen weaving became famous and was widely exported. The French produced the finest linen weaving.

1812 – linen was produced by mechanization, although much was still hand-woven. The first mill for the mechanization of the production of linen textiles was built in 1812, much later than that of cotton. The process is similar to hand methods, and includes the softening of the flax stem by soaking and boiling; it is rippled, retted, scutched and heckled. Heckling consists of drawing a handful of flax stems through steel teeth several times with progressively finer teeth, to disentangle the fibres and bring them into line. The longer-length staple is known as 'line' and is considered the best; 'tow' is the shorter ends. The flax line is then sorted for quality and prepared for spinning by spreading, drawing and roving. The coarser linen threads are dry-spun and the finer wet-spun. Further processes make a smooth lustrous thread for weaving. It is sometimes treated with lime, soda and starch, and mangled to give a high stiff gloss.

1943 – a report shows that during the war nearly 250,000 acres were cultivated with flax in Ireland and England, as supplies of cotton were cut off by German U-boats.

1950 – linen or flax cultivation declined in England and Ireland, and it was imported as tow from France, Belgium and Holland.

1981 – not one acre of flax was grown for linen production in England or Ireland.

1985 – a fashion revival is predicted in the late 1980s for the relaxed beauty and crumpled softness of linen, when the flax industry is to be redeveloped using new technology and chemical retting, and with a probable 1,000 acres of flax under cultivation.

The luxury represented by a return to high-quality linen bed sheets and dress, in spite of the fickle and precarious nature of fashion, is indicated by the fact that a pair of kingsize sheets in linen cost £270 in 1984 and £495 in 1987.

Terms associated with linen

Some well-known names of linens hold historical interest, such as:

Cambric – the name derives from

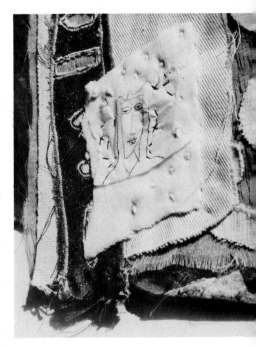

147 *A sample of layered materials using cotton velvet, twill, repp, rayon slub brocade, gauze, felt and paper. 1985. Worked by Lindy Richardson.*

148 *Experiment on freely made net, with stitchery, applied herringbone material, and cotton velvet with hand seeding and machine stitchery. 1985. Worked by Lindy Richardson.*

Cambrai, a town in the département du nord, France. A beautiful linen textile of various types, it was introduced into England during the reign of Elizabeth I. Lancashire and Scotland produced imitations in cotton, at a much later date.

Cambric muslin – fine cotton, used for Ayrshire embroidery.

Irish linen – a fine linen of highest quality. The flax grown in Ireland produced the best natural fibres and rivalled that of Chambray, France, which had the highest reputation of all for growing conditions. Even threads, soft texture, smooth surface and flexibility were due to the quality of the flax, and Belfast, Carrickfergus and Londonderry were the main centres of production.

Lawn – lawn with cut work, silver and spangles is recorded as a gift to Queen Elizabeth I. It would seem to have been a typical ruff with the additions of silver decoration to make an impressive present. Shirts, ruffles, and ceremonial handkerchiefs were also made of this material. Lawn overlaps to some extent with cotton muslins. The term lawn probably derived from the French *linge* (linen), and is now often applied to cotton.

Linen damask – a fine twill and satin-type weave, with a design of flowers, stripes or ciphers, woven into the ground and reversible. The right side is identified by the satin-weave to the design. Double damask is reversible, that is, satin both sides.

Damask linen was used for tablecloths and napkins and was produced mainly at Lisburn in Ireland, Bradford in England, and Dunfermline in Scotland, all famous centres. See *Huckaback*.

Silk

Silk is a natural fibre, obtained from the cocoon of the moth *Bombyx mori*. The worm produces a filament from an orifice or spinneret in the head, and this is worked round the worm in a figure of eight to form a cocoon. A gum-like substance attached to the filament helps to set the cocoon. The worm or grub turns into a chrysalis in the cocoon and emerges as a moth, breaking the cocoon with an exudation of acid. The moth then lays eggs and these develop into the worm, to repeat the three-monthly cycle. The worms feed solely on the young leaves of the white mulberry tree, and therefore silk comes from countries where the tree flourishes – mainly

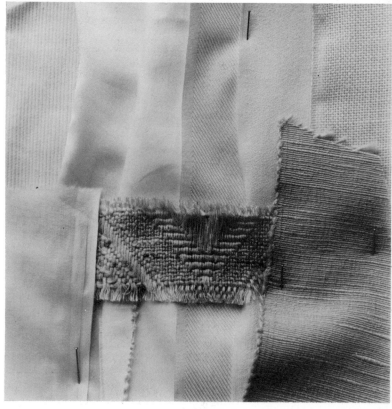

149 *Fine white materials.* Top row, from the left: *cotton piqué, silk satin, cotton sateen, twilled silk, fine wool crêpe and evenweave linen.* Below: *fine cotton weave, furnishing fabric, slubbed rayon.*

China and also Japan, India, Asia Minor, Italy and France. Lyon in France, and Venice in Italy became great European silk centres. Figs 4, 5, 64, 65, 84, 132, 164, 180, 244, 245, 272, 350.

Properties and characteristics

Silk is a very strong fibre and makes the richest and probably the most luxurious (and expensive) textile in the world. It is smooth, soft, warm, lightweight and comfortable to wear, and is often mixed and blended with other fibres to reduce costs.

Silk is not a good conductor of heat and so, when worn, body warmth is kept in and cooler, or hotter, air does not easily penetrate. Silk is therefore a good insulator against cold. It is resilient and does not crease easily, and is slightly elastic and also mothproof, but may rot and decay in bright light and hot or very humid conditions. It requires a dry even temperature and

care in handling, and should be stored on a roller or flat when possible, but not folded as it tends to crack at the crease lines.

Articles should not be allowed to get heavily soiled, as silk is liable to stain easily. Stains should be treated with as little delay as possible.

Dry-cleaning is considered the best method of cleaning, but washing of silk underwear (lingerie) and blouses should be carried out with a mild liquid detergent. Soap tends to leave a film on the fibres. Excess moisture may be absorbed by patting with a dry towel of cotton or linen. Press with a warm iron while damp or use a slightly damp cloth.

Silk does not shrink but may appear to contract, which is usually due to the type of weave, such as that of crêpe de Chine. It accepts dyes easily to show colours of glowing and vibrant brilliance.

Sericulture

Sericulture is the process of breeding silkworms to produce a silk textile. As with other textiles, most processes are now mechanized versions of work previously carried out by hand.

To obtain silk for spinning, the worm has to be stifled by hot air so that it does not emerge and break the cocoon. The cocoon is then soaked and softened in warm water to loosen the gum and allow the filament to be unwound in as continuous a line as possible.

Silk thread comes from reeling together the filaments of approximately seven cocoons, which are lightly twisted together for a warp or warp-ing. Reeling, or unwinding the cocoons, is the main process of silk production or sericulture. A continuous filament is usually about 300–350 yards; the remaining broken filaments are used as staple fibre and spun into a yarn or thread which is used in the weft, or sometimes as a warp. The total length of filament composing the cocoon is approximately 500–1,000 yards.

The gum is continuously disposed of throughout production, yet even the woven textile is stiff with traces of it. When the gum is finally dissolved and washed away, the gleaming brilliance and softly falling, fluid qualities of silk are revealed.

151   Detail of fig. 150.

150   A development of sheer material, with cut pieces for texture, and various materials such as leather, synthetics and ceramic beads, French knots, padding, seeding and eyelets. The foundation is worked on the shirring machine. 1985. Worked by Sue Herbert.

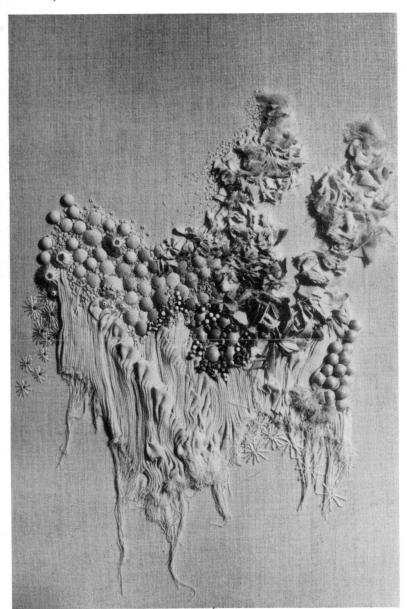

The sheen of silk is particularly good for quilting, and especially so in white, as the shadows made by the stitching make a subtle contrast. Knotted stitches, contrasting with satin stitch, are also typically effective.

History

The history of silk gives one repeated fact, that the production was kept a secret in China from approximately 3000 BC to AD 400, when it reached Korea and Japan by being smuggled out with refugees. Some eggs of the moth were hidden in the hollow of bamboo canes and brought out of China through Byzantium (Istanbul), and from these eggs sericulture developed in the West. It reached India and Asia and then Italy, France and England by the fifteenth century.

There are other well-known romantic stories, one of a Chinese princess hiding some eggs in bamboo canes among her wedding gifts when on her way to marriage outside China, and another of two Christian monks hiding eggs in bamboo canes attached to sacred scrolls.

is a time-honoured industry. Lavenham in Suffolk was an early centre, as were the South Downs and Devon. Bradford, in Yorkshire, is a typical later one. Figs 130, 149, 268.

Characteristics

Wool, like silk, is not a good conductor of heat and therefore is a good insulator as, when worn, it helps retain the body heat.

Wool is warm to wear, and hard-wearing, but is liable to attack by moth and mildew, if stored damp. It is resilient and springy and naturally crease-resistant, but tends to shrink if roughly washed. It is often treated with chemical resistants and shower- and stain-repellents; some pre-shrunk labels occur.

Production

The fleece is treated in the expert processes of the great woollen textile industry, upon which much of England's early prosperity was founded.

The cleaning processes include washing, scouring, beating and scribbling to remove dirt. Carding, on early machines such as the Licker-in and the stripper, combed the fibres into a smooth sliver of parallel untwisted thread, which was then stretched and twisted ready for spinning and weaving.

When the wool is combed the fibres are separated and the shorter staple is removed; the longer staple fibre of about four inches is used to form a very firm crisp yarn known as worsted. It forms a hard-wearing and handsome textile for suits and coats of the best quality. The shorter staple is also of good quality and is used to make an excellent textile for dress and lightweight garments.

Bleaching and singeing are among other processes which finish the final product.

The woollen industry is versatile and of a much longer establishment in England than cotton. It is an involved and interesting subject, and a study in itself. Wool displays the weaver's art, skill and ability and also that of the tailor and dressmaker, but it does not have a great history in white embroidery, although white satin and velvet, beads, braids and trimmings make effective textures on soft white

Names associated with silk textiles

Derby– produced ribbons, famous for the weaving.

Flemings– Huguenots, refugees who excelled as silk weavers.

France – high traditional technique.

Italian – high traditional technique of early silk velvets and later brocades and damask.

Spitalfields – a district of London where Huguenots settled in 1685, famous for silk brocade and damask weaving.

Wool

Wool is a natural animal fibre from the fleece, or coat, of sheep. The animals are shorn and the fleece produces a short staple fibre of approximately four inches in length.

Other wools come from merino sheep, camel hair, the angora goat (often called mohair), rabbit, llama, alpaca and vicuna goat, a cashmere. All have a lustrous and longer staple fibre than sheep's wool and make a fine, lightweight, warm and luxurious wool, which is soft but not as hard-wearing as sheep's wool.

Sheep's wool traditionally comes from Britain, where wool production

wool for cloaks, capes, coats, dresses and suits.

Wool is used in many peasant and ethnic communities, with a range of processes for production, and often using a primitive distaff and spindle for spinning and a simple loom for weaving to a very high standard.

Embroidery threads

There is a very good variety of textures in wool threads, including knitting wools for experimental and inventive work and wools for the traditional techniques of canvas work. Individually made threads from basic fibres can add variety. Figs 123, 128.

Felt

Felt is a matted or bonded cloth and is produced mainly from unspun fibres. Its surface can be textured or smooth, and is open to scuffing, cutting and original treatments. Fig. 154.

Synthetic fibres

Synthetic fibres consist of mineral fibre with either:

1 some organic content or origin, such as wood pulp or cotton linters (waste), which when treated with chemicals are classed as cellulose and known as viscose (rayon or 'artificial silk'), first produced in the USA in 1905; acetate (rayon or 'art silk'), produced in 1920; and triacetate (similar to nylon), first produced in the UK about 1950; or
2 entirely chemical content, such as oil derivatives, which are classed as synthetics and known as polyamide (nylon) first produced in the USA in 1930; polyester (Terylene, Dacron), first produced in the UK in 1941; and acrylic (Acrilan) first produced in the UK in 1952.
Figs 131, 134, 143, 153, 156, 157, 233, 254, 300.

Characteristics

All synthetic fibre has been developed to have hard-wearing qualities with resistance to creasing, shrinkage, moth and mildew, and to be almost indestructible, apart from some which melt under excessive heat.

154 Pieced squares sample. Squares of iron-on backing, joined with hand stitching. 1985. Worked by Irene Ord.

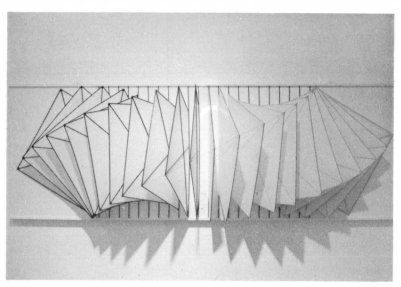

During the war of 1939–45, supplies of cotton and silk were greatly restricted and the use of synthetics expanded; for example, nylon replaced silk for parachutes.

After the war great advances were made in developing the industry with inventive use of chemicals, acids, solvents, starches, oil, and dyes, leading to giant plants and industries in as great a tradition as the wool, linen, silk and cotton mills.

Synthetic fibres have individual characteristics of their own and are

155 'Progression', 1983. Paper and enamel rods. Worked by Sally Freshwater.

Synthetic fibres are particularly easy to care for and most are drip-dry, non-iron and able to accept hot water.

An anti-static agent which overcomes the tendency to cling to the body because of static electricity, and also a flame-retardant against inflammability, are applied in the early stages of manufacture. Other treatments give absorbency and thermal drape for insulation, and dyes are all used in the fibre stage before spinning and weaving.

Viscose is mainly combined with other fibres in blankets, polyamide/nylon is used in underwear, sleep wear and shirts, polyester/Terylene for dress and duvets, and acrylic/Acrilan for soft knitwear. All are intermixed with natural fibre, and garments are carefully labelled with the different proportions to comply with EEC regulations.

Production of synthetic fibre

When the raw material, which has had many chemical treatments, has formed into a glutinous liquid, it is passed or forced through spinnerets or fine nozzles. The liquid is set as a fine filament or thread by the action of a setting agent, which for viscose is acid, and for acetate, hot air. Polyamide and polyester have similar processes, and all are highly involved chemical techniques.

The filament may be cut into staple

fibre and spun into a yarn, as in natural fibres.

The staple fibre mixes and blends successfully with all fibres, natural and synthetic, and the average length compares with cotton at 28–60 mm, wool, 40–100 mm, and worsted, 50–200 mm. They may also be textured by shaping them with heat. Thermoplastic shaping helps to hold the air and this makes for absorbency and insulation.

Tufted, melded and bonded cloth can also be manufactured by massed fibres set with heat in a process of lamination. Fig. 143.

History

The early synthetic fibre of the 1920s,

156 Free-standing shape in nylon. 1984. Worked by Cathy Merrowsmith.

developed to fill a wide range of uses for industry, such as tyres, carpets, and computer ribbon, as well as textiles. In the 1950s triacetate was a substitute for nylon, which was then made only in America.

The fibres are all blended and mixed with each other and with natural fibre, and their main use is to supplement natural fibres, which cannot meet the demands of the population. From supplying demand during and after the war when other supplies were cut off, synthetics have virtually replaced the great cotton and wool

157 Free-standing dome shape in fine nylon. 1984. Worked by Cathy Merrowsmith.

industries of England, where the mills now stand empty or serve as museums.

Nowadays most synthetic fibres are able to be treated to acquire qualities of natural fibres, for instance soft fluffy or bulky wool (acrilan), permanent pleating and the pliability of crêpe de Chine (terylene/polyester), the slubbed weave of linen (viscose) and the matt surface of cotton (polyamide/nylon), yet they retain the advantages of hard wear and easy care.

Nevertheless it is often thought that synthetic fibres have an unsympathetic quality and lack natural comfort and beauty.

This is shown in embroidery, where synthetic fibre does not integrate in the same way as natural fibre, although it has an acceptable character

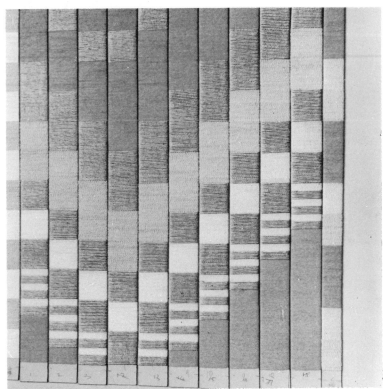

158 Detail. 'Escalator'. Wrapped threads. 1985. Worked by Constance Howard.

makes hand embroidery appear out-dated or nostalgic.

Paper Figs 126–9, 133, 134, 141, 143, 144, 147, 155.

Paper can be made from a variety of fibres and gives a range of interesting textures.

Hand made, both professionally and by experiment, it adds a personal quality to investigative embroidery.

Care of fibres and embroidery

Conservation

Conservation aims to preserve what remains of an item or object and, as the fibres are often very fragile and brittle with age and also discoloured, great care may be needed to give the correct support.

All fibres will eventually deteriorate and discolour with age, and poor climatic conditions and strong light hasten the process – particularly light, as it is so generally accepted for visual purposes when the other considerations have been taken into account. A changing display helps on this point both in public exhibitions and private and personal collections.

Discoloration and some damage and stains often have to be accepted, as the article may well be too fragile to treat or, in other cases, the treatment may be too drastic or extensive. Some stains may be locally treated and, if not removed entirely, made less apparent but the chemicals used for cleaning and stain removal may cause further damage, unless used in correct proportions.

It has been found during a monitoring programme of washing and treating white work and lace that some of the original whiteness may return for a time, but that the fibres will gradually discolour again, and in the process some loss of body occurs to the fibres. With this background knowledge, the use of many recipes for the care of textiles, either from the past or present day, should be considered with great caution and even discounted. There is a great desire to return old embroidery to its former glory, but many treatments, such as covering the area with powdered bi-carbonate of soda, potato, flour, or talcum (supposedly to absorb grease, dust and dirt), which are then all knocked or patted off from the wrong side, have unfortunately not proved successful. This type of treatment is

159 Detail. Free-standing form in gathered heavy cotton. 1984. Worked by Beverley Clark. Figs 184, 349.

for dress, especially with machine embroidery, which offers speed and inexpensiveness to make available to everyone what was once considered a luxury, and which to some extent

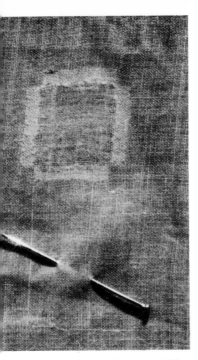

160 *This small darned patch is hidden away almost unnoticed in an Ayrshire robe – always an interesting detail to discover. 1.2 cm ($\frac{1}{2}$ in.) square.*

definitely frowned upon by professional conservators. Traces of any of these elements left in the embroidery may result in even more damage, and fragile articles may fall into pieces with firm patting.

To conserve old textiles, and in particular white work embroidery, the first step is to ensure that the item is clean and remove, if possible, any unsightly stains. It is therefore helpful to ascertain the composition of the fibre of the article and, if possible, the nature of the stain, as removal depends on the properties of both.

When in doubt, or if the article is valuable and the staining strong or extensive, cleaning should be carried out by an expert or specialist firm and the advice of a museum curator or professional conservator should be sought.

Restoration

Restoration aims to replace worn areas with completely new work, matching threads exactly in colour and texture for embroidery, lace and weaving. This is not always effective since many conditions of the past in spinning, weaving, dyeing, in the water used for the washing, atmosphere and the cultivation of the raw

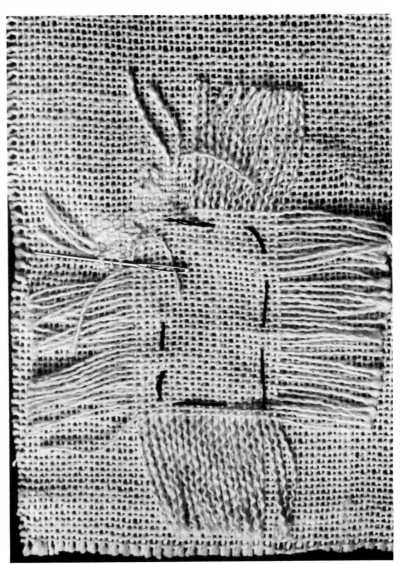

materials, however carefully considered, are changed and often elusive to copy. This also applies to study of past embroidery techniques.

Restoration does, however, give a brand new look to articles, and it is revealing to see how brash the taste may have been in the past which time has imbued with an uncharacteristic subtlety.

Repairs

The value of repairs is doubtful, as more damage is often caused, and darning into weak material does not necessarily strengthen, as it pulls away from surrounding weak areas only to increase damage. (A darned patch for a small hole in good material is a nearly invisible repair and may be found in valued garments.) Figs 160–63.

161 *Method of working a darned patch. Insert the needle into the ground of the garment and then insert a thread from the patch into the needle and draw through. Repeat until all threads have been used. Trim and press.*

Before cleaning and washing, it is advisable to back weak areas with fine net, usually of nylon, as it is strong and does not shrink. The net may be tacked on both sides of fragile embroidery during cleaning, and before the repair is carried out. The net is then removed and replaced, if required, at the back of the article to support the darning or a run stitch, worked in a fine thread, through both materials. The net should cover the whole area, or from one seam to another. It is advisable to match materials for repair in age, colour,

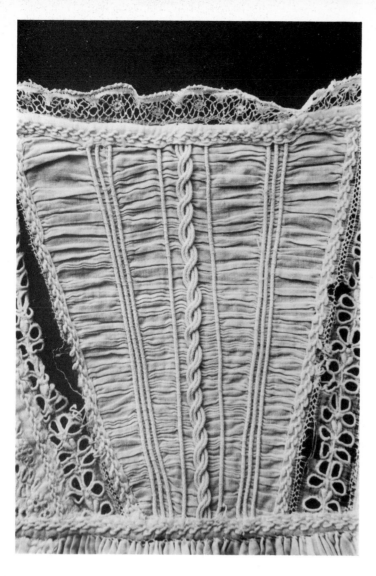

162 Bodice showing cords arranged over ruching. Note Valenciennes lace at neck, feather-stitched edges, and the skirt attached with oversewing and a folded gathered edge. The insertions at the side need the support of fine net. (Constance Howard).

texture, weave and fibre. New material, if there is no alternative, should be soaked and washed before use. Jap silk may also be used as a backing for a more solid repair.

The opinion of a professional conservator, either to carry out the repair or for a consultation, is always informative.

Cleaning

Dirt and dust are harmful and abrasive, and may be removed by rinsing and washing, using distilled or deionized water, and allowing the object to soak in several changes of water.

In white work embroidery, where cotton and linen are used so extensively, careful washing is usually a safe method of cleaning. In all cases a test is advised to note reaction to water, which should be cold, since hot water sets stains. Always use distilled or softened water whenever possible.

Stains

Waxy, greasy, or milk stains – may be treated with white spirit, lightly applied with a pad of cotton wool. Before treatment dampen, with the spirit, the area around the stain to reduce or avoid a ring mark after treatment.

Wax – excess may be lifted from the surface and the remainder covered with blotting paper and a hot iron to melt and draw the wax into the paper. Repeat, if necessary, with clean blotting paper. A dusting of fullers' earth may help absorb some grease on heavy fabrics. (*Note*: always use white spirit away from heat or fire and in a well-ventilated space, such as near an open window.)

Gravy, spots of fat, tea, coffee, and fruit juice stains – if treated immediately, and before drying, may be successfully removed by covering the area with a cotton or linen cloth or paper tissue and squeezing it very tightly, so that the stain soaks into the cloth. Otherwise when dry treat with perchlorethylene. Alternatively, these stains may be lubricated with glycerine applied with a cotton wool pad, and then washed.

Some inks, blood and rust stains – may be treated with salt and washed in a weak (5%) solution of oxalic acid. Blood before it is dry, for instance from a pricked finger, may be removed by lightly touching with the tip of the tongue or saliva of the same person. Hold a cloth behind the mark to absorb the stain. The enzymes of the saliva dissolve the blood. Boiling and bleaching are destructive.

Iron mould – may be treated with oxalic acid solution; when linked with damp marks, use distilled water and very weak solution of detergent. Dab with cotton wool or paint brush. Rinse in distilled water.

Lipstick, ballpoint pen and fruit – dab the area with cotton wool soaked in perchlorethylene – to be found in proprietary cleaning preparations sold at chemists and stores. Note the contents on the bottle.

Nail varnish – treat with acetone.

(*Note*: white feathers may be dusted with magnesium carbonate powder.)

Rinsing and washing

This method applies to cotton, linen, silks and some wools.

1 Lay the article flat on a sheet of polythene to support it, and to avoid frequent handling, in a clean container large enough to accept the article covered with water – a plastic bowl or (clean) seed tray is ideal. Lift the article in and out of

163   Net, conserving the fragile insertion, is attached at seams on each side of bodice. Note the net to be trimmed away at the neck. The most effective treatment of ruching is to remove it from the bodice, undo the gathers, and clean and stretch the cotton. Renew the gathers and replace in the bodice. Textured surfaces all need care. Crinkle fabrics, bouclé and crêpe require tacking and measuring to keep the original appearance. Professional advice is essential.

the tray on the polythene to keep it flat. Fig. 164.

2 As hot water sets stains, rinse the article several times in cool or cold distilled water, or water from a water softener, leaving it to soak for half an hour. Longer soaking may allow the dirt to redeposit.

3 After cold rinsing, further treatment with a solution of a mild, good-quality liquid detergent is recommended, as soap tends to leave a film on the fabric.

4 Keep the article flat and agitate the water around it.

5 Lift out the article on the polythene sheet and rinse out the detergent, either by gentle running water or several changes of water in the container. Use distilled or soft water.

6 Excess moisture may be soaked up by resting the work flat on the polythene and lightly dabbing or patting with a towel or white kitchen tissue.

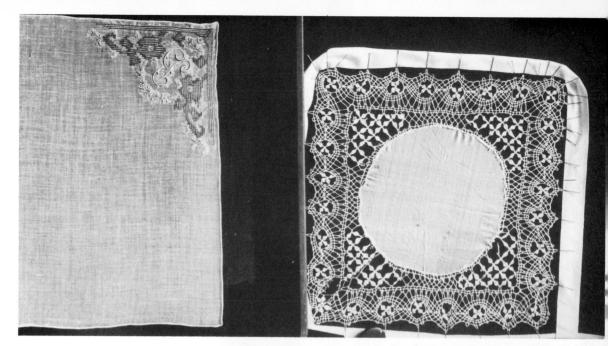

164 Left: *a wet handkerchief pressed out to dry on a sheet of glass in order to avoid ironing, which might flatten the texture. Behind the sheet of glass is a shallow seed tray, suitable as a receptacle for washing articles flat.*
Right: *a lace-edged doily pinned out to dry. (The tape is a prop to display the pins.) The silk centre is disconcertingly off the straight grain, but the outer edge should be pinned square (i.e., with right angled corners). A clean plastic sheet over a soft board as a base may be used for lace.*

Stretching

Both of these methods avoid flattening or distorting embroidery with an iron.

1 Small flat items or fragments, such as handkerchiefs, may be pressed or eased out on a clean glass or formica surface, gently pulling into shape with the threads or grain of the ground at right angles. With occasional checking, leave until dry. Rural pictures of the past showing articles stretched out on bushes or the ground to dry are not an indication of slovenly work, but show a sensible and inexpensive

165 *Knitted lace pinned out to display pattern, in the method used for lace. Each point has a pin. The work is dampened, and when it is dry and the pins are removed the points stay in position, as shown bottom left.*

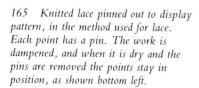

method of smoothing out creases.

2 All lightweight textiles, such as muslin, net and lace, are most successfully finished if they are not pressed with an iron but laid on a soft thin blanket while damp and pinned round the outer edge with brass pins upright into the blanket. Keep the threads and grain at right angles, and treat with care any curved or broken edges.

When dry, the pins are removed and the article will be found to have had much of its original crispness and vitality restored. (*Note:* this method is particularly successful with lace and bridal veils. In the case of a veil, lay a sheet over carpet, and with a box of pins to hand, pin out four sides of the veil while it is damp. If left overnight in a place where the carpet will not be trodden on, the veil can be lifted in the morning renewed.) Each curve, point, picot or scallop of the edge should be shaped with a pin and the whole outer edge should be checked for shape – for example, right-angled corners if it is a square.

Stretching by mounting into a frame is another method, but care is needed as the work may split and tear under too strong a tension.

Pressing

Pressing the wrong side of embroidery on cotton and linen may be successful when care is taken, as pressing with an iron is different from ironing.

Pressing is used for embroideries, needlework and dressmaking processes. It is usually carried out with a pressing cloth between the article and the iron. The main difference between pressing and ironing is that the iron is pressed on to the material and lifted and pressed again, firmly but without leaving the impression of the iron on

167 An ironing pad made of eight thicknesses of soft towelling covered with several thicknesses of old sheeting for a smooth surface when pressing embroidery. Note the insertion with beading on either side and plain material for a seam.

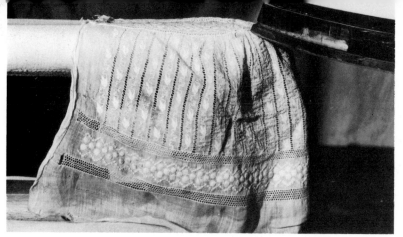

168　The sleeve board is helpful for shaped articles like a bonnet or sleeves, touching up points of gathers, and other details, to avoid creasing the article elsewhere. The front of the bonnet is incomplete; it would be finished with lace or frills and drawn up round the face. The drawstrings meet on the inside at centre front, and are released for laundering and pressing. A damp or dry cloth, as required, may be used between the iron and the article, but is not shown in the illustration.

the work. Tests and practice with spare material are strongly recommended.

Embroidery should be pressed on a firm surface covered with several layers of soft towel or blanket, under a smooth clean sheet. The blanket allows the raised surface texture of the embroidery to sink into the softness but the firm surface allows the iron to press out creases. Attention should always be given to the grain of the material. Keep the threads of the background, which are vertical and horizontal, always at right angles to each other as the pressing proceeds.

Ironing

Ironing is a laundry method and technique, where the iron passes over the material, often while still damp from laundering, in gliding movements. Take care not to distort the grain and the shape of the article and always aim to iron with the direction of the grain.

Getting up an article

When getting up a garment for display, the order of pressing, to avoid creasing as much as possible, is as follows:

(*On the wrong side*)

- Frills, collars cuffs. (A sleeve board and a padded roll are useful aids for invisible seams and for detailed work such as easing the point of the iron into the gathers.)
- Waistbands, shoulder yokes, yokes, sleeves, back and front of skirt, back and front of bodice.
- Re-check collar and any detail, such as frills, last.

Protection

When storing embroidery or textiles, protection is necessary from dust and

169　The sleeve board enables the iron to work up closely either side of a seam allowance without marking the garment on the right side.

dirt, strong light, sunlight, heat, damp, mildew, warmth, moth and stagnant conditions, since all these contribute to rot and decay. Insect repellent strips, mothballs or crystals of tetradichlorbenzine may be hung

to circulate in the air, but should not touch the article or embroidery.

Industrial or city conditions set up sulphur dioxide in the atmosphere from petrol fumes and smoke and this is organically absorbed by the stones and wood of buildings, and by textiles. A simple and successful protection is to wrap all articles in acid-free tissue paper. White is recommended, as the colour tends to run very easily with a spot of water.

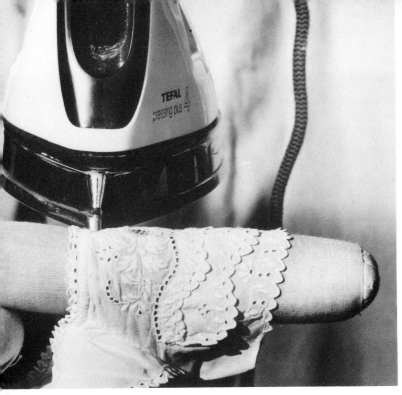

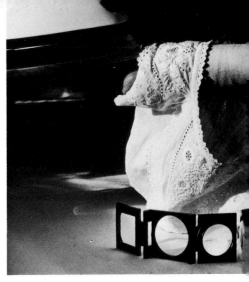

170 A roll covered with soft cloth and smaller than a sleeve board is useful for touching up.

171 Pressing small frills and similar details. A finger may hold other material out of the way. Note the magnifying glass known as a 'linen tester', as it is marked with measurements and has a glass powerful enough to count the threads of the background. The magnifier also opens out to be used for other purposes. It is a worthwhile piece of equipment and can show up revealing details of workmanship. See also figs. 172, 173.

172 The use of a covered roll, enabling layers of frills to be pressed without unnecessary creasing. Start with the top frill, as in fig. 166. Note: (i) Acid-free tissue paper for storing and packing. Coloured paper is not dye-fast. (ii) Prickers for marking out designs, lace charts and prickings. One is a modern needle vice (from tool shops); on the right is an antique mahogany-handled pricker. (iii) Three magnifying glasses. The large familiar reading glass is fairly satisfactory, and helpful for details. The small antique tortoiseshell botanical glass is also good. The linen tester mentioned in caption 171 is a useful tool.

Rolling

The most successful way to store large flat items is to prepare a roller of hollow card, or possibly of wood, and slightly wider than the article. Cover the roll with acid-free white tissue paper and then roll the article on to it, with the right side of the embroidery outside. This avoids crushing the embroidery and keeps the surface smooth and very slightly stretched. The roller extending slightly beyond the work protects the edges. Sheets of the same tissue paper may be rolled in with the embroidery. Fig. 173.

Folding

Articles such as dresses or robes which are not suitable for rolling should be folded with rolls of paper at the folds to avoid permanent creases, as sharp creases or folds tend to crack the fibres for the early stages of rot. The items should then be placed in a conservation box.

The centre of the work, where the main design is usually placed, and where the eye is naturally drawn, should not be folded. It is an ugly distraction if there are creases quartering the centre in any textile. This may be avoided by folding the article into three both ways. This leaves the centre, or area of greatest interest, uncreased. If the main interest is asymmetrical, the folds should be arranged round it.

Storing

Wrapped and folded articles are best kept in a cool dark cupboard away from light and warmth, with sliding shelves or drawers or with close-fitting doors to avoid infiltration of dust. A velvet edging stuck to the edges of the doors will provide dust-proofing.

An important feature when storing textiles is to air the items regularly every four to six weeks in a light airy atmosphere to review their condition. Although darkness protects the textile, it also offers suitable conditions for moths to breed, and airing is a vital precaution.

Mounting and display

A stretcher, either made from wooden battens, approximately 1 × 1 in., or bought from an art supplier and then mounted with backing, is a suitable basis on which to display embroidery, lace or fragments of textiles. Ensure that the corners are square, i.e. at 90°. The stretcher should be 5–7.5 cm (2–3 in.) larger than the object so that it is not crowded by the frame. Figs 84, 174.

A neutral, fine-grain backing, either calico or linen, pre-shrunk, is suitable so that the background does not overpower the item concerned. Pull the backing firmly over the stretcher and secure with small nails, or staples using a staple gun. Match the grain with the edge of the stretcher. Work in the following order: (i) the base, (ii) the top, (iii) one side and finally (iv) the remaining side. Begin at the centre of each edge.

A further lightweight material may be used to cover the backing to highlight white openwork, lace or embroidery, or to suit a particular room setting, such as a light blue or rose-coloured satin. Dark or light colours may be chosen, and pale blue is a popular choice to set off white. Secure this decorative backing with evenly spaced overcast stitches into the basic backing.

A woollen backing, although easy

173 A roll of card or newspaper covered in acid-free tissue paper, used for storing embroidery, with the article rolled round it right side out, and with a layer of the same tissue paper between. Note the linen tester in situ at the correct distance for viewing. The botanical magnifier is closed. On the left is a pack of acid-free tissue paper.

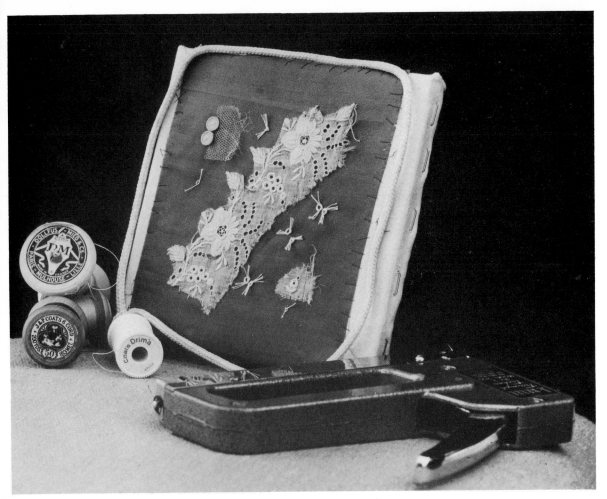

174 Small collage of conservation items, showing fine linen secured on a stretcher with staples, and an extra silk mount secured with spaced stitches. The conserved objects of Ayrshire embroidery and two Dorset buttons are lightly stitched in place. A cord laid in place for stitching illustrates a simple method of raising the glass from the surface of the embroidery when framed. Note the threads suitable for this work, and the staple gun.

to handle, tends to attract moth, and silk alone is not strong enough. Linen is suitable, without an overpowering weave, but synthetic fibres are often harsh and unsympathetic to natural and old textiles.

The embroidery is lightly stitched on to the backing, matching both warp and weft grains. Pin at suitable points with an upright pin. The uneven edges of fragments are particularly attractive and appealing, and so need not be cut and trimmed to a straight even edge.

When the mounting is completed, it is advisable to secure a board over the back of the stretcher or frame, as this helps to keep out dust and dirt, and definitely preserves the textiles, as has been proved by work protected in this way. Alternatively, the work may be carefully removed from the stretcher, mounted over strong card as for new work, and then framed for protection.

A glazed frame may complete the protection of the mounted work. An inner frame to lift the glass from resting on raised embroidery is recommended if this can be arranged; otherwise a cord sewn round the outer and top edge of the mounted work is a good guard and raises the glass. The cord is hidden by the edge or lip of the frame.

A further method is to cut a window in a card mount and cover this with material which has a smooth fine subtle weave, such as calico or silk, and does not conflict with the conserved subject. Insert the subject from the back, without the stretcher or card, by means of stitches or adhesive. Cover the back and set in a frame with glass. The thickness of the mount protects the embroidery from the glass.

Tacking or light stitches should be substituted for pins when mounting historical work.

What may seem a pathetic piece of work, when it is got up – that is, rinsed, stretched and mounted – often displays fine features of genuine interest. The fragmentary nature of some specimens intensifies a charm which perfectly preserved professional examples may not have.

FIGURED MUSLIN

Muslin decorated with dots, spots or trefoils.See *Fibres*.

FIL

French term for thread.

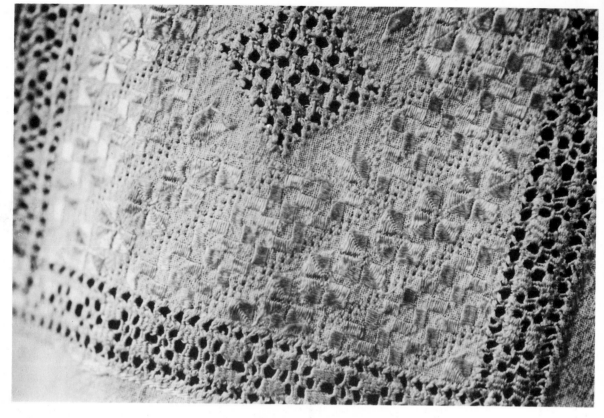

175 *Example of floss embroidery with counted satin stitch and eyelets, punch stitch, flat stitch with drawn thread work and needleweaving bars. Note the change of light on the silk. (Lise Mossery).*

FIL DE TRACE

A couched thread outlining the design on the usual firm base of paper or linen in the making of needlepoint lace or reticella. The term also denotes the thread for this. Fig. 268.

FILET

A term fashionable in the nineteenth century for net darning and/or the making of net, known as lacis in the sixteenth and seventeenth centuries.

FILLINGS

The use of stitchery, and particularly buttonhole stitch or needle-made fillings, darning, counted satin stitch and counted patterns, to fill areas of a design such as leaves and petals or open areas.

112

FISHERMAN'S KNOT

Square netting secured at intersections with knots. See *Net.*

FLOSS SILK EMBROIDERY

Floss thread is an unspun silk of oriental origin, for instance from India, China, Japan or Turkey. Typically, the work uses white on white and generally displays the high gloss of silk in counted stitch patterns, needleweaving and flat stitch on table mats or blouses. Short lengths of thread should be worked to avoid fraying of the thread. Figs 175–80.

Although carded and drawn out as a thread, floss silk is not spun and twisted. The outer covering of the silk cocoon is sometimes used, and the shorter lengths are worked together for floss thread. Better-quality silk comes from the centre of the cocoon, where the thread is more continuous. Stout floss is used for laid work, particularly in church embroidery.

Floss threads are used for flat stitchery such as fishbone stitch (see figs 176–9), which is one of a group of stitches sometimes referred to as 'Oriental' when worked in silk and includes:

Basket stitch

Cretan stitch and open cretan stitch

Double back stitch – a slanting form of herringbone.

176 *Fishbone stitch or flat stitch composite with eyelets. 1 Work an Algerian eyelet of eight stitches over two threads and bring needle out in same position as last stitch. 2 Insert needle three threads down and bring out under two threads, slanting one thread up. 3 Insert needle three threads across and bring out under two, straight up. Continue as in (2), increasing a thread each time until there are five stitches on each side. 4 Position needle and thread as indicated and draw thread through. 5 Work an eyelet as indicated, omitting top left stitch. 6 Repeat (2), inserting needle three threads across and bringing it out under two threads and slanting one thread. 7 As (3).*
The space between the top motif and the lower surrounding motifs may be increased by inserting the needle as in (4), but bring it out more than two threads down and then complete the eyelet as at (5) and continue onward.

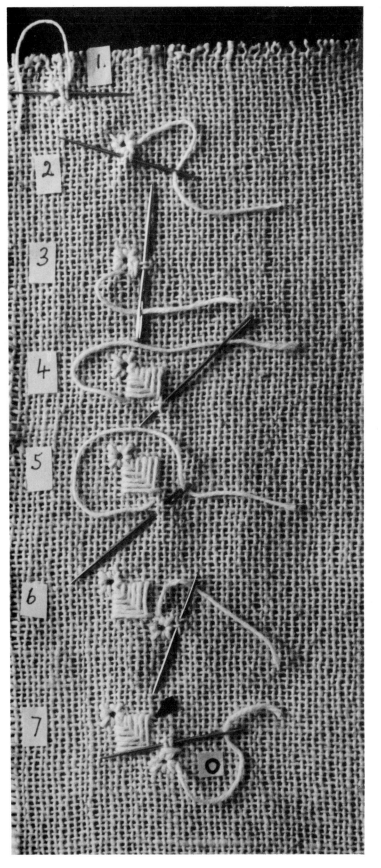

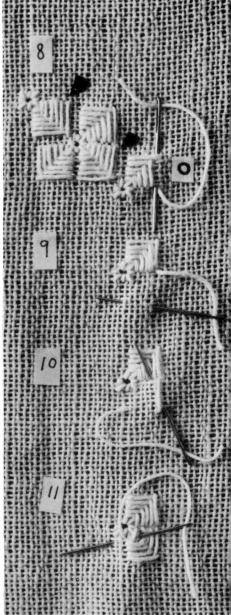

177   8 Indicates motif may be worked
with a larger number of stitches, but the
process is the same. Pointers indicate the
repeat of the top motif. 'O' indicates
continuation point from (7) (fig. 176)
and position of needle for next motif.
9 Insert needle seven threads down and
six threads across, slanting one thread
up. 10 Insert needle seven threads
acrosss and six threads up, slanting two
threads up. Continue reducing one
thread until there are five stitches.
When familiar with the work, you may
find that there are alternatives to this
stage of working the motif. 11 Position
needle as indicated. Note overlapping
stitches.

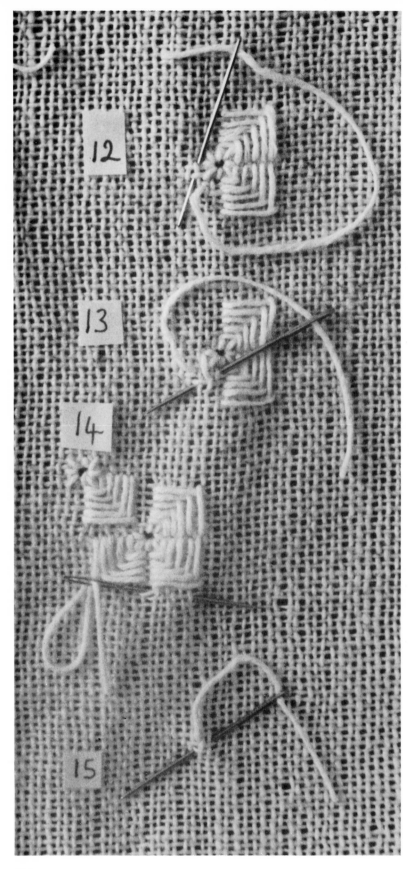

12 *Insert needle three threads straight up and bring out under two threads, slanting one thread across.* 13 *Insert needle three threads across and bring out under three threads, slanting two threads down. Repeat (12) and (13) for five stitches.* 14 *Bring needle out as indicated under six threads and slanting down two threads.* 15 *In position for working the first stitch of the next eyelet.*

179   Experiments in flat stitches.

Fishbone stitch, open fishbone stitch and raised fishbone stitch – slanting stitches.

Flat stitch – like fishbone and with horizontal stitches overlapping on a centre line.

Leaf stitch

Ladder stitch

Roumanian stitch

Vandyke stitch – no centre stitch on reverse.

Mrs Christie's *Samplers and Stitches* shows ladder stitch as different from both the composite white work ladder stitch and the simple open chain stitch, which is sometimes known as ladder stitch. For examination purposes, students should perhaps provide information such as a description or a mention of the purpose and use of the stitch, to avoid any doubt. Many stitch names, as has been noted, were evolved by the Victorians, and are now sometimes duplicated. Oriental stitches, like darning, are well integrated with the background, which keeps the silk in good condition, and the sheen well displayed by the smooth surface of the stitch.

Although floss silk embroidery

looks rich in colour, white has a particular brilliance which accentuates the stitchery. The stitches are frequently found in work from areas where silk is readily available as an embroidery thread, such as Turkey, the Mediterranean, India and China. Other features of the work are:

- fundamental and expert understanding of the stitches;
- suitability to purpose;
- exploitation of the thread so that the greatest amount shows on the top surface;
- work which is almost reversible;
- strong and integrated stitchery;
- smooth interlacing or overlapping stitches of a greater subtlety than counted satin stitch.

All activity in stitchery is useful for assessment and consideration when discovering methods of the past. Oriental and early patterns are frequently complex, and indicate the slower pace of life, before the speed of machine work.

Forethought is required when attempting stitches from historical examples, so that the needle finishes in the correct position for continuing the next movement. Many alternatives may be found.

An interesting composition of fishbone stitch, or Oriental fishbone, and Algerian eyelets in floss silk, is used for motifs in a continuous sequence of working and also forms a reversible pattern. Each motif may be worked individually, as a possibly easier alternative, but it is then necessary to turn to the back of the work, in order to run the working thread through the back of previous stitching and arrive neatly at the centre for the next motif. A counted satin stitch motif may appear to be even simpler, but it gives a different character, as the sharp divisions show some background threads.

The use of a frame is optional but helpful for counting threads and checking repeats in the pattern. A tapestry needle avoids splitting working and ground threads, and is very useful when unpicking and reworking becomes necessary.

FLOURISHING THREAD

A nineteenth-century name for a fine linen thread, silky and shiny, for repairing damask linen. It may be found wound on cards, left over from work, when searching old work boxes.

FLOWERS

See *Satin stitch*

FOOTING

See *Heading*

FRILL

Frills are a feature of white embroidery, for pillows and cushions and particularly for dress decoration, as an accessory at the neck and wrists of a garment and also as part of the design and construction, such as on wide frilled skirts or down the front bodice or round the shoulders. Frills may be added to frills for skirts and collars, or inset as rows of small frills for decorating skirts, sleeves and bodices, and as edgings and linings to petticoats to give body and fullness. When used as a lining or protection to the train of a dress as in Edwardian times, the term *balayeuse* or 'sweeper' was used, and the rows of frills bought commercially for the purpose were called *balerino*.

All materials can be used.

Frills are usually twice the length of the finished area, otherwise the fullness appears meagre and the frills fall flat. In fine material more fullness is required, as much as four times the finished length. Figs 15, 29, 59, 182.

To set the frilling evenly, mark the edge which is to receive the frilling into four with pins, and divide the frilling also into four. Draw up the fullness, match the pins and tack into place. Stitch either by hand or machine, according to design.

The gathering used to draw up the fullness helps to keep the frill standing crisply, but the stitchery of an embroidered frill also acts as an effective stiffener, as well as being an added decoration, particularly a buttonholed edge, as it is so firm. Tucks which run the length of the frill serve the same purpose of stiffening and decoration. Most embroidery techniques are suitable, particularly broderie anglaise and eyelet.

Embroidered cotton frilling became very popular with the onset of machine embroidery as it was much cheaper than hand work and also available in vast quantities.

FRINGE

In white work a fringe made from knitting is an important and typical feature of Mountmellick embroidery, and it is rewarding to find such examples, as they are frequently removed because of wear and tear.

Fringes are otherwise used as trimming as in other forms of embroidery, often on collars and the edges of capes, cushions and table linen; here

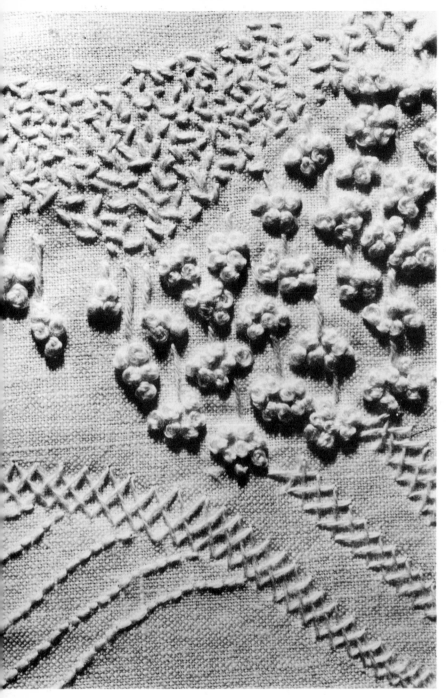

181 *French knots used in a sampler, with seeding at the top, and herringbone and back stitch at the base. 1980. (Tunbridge Wells Centre).*

FRENCH CAMBRIC

Very high quality linen cambric with a naturally silky finish, used for hand-decorated handkerchiefs and exquisite baby clothes, including exceptional examples of Ayrshire-style embroidery. Originally made at Cambrai, France, now a cotton material. See *(Fibres (linen)).*

FRENCH KNOT

A stitch used in white embroidery for texture to contrast with the ground material or other smooth stitches, such as satin stitch or stem stitch. Figs 14, 150, 181.

look for this process of construction when purchasing garments at sales, as it makes a considerably more delicate finish than a double yoke or a heavy binding sewn on the inside of a garment to hide the raw edges.

A rolled and gathered seam is another neat and attractive finish. Fig. 118.

Coilisse

Coilisse is a French term for gathering by a fine running stitch drawn up to pucker the surface with irregular wrinkles, yet it gives a uniformity of broken texture and offers scope for a subtle textured surface. Another treatment may be achieved by a gathered length of material drawn up and dampened and left to dry, with the gathering thread then removed; this makes a textured surface for textile work and a ground for further embroidery. It is possible to organize patterns in this way when gathered by hand.

Other forms of gathering are also introduced into present-day embroidery.

the type of fringe worked into the edge of the article by darning is perhaps the most applicable, as it launders well and is securely attached. Frontispiece, figs 55, 59, 234, 237.

182 Frill. Machine-embroidered dots and beading and hand-made tucks.

GATHERING

A row of run stitches used along a length of material which, when drawn up, fits a shorter length, such as a full sleeve into a cuff. Until recently this was done with great precision by hand, with two rows of identical stitches and often counting four and three threads of cotton or muslin to make very neat pleats. Figs 30, 183, 184.

In many examples the top edge of the gathered length was folded over once and the gathering thread run through the double thickness. The fullness was usually tightly drawn up, and this kept the raw edge in place and protected it. Fig. 58.

This made a simple method for attaching the fullness to a single thickness of material such as insertions, lace, or a light and embroidered yoke as in blouses and baby robes. The stitches pass between the fold of gathering to make a crisp and rounded finish to the fullness. It is interesting to

G

GADROON

Plaited trimming similar to braid, often in white as a fashionable finish for coats. See *Braid, Cord.*

183 Gathering stitches with beads on cotton seersucker. 1985. Worked by Irene Ord.

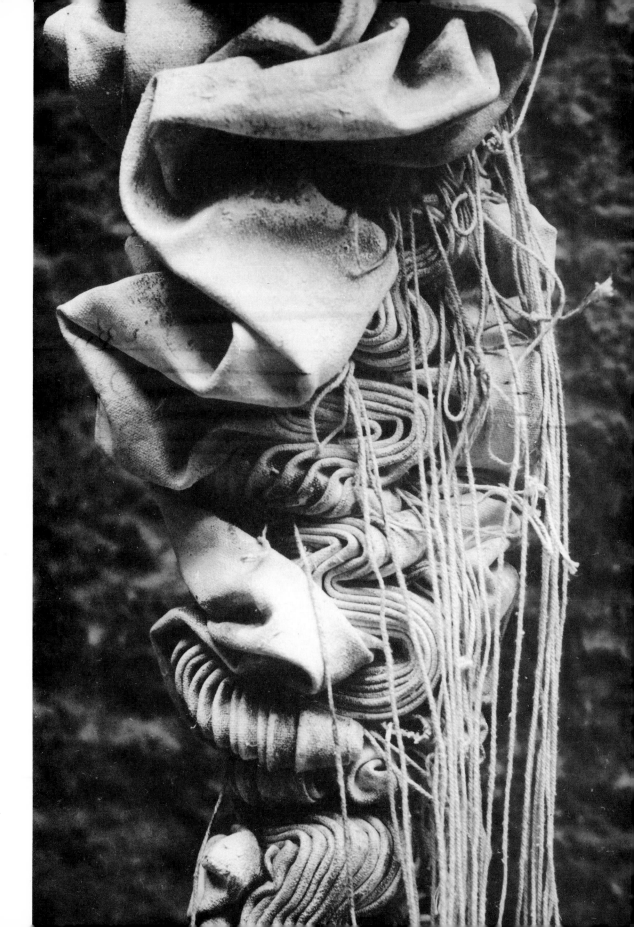

184 Gathering, in a free-standing form showing hanging threads and the cotton reinforced with paint. 1985. Worked by Beverley Clark. Figs 159, 349.

Stroking

Stroking is a step in the method of controlling fullness used regularly in the nineteenth and early twentieth centuries to set gathers exactly into the band of a skirt, yoke or cuff, by passing a blunt needle down between the gathering stitches to make small pleats to stitch between. The work was frequently attached to a hemming bird.

The nineteenth century saw the invention of a machine for gathers which made 2,500 stitches per minute, known as gauging or shirring.

Nowadays gathering is usually worked in single thickness and on the sewing machine by loosening either the top or the lower tension of the stitch and then drawing up the loose thread. The fullness is then stitched on to the yoke or sleeve band, also by machine, and this gives a very flattened appearance in comparison with the stroking method. Figs 58, 61.

Smocking

Smocking is a decorative form of fullness which relies on careful gathering in the form of temporary tacking to form pleats which make a foundation for smocking stitches.

GAUGING

A decorative texture to textiles, consisting of parallel rows of running stitches drawn up to form pleats, but not so closely as in gathering. Usually used in dressmaking, but also in embroidered wall hangings and structures. Fig. 183.

GAUZE

A somewhat outdated term for a transparent silk material, now known as organza, and often with the weft a different colour from the warp.

It is a very fine evenly woven silk which originated in Gaza and was sometimes termed 'gossamer' in the seventeenth century. Today it has been generally superseded by man-made fibres.

White silk gauze was used for early nineteenth-century darning samplers, and early examples may be found of gauze pulled and oversewn or whipped together as a mesh or net. Fig. 299. See *Fibres (silk)*.

GIMP or GUIMPE

The term 'guipure' derived from the thick thread or gimp used for outlining in lace and embroidery. A gimp is also considered as a braid or cord for edges in upholstery. The term *passementerie* was once used for openwork edgings made in the manner of lace but using cords, gimps and metal thread for decorating formal dress, coachwork and upholstery. See *Card, Lace*.

GREEK POINT

This is a type of embroidered linen, thought to have been passed down from the early Greek civilization, where the skills of working linen eventually spread to other parts of the Mediterranean, especially Italy.

It is now considered a coarse imitation of needle-made laces worked in Venice from a book which Vincola published as a pattern collection in 1587 of 'cutworkes', or reticella and punto in aria.

Greek point was revived by studious embroiderers and craft societies of the nineteenth century, particularly in the Lake District, for purchase by Americans touring Europe.

GROUNDS

1 Background or base material for embroidery.

2 The ground of lace, either composed of bars or net. The net may be formed of various meshes: hexagonal, honeycomb or diamond.

GUIPURE

Historically the term derives from the gimps, or cords, used as outlines for a coarse lace held together by bars. Over the centuries the name was applied to needle-made lace as well, and areas of the design richly padded.

Although today guipure often means all work with a background composed of bars, instead of net or réseau, it also refers to a bold form of machine embroidery using padded satin stitch in a strong design, often in imitation of a coarse lace. It is a chemical lace made on the machine in large quantities and sold by the yard for dress wear.

A form of cut work in hand embroidery, with bars and padded satin stitch, is also sometimes classed as guipure.

In the nineteenth century a form of tape lace held together by bars also occasionally came under this heading, and another variation called 'guipure d'art' consisted of elaborate embroidery on square net, with stitches of various kinds such as knot, stem and chain worked on a basis of darning and loop stitch to give a raised surface. A further strange embroidery was developed called 'guipure Renaissance'. It is made of cheese cloth, cut and folded into squares and triangles or moulded into curves for the design motifs and held in place with cords and bars.

This work is perhaps most interesting as an example of the influence of domestic activity on materials used for embroidery. In the nineteenth century, a great deal of food was produced at home, such as cheese and smoked and preserved meat, and many foods were strained and wrapped in loosely woven white cotton cloth, not used today. Mutton cloth and cheese cloth are, however, still well-known terms, sometimes as a cleaning cloth and sometimes as a fashion material.

The tradition continues into the twentieth century, for during the 1939–45 war flour bags were substituted for a background, in the 1960s nylon net containers for vegetables were used, and in the 1970s 'found' objects reflected a spirit of spontaneity and inventiveness.

Guipure, like many other terms, has lost its real meaning and it is clearer to describe work by its technique, such as buttonhole bars and cut work, or machine embroidery with openwork and satin stitch.

GUSSETS

These are sometimes worked in buttonhole stitch as a decorative reinforcement for seams, such as the side seams of shirts. Fig. 252.

H

HAIRPIN

Hairpin work is a form of decorative interlacing threads. Fig. 216.

HAMBURG POINT

An early coarse lace; it later referred to a type of pulled work in the eighteenth century, and then in the nineteenth century the name was applied to a machine-made white embroidery and exported to America.

HARDANGER

Identification

Hardanger embroidery is identified by small rectangular blocks of counted satin stitch which form an overall pattern as well as an outline to open areas of design, and which are arranged in groups either vertically or horizontally on a coarse heavy evenweave background. The blocks are known as kloster blocks.

Further blocks of varying size, but always rectangular, form a regular geometric design to enrich the background and give a weighty and glossy all-over pattern.

At first glance there is a similarity to drawn thread work but the blocks

185 Hardanger sample, showing satin stitch kloster blocks and a variety of centre fillings. On the left: picots. On the right: loop stitch. (Embroiderers' Guild).

of satin stitch are easily distinguishable, making rich heavy borders or all-over designs. Bars divide the openwork. Figs 185–8.

History

Hardanger is a regional form of linen embroidery from the mountains at the head of the Hardanger Fjord in Norway. The embroidery seems to have kept its character without being debased by outside influences, perhaps because of the isolated and inaccessible position geographically of its place of origin, and its simple strength of design and technique.

Designs

Designs are geometric and planned on squared paper, and are often built up from a central block. The play of light on the different directions of the satin stitch blocks provides a showy texture and is a consideration for designing as too many may be distracting, too few insignificant.

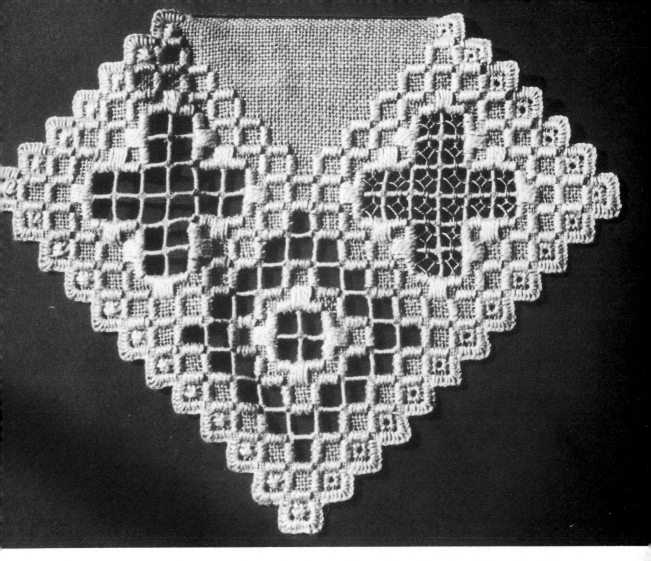

186 *Hardanger, showing diagonal blocks of satin stitch and the use of buttonholed edge and eyelets on the right, and raised cross stitch on the left.*

Ground

A heavy coarse evenweave linen is used, usually with a double evenweave where the threads are easy to count and also allow the working thread to rest easily between them.

Technique

Tools – scissors with a sharp and pointed blade.

Frame – optional.

Transfer of design – tack (baste) line.

Needles – tapestry with a rounded point and large eye.

Threads – linen or as available, slightly thicker than the threads of the ground and with a shiny surface, such as mercerized thread, to display the satin stitch blocks. A finer thread for loop stitch and open fillings, such as one strand of stranded cotton.

Join on/off – a double stitch where it will be worked over by the embroidery.

Process – stitch.

The kloster blocks of satin stitch are composed of an uneven number of stitches counted over an even number of threads of the background. Four threads of the background require five satin stitches; this is an average size. Kloster blocks may be worked vertically and horizontally, i.e. warp or weft.

Diagonal lines are formed by steps.

The openwork area of the design is marked out or edged with kloster blocks alternately with plain ground.

Always leave four threads between each block.

Additional blocks may be added to make an impressive design and stitchery such as back stitch, chain stitch and Algerian eyelets may be worked for elaboration.

The embroidery and the kloster blocks should be completed before cutting away any threads.

Cutting

Use very sharp scissors to get a clean cut. Threads are cut away close to the satin stitch block.

Threads between the blocks remain, and these are darned, woven, or overcast to form bars securing the openwork, which is now a coarse type of square mesh. This completes the basic embroidery.

Enrichment may be given to:

1 the bars of the openwork by mak-

121

187 *Small pin cushion in hardanger. French knots for texture at cross bars. 16 cm ($6\frac{1}{5}$ in.) square.*

ing picots as the darning proceeds;

2 the openwork mesh by incorporating loop stitch as the darning (or interweaving) proceeds;

3 the square of openwork by incorporating loop stitch or interlacing stitches with the bars. This should be planned at the beginning of the design for greatest effect.

It is possible to add loop stitch as in other embroidery, but it is more time consuming and, if planned at the be-

ginning, it is most easily incorporated as the work proceeds. (*Note:* typical additions are wheels or spiders.)

HEADING

A term used for the straight edge of lace which is attached to garments. The shaped edge, such as a scallop, is known as the footing.

HEADDRESSES

See *Bonnets.*

HEDEBO

Identification

Hedebo embroidery today is recog-

nized by a design of cut-out shapes filled with approximately one half in a buttonhole stitch filling and the other half with buttonhole bars arranged in a pattern of scallops, wheels, and lines.

Early hedebo embroidery of 1750–1850 has floral designs of open areas of a square mesh, made by cut and drawn threads or pulled together, and surrounded by rows of chain stitch and back stitch. Chain stitch also interprets the greater part of the design. Figs 189–194.

History

Hedebo embroidery originated in

Denmark as a peasant embroidery and, like many other embroideries, followed the typical development through outside influences, until it became the work as it is known today.

In the early eighteenth century hedebo flourished in Denmark, as Dresden work flourished in the neighbouring German states of Saxony. Techniques included pulled stitches, and the work was similar to and sometimes termed opus tiratum, punto tirato, Hamburg point, Dresden point, broderie de Nancy or Indian work. The embroidery was bold and strong and did not have the high standard of fine craftsmanship of Dresden work, but it achieved a quiet and simple unity. In the early nineteenth century the fashionable revival of reticella is to be seen in the squares of openwork added to the design, and with the simple early openwork and stitchery it is organized in borders. This gives importance and interest but not necessarily added charm.

189 Detail of hedebo work, showing buttonhole filling and buttonhole bars to complete heart- and crescent-shaped flowers.

190 *A design in the style of early hedebo, showing open pulled stitch fillings to leaves which are outlined in chain stitch and back stitch. This sample was probably worked in Turkey for export to the European market. 18 cm (7 in.) diameter. (Lise Mossery).*

Later the simple mesh, outline and surface stitchery became obsolete and were replaced by involved shapes such as hearts, crescents, circles, leaves and tulip-shaped flowers outlined in buttonhole stitch and filled with surface buttonhole fillings, bars, scallops and wheels. The fillings were not worked through the ground but were attached to the buttonhole outlines. The ground material was then cut away from the back on the wrong side of the work. The presence of the ground material acts as a support to

191 Detail of early hedebo. (Lise Mossery).

the curving shapes during the process of work, but additional paper may be tacked to the back.

The somewhat quasi-peasant style of motifs formed in conventional hearts, tulips, crescents and other idiosyncratic shapes decorated the corners and centres of tablecloths and, although inventive and very well executed in detail, the effect is of an isolated and sparsely decorated appearance, since it does not have supporting or connecting surface stitchery. By the twentieth century this last type of work became known all over Europe as hedebo, and, in spite of having no local background, it was commercially successful and frequently reproduced in magazines for dress and table linen to be worked at home. In some examples the open spaces are filled with tatting or crochet, replacing the buttonhole fillings and generally debasing the original work. In Denmark, however, there was a conscious return to the integrity of early work.

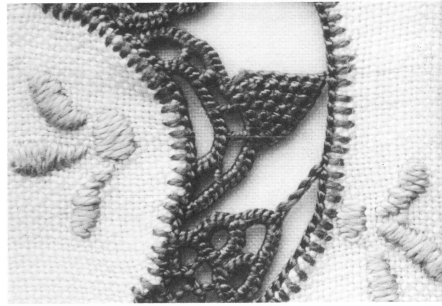

192 Detail of twentieth century work, showing use of mercerized thread. (Lise Mossery).

The buttonhole fillings in hedebo are very coarse in comparison with lace or Ayrshire fillings on muslin.

Design

The design of hedebo embroidery ranges from the simple bold conventional flower shapes of the early work, through borders incorporating reticella, to motifs of openwork in curving shapes and crescents, flowers, leaves and hearts. Figs 189–92.

Grounds and threads
The early work is on a coarse linen and worked in heavy white embroidery thread. Later fine linen, suitable for afternoon tea table linen, was embroidered using a fine linen thread or sometimes a firmly twisted mercerized cotton thread.

Cotton backgrounds and cotton muslin were also used as they became readily available.

193   Tea cloth worked in hedebo embroidery, using a tinted thread. Mid-twentieth century.

Techniques
A square mesh is made of cut and drawn threads of the background from warp and weft, which are then overcast. On to the mesh simple darning patterns are worked in the form of checks or diamonds, crosses and loop stitches. Other techniques include buttonhole bars, wheels, scallops and fillings in open cut work.

Hedebo buttonhole stitch is sometimes worked with a twist for extra stability. Satin stitch, eyelets and selective use of French knots are occasionally added.

Edges may be finished with simple buttonhole, Antwerp edge, or Armenian edge.

HEMSTITCHING
Hemstitching is used in drawn thread work, to group threads together at the edge of open borders, or to secure a hem where one or two threads have been withdrawn for decoration, as is typical in handkerchiefs. Hemstitching became a feature of drawn thread work during the passion for detailed finish of the nineteenth century.

In the early twentieth century 'hemstitching' was a term for drawn

194   Hedebo collar worked in white on cotton, showing a typical shape of the early twentieth century. Note involved edging. (Embroiderers' Guild).

195 Sampler of hemstitching. 1985. Worked by Margaret Potts.

thread work, as it was considered essential for working the open edges, but early work was not always reinforced in this way, and it is often omitted nowadays. A tapestry needle is used as it slips between, and avoids splitting, the threads. Fig. 278 (F1–2, Y-2).

Italian hemstitching can be seen on historical examples. Figs 94, 195. See also *Drawn Thread Work.*

HEMMING

Hemming is a construction or finishing stitch used for plain edges on single material for articles in dressmaking and needlework. The folded edge is often trimmed with decorative stitching or lace. Hemming is a very close stitch and does not allow any play, so it is not used for the hems of dresses. Slip hemming, or blind hemming, is used, as well as for appliqué with a folded edge. Rolled hems are also frequently used. Figs 3, 118, 164, 332.

HERRINGBONE STITCH

Another well-known stitch is sometimes called double back stitch as it forms two rows of back stitch on the reverse side. It is used in shadow work. Frontispiece, figs 317–21, 266.

When working on a curved line, aim to radiate the stitches, or work twice into the stitches on the inner curve, spreading those on the outer edge.

Herringbone may be threaded and interlaced.

It is widely used in embroidery at the present time and in white work for shadow work.

HOLBEIN STITCH

This stitch is effectively used in white thread on white ground, though it was originally worked in black on white and is shown decorating costumes in many of Holbein's portraits. The stitch is run stitch and worked so that both sides are alike. A horizontal, vertical or diagonal run stitch is worked in one direction, leaving even spaces between. The work is then turned and the spaces filled on the return to complete the design. Thought needs to be given to the back of the work as progress is made, so that the threads are not pierced. Fig. 304.

196 Detail of a strip of hollie point for a bonnet. Note design of pot of flowers, symbolic of the Annunciation. (Embroiderers' Guild).

HOLLIE POINT

A mystique often surrounds the formation of this buttonhole stitch filling which is considered a type of lace, often explained as a buttonhole stitch with an extra twist or with an extra knot. The purpose is to give strength to the work, which is often limp and easily pulls out of shape.

Although research seems to open every secret of past working methods, the actual manipulation of the thread in the past often gives a different

197 Hollie point. A Chain stitch (or couched) base or scaffold. B Bring thread up on right-hand side. Insert on left for laid thread. Bring up on left and pass needle under loop of previous stitch and laid thread, and form the working thread as indicated. Do not work into ground. C Finished stitch. D The stitch in a different thread. E Buttonhole stitch for comparison. F Variations of buttonhole crossed, vandyke, and the simplest buttonhole filling.

appearance and evades work of today, possibly because of the changed methods of producing the working threads.

Hollie point is considered indigenous to England and it is work that students and collectors are particularly pleased to find and own.

Originally used in churches, it is a buttonhole filling worked in straight rows and appears as a cloth. The early designs show biblical subjects, such as Adam and Eve, the Tree of Knowledge, the Holy Dove and the lily flower in a pot, representing the Annunciation. Other flowers, initials and dates are depicted later on the cambric shirts, underwear and children's clothes of the seventeenth and eighteenth centuries where the lace is used for side seams, shoulder and armhole seams. The most famous and frequent use is in the form of a strip or the circle shape for the back of babies' bonnets for christening, or as insertion for robes.

When it was revived in the nine-teenth century, the Victorian avid love of information and impressive terms led to names such as Barcelona, Cadiz, and Expelier lace, as well as seaming lace or bandwork, being used. Later faggoting and punch stitches took over, as they were less time-consuming, and these were followed by machine insertions and plain seams sewn by machine. Plain seams, sewn by hand with minute stitches, vied for invisibility with the machine stitches.

However, hollie point was one occupation of the industrious and inquiring needlewoman of the time and there are amazingly detailed instructions for the designs, including verses.

It is useful to have a counted number of chain stitches as an outline base to work into, or work the buttonhole on a firm couched line as in reticella. Fig. 197 (A–D).

Work two rows of eleven buttonhole as a foundation:

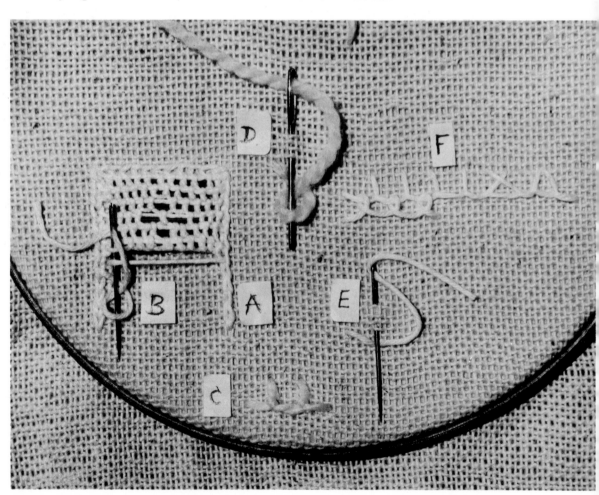

198 *Circular shape in hollie point for bonnet. Note the design.* (Embroiderers' Guild).

1st row – 5 buttonhole, miss 1, work 5

2nd row – 4 buttonhole, miss 1, work 1, miss 1, work 4

3rd row – 5 buttonhole, miss 1, work 5

4th row – work 11 buttonhole

5th row – work 11 buttonhole

6th row – repeat pattern from 1st row

Figs 196–8. See *Lace*.

HONEYCOMBING

A textured surface produced in fairly fine material by run stitch worked in parallel rows diagonally across the material and then in the opposite direction, and drawn up to produce partly puffed diamond shapes. Also a smocking stitch. Fig. 325.

HUCKABACK

Originally a coarse linen woven with small knots at regular intervals, making a rough absorbent surface for use as towels. Later a cloth with regular loops was produced which was suitable for embroidered hand towels.

Elephant towelling of the nineteenth century and Binka cloth of the twentieth century serve as a similar base for a form of counted decoration. Holbein stitches, darning, fringes, coarse lace and surface stitches such as chain and stem are used in a variety of decoration. See *Linen*. Figs 72, 216.

HUGUENOT LACE

Name given to a peculiar combination of muslin rosettes sewn on to net in the early nineteenth century.

I

IMITATION LACE

A popular early term for all machine-made laces produced in linen or cotton thread and in all widths. At the present time, nearly all lace generally available and sold by the yard is machine-made in nylon or synthetic fibre, with designs copied or adapted from hand-made lace. Some can only be detected as imitation by scrutiny of the solidly worked areas, where there are no clearly interweaving threads.

Other work, occasionally and incorrectly, is included in this term: cut work, work with buttonhole bars, broderie anglaise, tape lace sewn to net, or imitation Spanish lace. Swiss imitation lace is similar.

199 Detail of Elizabethan cushion, showing insertion stitches for a decorative join. Note use of tassels. (Hatfield House Textile Conservation Rooms).

INDIAN FLOSS EMBROIDERY

Rich floss silk embroidery in white or cream on white or black net for dress or mantel hangings, but not hard-wearing.

INDIAN LACE

Pulled work of the eighteenth and nineteenth centuries, and possibly lace taught by nuns or missionaries.

INSERTION

In textile terms a strip of material, usually embroidered, or lace with straight edges, inserted into a garment for decoration. Often used in yokes of children's dresses for decorative seams. Figs 61, 62, 106, 163, 167.

Insertion stitches

Plain oversewing frequently secures the edge of a decorative insertion, as it does not distract the eye. Figs 60–62.

Other insertion stitches are a range of decorative openwork embroidery such as buttonhole bars or herringbone, which connect two pieces of prepared fabric. Sometimes whole garments are made of narrow strips of material or rouleaux which are then stitched together with insertion stitches. See *Faggoting*.

IRISH CAMBRIC

A fine linen cloth produced in Ireland which rivalled the high quality of French linen or cotton.

IRISH EMBROIDERY AND IRISH LACE

Irish embroidery and lace developed in the nineteenth century as an introduced industry to help provide an income during the famine crisis of 1846. Previously, the national costume of a cloak of strong tweed, a thick plaited or knitted vest or pullover (Aran knit), trousers and skirts of tweed, knitted shawls and stockings and clogs or brogues was generally worn. There was little popular demand for decorative embroidery or lace and a small quantity of imports satisfied the fashionable or wealthy.

The white embroidery had all the characteristics of Ayrshire work but gradually, with fewer buttonhole fillings and less satin stitch on the muslin and cotton grounds, it became known as 'sprigging'. Women involved in the embroidery business in Scotland and England taught Irish women who then worked in groups at each other's houses to save light and heat; this procedure became a typical habit of work. Nuns also taught the work in schools and convents, and the products were sponsored and encouraged

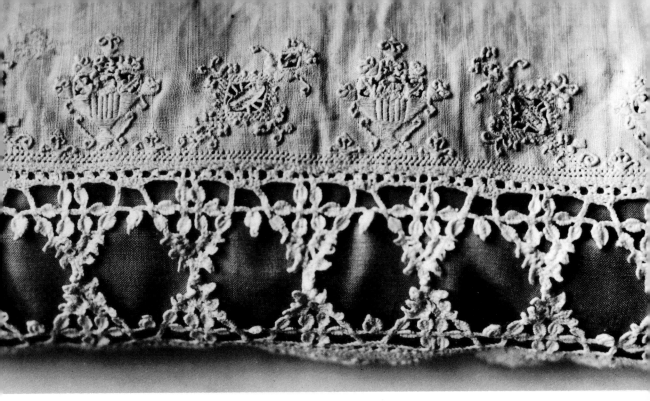

200 Bold insertion for the side of an Elizabethan cushion. See also fig. 106. Similar to woven picots, fig. 84. (Hatfield House Textile Conservation Rooms).

by influential people in England and abroad. Figs 24–8, 326–30.

Another type of embroidery was carried out at Limerick, on the newly produced machine net. A school was founded in 1829 for embroidered or tamboured (chain stitch) net, and led to darning on net in counted patterns. It developed and sold abroad, becoming popular for use as stoles well into the early twentieth century. Figs 74–6, 222, 252, 296.

Mountmellick and Carrickmacross are well known; the latter has fine muslin appliqué on net. Wide collars, about 20 cm (8 in.) deep and a metre (39 in.) long, known as bertha collars and worn with dresses widely cut at the shoulder, are typical examples of the work. Figs 51, 52, 234, 237.

Curragh point represented a type of tape lace with a cord outline laid on net or held with worked bars, and was typical of work produced in many countries at the time. Figs 73, 107, 215, 243, 340.

Crochet became a famous and particularly attractive product, worked to a very high standard of craftsmanship and design, with free raised petals and padded buds and minute picots worked in a fine white linen thread, giving a beautiful textural quality. Lace-like effects of crochet are seen on delicate cotton chemises, blouses and baby clothes. The crochet achieved a great reputation in imitation of Honiton, Venetian and Spanish lace but later developed into coarse wide borders, in the style of torchon lace, for use on afternoon tea cloths. This last type of crochet was worked extensively in Europe and America and countries under their influence. See *Carrickmacross, Mountmellick.*

ITALIAN CUT WORK

This term refers to cut and drawn thread work, known as reticella, of the sixteenth and seventeenth centuries, as distinct from the cut work of the nineteenth and twentieth centuries.

In Italian cut work the solid areas are of buttonhole stitch forming a geometric design. In cut work the linen ground is used for the solid areas of the design, which is mainly floral and secured with worked bars as the ground is cut away. Figs 102–6, 283. See *Cut work.*

ITALIAN DARNED NETTING

An early lace possibly made in Sienna, known as Sienna point. By the sixteenth century it was worked all over Italy. A thick thread is darned on a hand-made knotted square mesh net. The early work had only one or two variations of stitch in a simple, bold design.

ITALIAN HEMSTITCHING

Italian hemstitch is seen on many antique and early linen embroideries and is often found combined with drawn thread work, pulled stitches and punch stitch.

The stitch was eventually replaced by the more familiar hemstitching used today, and so prolifically and industriously in the late nineteenth and early twentieth century.

Other stitches related to Italian hemstitching are alternate back stitch, mock hemstitch and pointe turque, which is a simple open filling in a punch stitch Fig. 201 (C1–3).

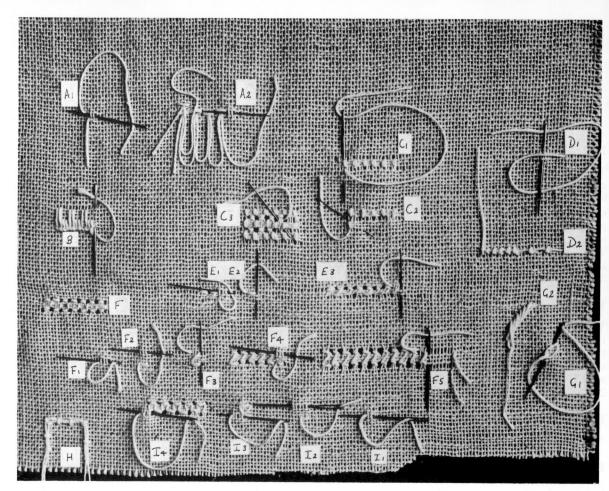

201　*Working sampler showing Italian hemstitching for comparison with other stitches. A1–2 Turkey rug stitch on two threads of canvas. A1 The needle shows the first stitch with a loop above (to allow the needle to be inserted). A2 The second stitch. Pull top loop securely into place. Repeat as in (A1), leaving a loop of approximately 2.5 cm (1 in.) below for tufts. Work from left to right. Commence at lower edge and work upwards. When area is completed, cut loops quite short for tufts. B Sorrento edge. A decorative buttonhole stitch. C1–3 Pointe Turque. A simple pulled stitch filling. C1 Work from right to left. C2 Then left to right. C3 Turn work and repeat as a filling. D1–2 Coral stitch. Lay the working thread along the line to be covered in the direction of work (right to left), and bring the thread round to the right, below line. Insert the needle at right angles above the thread and bring out below into the loop (D1). Draw the needle through the ground and draw up the thread upright at an angle to the stitch to make a well-formed stitch.*

E1–3 Imitation hemstitch. No threads are withdrawn. Work from left to right. F1–5 Italian hemstitch. A method of punch stitch often used in historical embroidery. A single thread may (F5) or may not be withdrawn (F), as required. Work from left to right. G1–2 Rope stitch. Work a chain stitch and then insert the needle as in G1, continue in this way as in G2. Good for use on a curved line. Somewhat similar to twisted chain, but worked more closely. H Corners in couching. I1–4 Double backstitch (as a pulled stitch). No threads are withdrawn. Work from right to left.

stitch in floss silk. In general it followed the Chinese. Figs 54, 55. See Chinese embroidery.

JOINING

Join with weaver's knot or lace knot for netting, plaiting, needleweaving or darning.

Join on/off – usual method. Start working thread by run stitches into working line or with a double stitch where it will be covered by subsequent work. Fig. 275.

Finish thread by passing thread into back stitches already worked or by run stitches or a double stitch on working line, where it will be covered by further work. Figs 2, 222.

J

JAPANESE EMBROIDERY

Usually in colour but occasionally white only is used, exploiting the textures of different directions of satin

K

KNITTING

This occurs in the knitted fringes associated with Mountmellick embroidery. It is sometimes included as a contrast texture in appliqué, as a ground for embroidery, and as a substitute lace by working open patterns. There is a great area of white knitting as shawls and baby clothes. Figs 165, 203, 223, 234–7.

KNOTS AND CORDS

When worked in white, knots and cords give a tough, bold texture for trimmings and outlines, as do knot stitches like coral stitch and French and bullion knots. Figs 2, 49, 99, 202, 236. See *Cord*.

KNOTTED LACE

Now known as macramé.

KNOTTING

Examples of knotting in eighteenth century white work are the result of a famous mania among ladies, including those attached to the royal court. The simple work of knotting yards and yards of thread, probably linen, possibly cotton, with closely spaced small knots of even size, was not very demanding and very easy to carry about. The thread could be worked in carriages on journeys, as well as in all leisure hours. Mrs Delany, the indefatigable letter writer, paper-flower-picture maker and embroiderer, turned her talented hand to this work. There is a handsome example of a large cot cover made for her godson in 1747 in the Ulster Museum, Belfast. It is referred to in her correspondence and is well authenticated by a contemporary label. The design was first traced out finely in ink, or a fine black oil paint line, on to linen, and then the knotted thread was simply sewn over with couching stitches to keep it in place.

The design for this particular cover is very full, having a repetitive design over the whole area similar to a quilting design and with a centre of flowers surrounded by small flowers. Part of the central motif is repeated in the corners. The design may have been her own or drawn out for her, and required months of work to complete, comparable to the time involved in making a quilt.

Other knotting appears in white work in a form of lightweight macramé, which was mounted over bright silk or cotton for cushions or bags and parasols and used particularly for garden furniture including hammocks, in the nineteenth century. Figs 2, 99, 201, 202, 236.

202 Samples of knotting, adaptations of which have been used throughout the centuries, and in fine thread for dress decoration.

L

LACE

Introduction

Lace is used in conjunction with white embroidery in such a large number of examples that a very brief record seems relevant, especially as lace enriches white embroidery as a trimming, and it becomes interesting to identify it.

In the nineteenth century, so many concoctions of white work and lace were contrived that unless carefully authenticated by writings and notes it is difficult to give a totally accurate designation. An opinion may be given, however, with consideration of factors such as trade and travel, interchange of ideas, employment, country, districts and fashion, and these make a most interesting and informative assessment.

The Victorians added machine-made lace to earlier hand embroidery and early hand-made lace to later machine embroidery.

Lace in many ways is the inspiration for much white embroidery, which attempts to capture or imitate the costly, flattering creation. Yet white linen embroidery was also an inspiration of the beginning of lace, in work such as drawn thread work which evolved to reticella and then to

*203 (Opposite) Two examples of
Raschel machine knitting. Left: 1980.
An elastic knit in synthetic threads.
Right: 1900–1910. A silk shawl.*

*204 A bonnet with Valenciennes
bobbin lace insertions and Ayrshire
embroidery on muslin, showing the
needlemade fillings, which also surround
the crown as free petals. The diamond
mesh of plaited Valenciennes is also
clear. (Embroiderers' Guild).*

*205 A fragment of nineteenth-century
embroidery from a professional
workroom, made into a collar and edged
with a machine-made lace, which is
somewhat incongruous with the fine
embroidery and was probably added
later. The top row shows fine satin
stitch flowers with buttonhole fillings
typical of later Ayrshire work, and also
trailing. The centre row has a
background of cut and drawn overcast
square mesh, with darning in the form
of stars. The lower row shows two*

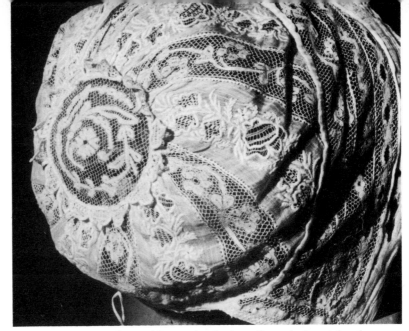

*pulled stitch patterns of great delicacy. A
filling of very fine drawn thread work
with overcasting is also used in the*

*border to form a background to the
flowers and leaves. 12 × 36 cm
($4\frac{3}{4}$ × 14 in.) overall.*

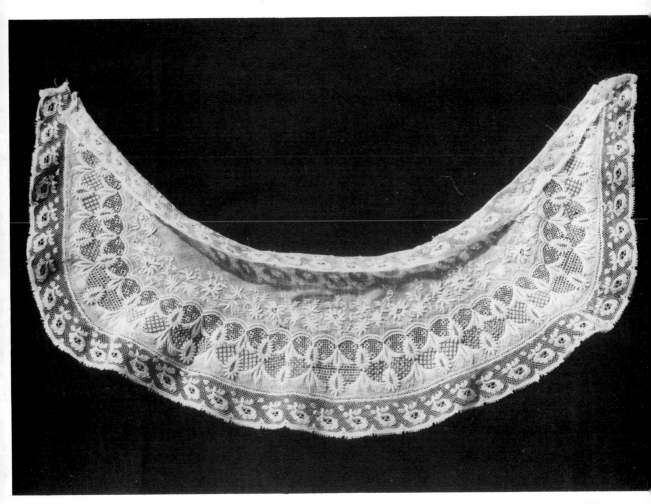

206 *Detail of patterns in the collar from fig. 205.*

207 *A cushion which shows part of a border depicting a shepherdess with big puff sleeves surrounded by four sheep between geometric motifs, all in reticella, drawn thread, darning and buttonhole. The borders also contain sheep. The outer borders are of buttonhole with the narrow borders in needleweaving. The square grid of the ground threads may be seen throughout the work. Probably early seventeenth century. Cushion 58 × 38 cm (22⅘ × 15 in.). Border with figure 15 cm (6 in.) wide. (Hatfield House Textile Conservation Rooms).*

needle-made lace. In the same way knots, fringes, cords, and plaiting and twisting of the threads at the end of woven linen became a basis for bobbin lace worked on a pillow (see Frontispiece). Most lace is made of a linen thread which is stronger when wet and so is excellent for laundering; the fine threads of linen then dry crisply and a little stiff to set off detailed patterns.

As needle-made lace is composed of buttonhole stitch it is easily associated with embroidery, and today, when embroidery is developing beyond the boundaries of stitching, the plaiting and twisting of bobbin lace is also a relevant interest. Net darning is also interrelated. Figs 102–3, 143.

There are no real facts as to which type of lace came first, needle-made or bobbin, or in which country, but needle lace probably developed simultaneously in parts of Italy and Spain, coming from influences of Greece or Cyprus, where in the earliest times it is assumed that nuns carried out ecclesiastical linen work. Early surveys of ancient Greek civilizations of 2500 BC reveal that linen work existed in Greece and spread to the surrounding islands. In 1200 BC retting flax by the River Linaria is recorded (Linaria, linen) in Mycenae at Pylos.

By about AD 1500, and with the influence of the Renaissance, ecclesiastical lace, established in Italy, began to be used by the laity and for some secular purposes.

The rich trading merchants of Venice fostered its production and could afford to pay for the costly needlepoints for secular use. The breathtaking detail made impressive textiles, but in some cases they cost the workers their eyesight.

208 A sample of Venetian-style needle-made lace, possibly of the nineteenth century. Note the raised outlines and picots, spines sometimes called fleurs volants.

Inventories throughout the centuries show that lace was bequeathed as gifts, for it was worn with lavish extravagance and as a great status symbol, for men particularly.

Not so well-known is the fact that the term 'lace' did not appear until the end of the seventeenth century and that the terms lacinia, fringe, or lacez, described the work. The word *dentelle* (French for lace) appears in an inventory of Mary Queen of Scots. In 1660 dentelle generally took over from punto or passement aux fuseaux or passement à l'aiguille. Lace makers were known as passementiers, and this included braids and the working of metal threads.

Both Italy and Spain became great lace centres and exported large quantities to Europe, including France and England, to be worn as ruffs until about 1614 and by 1640 as flat collars. Figs 202, 217.

Italian lace

Reticella

The earliest laces of the sixteenth century, now known as reticella or Italian

cut work and made with a needle, developed from intricate forms of drawn thread work, and incorporate darning and buttonhole design in curves and angles, and buttonholed over, darned or interwoven to give strength. From this process, basic threads were couched on to a design marked out on parchment and then worked over with buttonhole and darning. The couching threads were cut and released from the back of the parchment, and the remaining pattern of buttonhole stitches lifted off, later to be known as punto in aria, being completely free from any background linen. Figs 102–3, 209, 283.

Punto in aria

Punto in aria, or stitches in the air, could be worked in single motifs or in a continuous strip and so could be gathered and attached to curved edges.

Venetian

Famous laces which followed in the early seventeenth century include styles such as gros point, rose point and pointe de neige. Venetian lace had

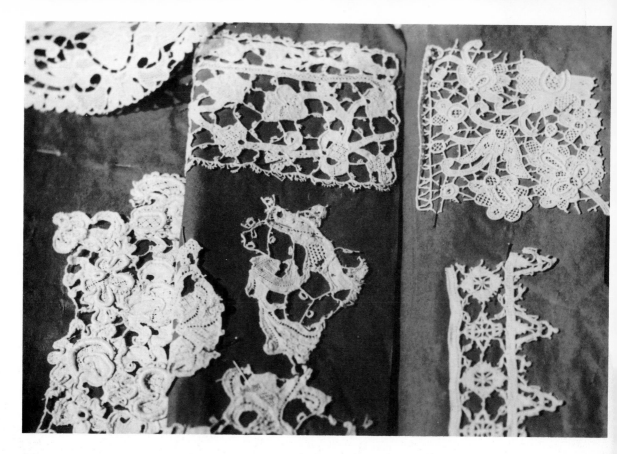

209 Samples from a notebook showing needle-made laces, reticella and punto in aria of the nineteenth century. At the top left, chemical lace edging showing typical bars of the work.

conventional flower designs which became padded. The outlines, or cordonnet, were decorated with two or three rows of picots, and later the padded motifs were similarly decorated and also with spines and thorns made of miniature bullion knots. It is a real and inspiring joy to study, as so much detail is so lightly carried out. The motifs gradually became more widely spaced in the design and gimps and bars were introduced, to become 'guipure'.

Venetian lace of this time is always valuable, and of the greatest beauty in design and the highest quality of workmanship. Figs 208, 209.

French lace
See *Bar, Picot*.
In 1660 Colbert, a French politician, passed laws against the import into France of Italian lace, because so much money was leaving the country to buy it. He instigated a new lace industry at Alençon, in spite of an already established centre producing a lace known as pointe de France. Fig. 210.

Pointe de France
A lace somewhat like Italian gros point, and worn at the French court before 1660.

Alençon
The name for the new lace of 1660, which became renowned as light and fragile, and fashionable after the heavy gros points. It is composed of buttonhole stitch and is a world-famous French needlepoint, or needle-made, lace of great delicacy.

Buttonhole stitch is used for all needle-made or needlepoint lace, for the solid and open fillings, over the cordonnet outlines and for the mesh or net ground, i.e. réseau.

Fine white linen lace thread known as fil de trace is couched over the lines of a design drawn out on firm paper. Buttonhole filling is worked on the couched foundation in the appropriate spaces, to form small motifs, and these are connected with the réseau as the work proceeds, rather than added later. It is strengthened with another thread twisted in and out of the mesh.

Argentan
A lace which rivalled Alençon lace; together these are the only true French laces. Both have a hexagon or six-sided mesh of buttonhole stitch, which in Argentan is (amazingly) worked over with buttonhole stitch for strength. The small-scale work is best seen with a magnifying glass.

Although embroidered cotton muslin was the craze of the eighteenth century, lace of the finest quality continued to be made and worn at court, and at the end of the century the lace workers, as well as the wearers, were indiscriminately guillotined during the French Revolution of 1789.

Valenciennes
This is the name of a town on the ever-changing political border between France and Flanders; early Valenciennes came from Flanders while the well-known later bobbin lace of the nineteenth century is considered to be French. It has a characteristic dotted outline of small holes to the design. The lace was used extensi-

vely for trimming edges and for frilling, as it is hard-wearing because of the closely worked design. It also became a favourite with Queen Victoria. Figs 162–204.

Flanders and Brussels lace

While French needle-made laces sustained a standard of delicate refinement, bobbin lace developed in the northern parts of Europe, including the Netherlands, or Flanders, where Brussels became a celebrated lace centre. Figs 210, 211, 245, 247.

210 A notebook showing French Mechlin and early Honiton lace (right). Note its delicacy compared with the Venetian lace on the left.

It is misleading to term lace as Brussels, unless it is authenticated as coming from that particular city, or very nearby. Lace was produced in great quantities throughout the Flanders region and, like Italian and French laces, is an extensive study.

The bobbin lace achieved great richness and lightness, equalling the French needle-made lace, and it became very popular, as it was quicker to work than needlepoint lace and therefore less expensive. It is valued for design and craftsmanship and is classed with the finest of laces, in the finest thread. Famous names over the period of production and into the twentieth century are as follows:

Antwerp

This is a bobbin or pillow lace, but sometimes appears to be an embroidery because of the cordonnet.

At one time exported to Spain and later coarsely worked by peasants, it is an example of the interchange of style and workmanship. The lace was large in design and originally included the Angel and the Virgin Mary, but degenerated into the now well-known Potton Kant design, showing a pot of flowers, an allusion to the lily's association with the Annunciation. See *Bobbin lace.*

Mechlin

A small area of réseau compared to the toile or design made an extremely

popular lace of the nineteenth century and was widely used.

Point d'Angleterre

No cordonnet, i.e. outline, but a very beautiful lace. It may have been so called to hoodwink the customs men into thinking it to be of English origin, and so avoid paying duty.

Duchesse lace

This was made in the early twentieth century with an ornate design of small bunches of flowers and with a raised centre vein to the leaves. Fig. 211.

211 Samples. Left: *Brussels lace – Mechlin.* Centre: *Honiton flowers.* Right: *point de gaz with free petals at the centre.*

Pointe de gaz

This is recognizable from intriguing free petals to the flowers, or wings to the butterflies, which stand free from the ground. Fig. 211.

Flanders or Brussels lace often shows the use of needle-made and bobbin methods in one piece of lace, and also of lace motifs applied to net in a method similar to Honiton.

English lace

Apart from hollie point, most lace in England, like other countries, was imported in vast quantities until it was banned, which led to a great deal of smuggling. Lace making was encouraged in England, and it developed as a bobbin lace.

The Huguenot refugees were experienced in both needle and bobbin lace making and brought their skills to England to enrich the craft, as they did in all countries where they settled.

English lace showed a good fine standard and was made in the Midland counties, including Bedfordshire, Buckinghamshire and Northamptonshire. The borders may be considered simple but they are exquisitely worked in fine thread, and were given names such as 'Bucks Fan', 'Bucks Kidney Bean', 'Bucks Pea' and 'Winslow Kitten'. Bedford laces are associated with names such as Maltese and torchon. Figs 211–13, 245, 247.

Hollie point

This is a simple needle-made lace and considered to be indigenous to England. It consists of rows of buttonhole filling worked either in bands, rectangles or circle shapes, with the pattern achieved by leaving regular spaces between the stitches. The number of stitches is carefully counted as a chart on squared paper. The lace may be worked on a firm backing using an outline of couching, in the usual way, or on a basis of

212 *Page of Midland Counties lace: torchon on the left; Bucks on the right. The label states the price per yard of the samples on each page. English.*

carefully counted chain stitch. See also *Hollie point.* Figs 196–8.

Midland counties
A bobbin lace in the form of borders or edgings and small articles, with typical designs which include a spotted ground. Figs 212, 213.

Devon or Honiton
A well-known centre where bobbin lace was produced in floral patterns,

mainly as wide borders and as motifs for applying to net for dress and handkerchiefs. The motifs often display the emblems of the British Isles, with a rose for England, a thistle for Scotland, a daffodil for Wales and a shamrock for Ireland. Figs 210, 211, 216.

Torchon
The name given to a coarse type of bobbin lace, possibly originally from France or Saxony, also lace from Malta, known as Maltese. It came to be worked in most European countries, including England, and by craft lace makers of the last century and up to the present day. Figs 212, 232.

Machine-made lace
In the early nineteenth century net was produced by a machine invented by John Heathcoat, and this was used as a background for the application, or appliqué, of bobbin lace motifs as in Honiton and Brussels. Both laces became famous and popular as they now became more widely available.

Following the mechanical inventions in the weaving and spinning industry and that of John Heathcoat, the next step was taken by another young artisan-inventor from the Midlands, John Leavers, a framesmith and setter, who made his way to Nottingham. Stimulated by Heathcoat's initial success, he made up

5 Bucks "Pea"
6 Trou-trou

15 Bucks "Fan"
(Hdkf. 9" square 3/6.)

In 1846 an adaptation of the Leavers machine produced a type of woven square net with closer working for the pattern; this was used for lace curtains.

In 1855–60 Elisabeth Rachel, a fashionable French dramatic actress, started a vogue for draping wide lace stoles over the shoulders, and the demand for this fashion led to new inventions. In Leicester a lace producer, Redgate, developed a machine for a fine type of knitted lace, which was eventually called a Raschel machine, and a German company marketed the fashionable stoles produced by this method. Machine-made lace excelled at imitation of handmade lace, and all through the nineteenth century and into the twentieth more and more lace was used as it became readily available by the new machine methods.

In the early twentieth century the Barmen machine was invented, which produced extremely good imitations of torchon lace and other borders; today most lace of this type is produced by the Barmen machine.

In 1960 the Raschel machine, developed and refined, could produce extensive width curtains and material for dress and lingerie in a form of knitted lace, also net, and all had a slightly stretchy character.

After two world wars, and the fashions of the 'flappers' of 1920 and the sports girls of 1930, the lace industry was not so prosperous as before, but nevertheless continues in very successful production today.

Hand lace making became obsolete as a commercial proposition, because the cost of making and the care required for such delicate, extravagant wear were impractical. It became the interest of the studious and inquiring craft worker producing mainly borders in traditional Midland counties patterns, sometimes known as Beds, Bucks, Maltese or torchon. Experiments are also carried out, and show a style typical of the 1970s onwards. The foundation of the Lace

his mind to discover a method by which the pattern as well as the net ground work of lace could be combined in one process. In 1813 he solved the problem and thereby established in Nottingham an industry which flourished and grew to its present proportions.

The Leavers lace machine had a warp, beam and bobbins. The bobbins were flat discs which carried the thread, the beam threads outlined the warp threads and both hung vertically. The warp threads were spaced out marginally in front of each other

213 Bucks lace (Midland Counties).
From the top. Second row: *Winslow
Kitten;* third row: *Kidney Bean.* At
the left. Third and sixth: *Bucks Pea
(labelled 5);* Fourth: *Trou-Trou, for
threading fine ribbon (6). All examples
but three show honeycomb stitch, which
may be seen most clearly in the fan
shape second from the base.*

to allow the discs to slide in between and pass from the front to the back with a pendulum-like movement. The warp threads were pulled either sideways to make open areas in the lace, or close together for more solid areas with the thread from the discs. Sometimes there were as many as thirty-two discs or bobbins to the inch.

Lace worked on the Leavers machine was known as Chantilly, flouncing and all-over pattern, and designs were reminiscent of the eighteenth century; some designs were worked over with extra handstitchery. The Leavers machine produced a light dress lace with a net ground, easily distinguishable when compared with hand work.

The Leavers machine seemed a miracle of invention and was used and known throughout the world to give Nottingham and Nottingham lace its renown.

215 Compare the hand-crocheted collar, in Carrickmacross style design showing raised petals, with the machine-made border using the same details in a different arrangement. Note the change of direction of the picots down the centre of the filling between the rose and shamrock leaf; also the finely hand-worked monogram in trailing.

Guild led to an interchange of information and exhibitions for lace.

Examples of all types of machine-made lace make a rewarding collection, as of course do hand-made lace samples. The charm of lace also adds a recurring delight to fashion.

Other lace-like work such as hairpin work, knitted lace, Tenerife work or tatting should not be confused with lace. Figs 214–16. See *Machine embroidery, Net.*

LADDER STITCH

See *Punch Stitches*

LETTERING

Identification

White work embroidery is well known for linen marked with initials, monograms, cyphers, numbers and dates which are sometimes topped by or surmounted with a coronet for a titled family. Some consideration of the form and shape of each letter ensures that they all hold together as a harmonious set, that is, an alphabet.

An alphabet on white linen and worked in reticella (fig. 217) is part of a magnificent sampler which shows drawn thread work, counted satin stitch, punch stitch and Holbein stitch in white thread, and is typical of the seventeenth century. For collectors, these samplers can be difficult to find, but for students there are many museum examples. Letters are usually easily recognizable, but with age and wear may become distorted and need to be read with care. Initials are inter-

216 A sheet of decorative edges of the late nineteenth and early twentieth centuries. Top left: *hairpin work*. Top right: *circular motifs of Tenerife work joined together as a border*. Centre: *knitted lace*. Lower left: *Honiton lace, two examples showing different grounds*. Lower right: *handwoven huckaback linen from the Lake District of the nineteenth century, made into a mat with a crochet border.*

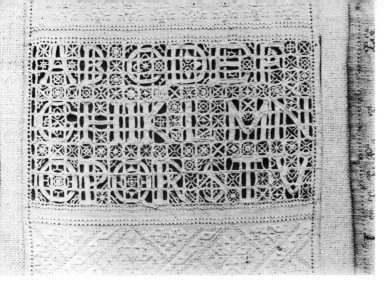

preted in an almost unlimited variety of white embroidery, with satin stitch on handkerchiefs the most popular and prolific. Figs 215, 217–22.

218 A fragment of a monogram with decorative border of leaves and birds in satin stitch. Size 11 cm ($4\frac{2}{5}$ in.) square. Possibly Swiss.

and devices which are sometimes incorporated in the design, positive identification of the family or the country of origin is nearly impossible. The work, probably taught or made in convents, is of a fairly universal standard. Figs 218, 219.

Nineteenth-century Irish work is celebrated for skill in embroidered lettering on linen handkerchiefs, and fine work included the stitches already mentioned. France, with a great reputation for handling silk in weaving and embroidery, excelled at lettering in white silk thread on a white silk ground.

The Swiss, well known for white embroidery and initialled handkerchiefs in hand work, came to show the greatest expertise in machine embroidery, producing world-renowned exports. Fig. 322.

England had saddle cloths and horse rugs monogrammed in white on heavy cloth, as well as the more usual work on cambric (such as handkerchiefs or underwear). Fig. 215.

Families with four or more children found marking linen essential at this time if garments were not to be shared and since, as a general rule, a washerwoman visited a household perhaps only once a month or less, it became necessary for each member to have several sets of clean underclothes and sheets to last until the next visit.

This accounts for the large inventories of linen for families and also for the large chests of drawers of the eighteenth and nineteenth centuries needed to hold such articles.

In the 1920s and 1930s it was fashionable to have initials or monograms embroidered on pockets of blouses, dresses, housecoats or loungewear, and machine embroidery was extensively used. Rich silks and soft crêpe de Chine were embroidered in satin stitch and punch stitch appliqué, using contrasting textures.

The handworked satin stitch for letters is sometimes replaced by rope stitch, as it is so much easier to work. Fig. 201(G). Feather stitch and trailing stitch are also popular. Other stitches for decoration included in designs are:
1 Pointe de Paris (dot stitch), a name for seeding.
2 Herringbone stitches often filled open areas, the edges of which are buttonholed as well as the threads of the herringbone, which act as bars. Herringbone as shadow work is used on thin material.

219 A religious monogram in satin stitch and seeding outlined in stem stitch. 3.5 × 4 cm (3⅖ × 1½ in.).

History

Letters have been used throughout the centuries in the form of monograms and cyphers in many different forms of embroidery and are to be seen on personal possessions and particularly on fair linen for the church, where IHS, PAX and saints' names are familiar examples. The work is of a professional standard, not always carried out by nuns.

Famous named antique examples are an apron dated 1717 by Mary Tykell at the Victoria & Albert Museum, a sheet for the Earl of Derwentwater dated 1716 at the Museum of London, and an apron of 1721 at the Burrell Collection, Glasgow. This work is not professional but produced at home by women and girls as an exercise or as an expression of affection and of a love of embroidery, and it is sometimes in a fresh and naive design.

During the nineteenth century stitches become more varied in an effort to find quicker and easier methods than the exacting and painstaking work of the early samplers. There are fine examples of satin stitch, flat and padded, set off with rows of stem stitch, seeding, French knots and other white work techniques. Intricate designs of initials are combined with flowers, ribbons and birds, particularly in the eighteenth century, but they are sometimes so involved that they are difficult to decipher. The craftsmanship is generally high, with exquisitely fine details using eyelets and punch stitches to form openwork.

Titled families have coronets over the appropriate letters and monograms, and all linen is marked in this way, including sheets, pillowcases, bed covers, towels, tablecloths, table napkins, underwear, shirts and shifts. Crowns are used by royalty, but also sometimes as a design motif or to show a royal connection.

The elaborate marking of linen was carried out all over Europe and, apart from clearly defined heraldic crests

3 Hemstitching in various arrangements is often included, with appliqué and satin stitch.
4 Decorative darning, counted and pulled stitches, are often used as a background to a letter left unworked.

These are clues to identification for a detailed collection; however, machine embroidery imitated these techniques with brilliant ability and is also interesting to collect.

Design

When wishing to embroider letters it is always a challenge and fun to develop a personal alphabet, to make a complete set of letters in relation to each other. There are many books to help with this important area of design. Perhaps the most basic and useful aid is squared paper, to give letters uniformity, because stitchery tends to introduce idiosyncrasies and give a certain amount of diversity. There are many nuances in the design of calligraphy, but the following basic suggestions might assist the real beginner. Figs 220, 221.

Size

Count the number of squares, for example:

Height – four squares for all letters.

Width – some letters will be four squares wide but no wider, and others will need to be only three or two squares wide, according to their outline.

Space

Adapt the space between letters to suit their different outlines, so that a balanced word is formed.

Letters of full width which fill the designed size require a clear space between them when they fall next to each other. Letters with a varied outline, and those of full width, when used with narrow letters require modified spacing.

Spaces between words need, on average, the width of one letter. Single or small words like 'a', 'at', 'to', require less space than longer words, otherwise they may appear to be lost.

Shape

Letters are most successful when kept quite simple, without fussy outlines or decoration.

A letter drawn with a single line is

acceptable as a design for interpretation in any simple line stitch, such as stem or chain. Thicker lines are required for appliqué. More involved lines develop with experience for particular methods, for example:

- for counted thread, counted satin stitch or cross stitch, squared paper is useful to balance the letters;
- for appliqué, the use of straight lines simplifies matching the grains of the material, as curves easily stretch out of place;
- for stem and line stitches, both straight and curving lines are workable.

Machine embroidery is an area that has great possibilities, according to the ability of the worker. Bold straight letters, flowing lines of script and intricate details are all suitable for experiment on the domestic straight and zig-zag machine, as well as on power machines like the Irish and Cornely.

Plan

When designing personal letters, or an alphabet, aim to have a unifying or continuous motif throughout, for example:

- all uprights (verticals) 6 mm ($\frac{1}{4}$ in.) wide;
- all crossbars (horizontals) a single line;
- all diagonals 3 mm ($\frac{1}{8}$ in.) wide;
- all curves 6 mm ($\frac{1}{4}$ in.) at widest part, reducing to a single line at ends.

Alternatively, add a personal motif to letters, such as a series of crosses, eyelets, knots or shapes such as a crescent, leaf, triangles and festoons, and then continue to a complete alphabet.

Monograms

A simple first step for a monogram is to:

1 Double the height and halve the width for one letter.
2 Halve the height and double the width for the second letter.
3 Arrange other letters into this basic design.

Scale

A further consideration for successfully embroidered lettering is the scale of the needle and the ground material.

Small letters look appropriate on a

fine ground worked with a fine needle, i.e. crewel 8–10. A heavy even-weave linen or canvas needs a larger needle, i.e. tapestry 18–20, and a larger letter.

Grounds

Lettering appears on material of all fibres: silk, cotton, linen, wool, synthetic and mixtures, varying from very fine muslin to heavy felt.

Techniques

Lettering may be interpreted in most white work techniques, including those already mentioned, such as:

Appliqué – hem in place or use punch stitch.

Darning, drawn thread work, pulled stitch, net – may be used to work an area of the background surrounding the letter in plain unworked ground, or simply to fill a suitably designed letter. Fig. 222.

Outline stitches – stem, rope, feather, chain, herringbone and knotted stitches, such as coral, are all good for interpreting the flowing lines of script. Fig. 201.

Contrasts can be exploited with satin stitch, French knots or shadow work.

LIMERICK LACE

A net embroidery introduced to Ireland, sometimes called Irish lace. It is tambour on machine-made net. Many of the early examples have the Regency quality of a classical design. The Edwardian examples of the early twentieth century are not so richly worked and are imitations of Indian tambour or chain stitch. Open centres are overcast and the net cut away and sometimes filled with an open lace stitch. Borders show several rows of chain stitch filling leaves or scallops. The design is traced out on paper and, with the net then tacked over the paper design, the outlines are worked in chain stitch and the fillings in close rows of chain. For machine work the design would be run stitched or worked on the Cornely machine.

Towards the end of the nineteenth century less chain stitch was used and counted patterns were introduced into the floral design; these are now considered typical of what is an attractive and popular type of embroidery. Figs 222, 252, 296, 336, 344.

SIZE *Letters of uniform height, but some variation in width to make a balanced letter*

ABCDEFGHIJ
KLMNOPQRST
UVWXYZ

SPACE *A space of one square between letters of full width, i.e. four squares. Vary spacing to suit letters of less than full width*

HUB MAP
KILT DEN
VOW QUE
ICE FOX
ZAG JAR
YES

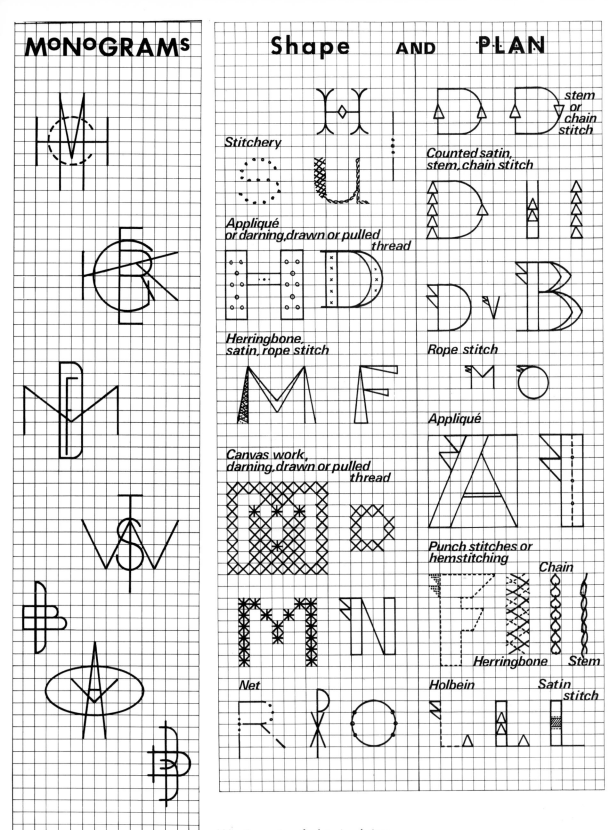

MONOGRAMS

Shape AND PLAN

Stitchery

Appliqué
or darning, drawn or pulled
thread

Herringbone,
satin, rope stitch

Canvas work,
darning, drawn or pulled
thread

Net

stem
or
chain
stitch

Counted satin,
stem, chain stitch

Rope stitch

Appliqué

Punch stitches or
hemstitching

Chain

Herringbone Stem

Holbein

Satin
stitch

220 *Suggestions for lettering designs.*

221 Satin stitch letter with decorative motif. (Constance Howard).

See *Carrickmacross, Irish embroidery* and *Irish lace, Net.*

LINEN EMBROIDERY

This work is often classed as Russian work, and sometimes German, and was also a term used in the eighteenth century when it decorated towels, counterpanes (bedspreads) and cloths. It is usually reversible, or alike on both sides. The design, on evenweave linen, has the background threads cut and drawn out at regular intervals, approximately six leaving two, from both the warp and the weft. The remaining threads are then overcast to form a mesh of even squares. The plain linen forms the design and is outlined in buttonhole stitch. The thread that whips or overcasts the mesh is often coloured in red, but frequently in white, and used for church work. Counted satin stitch is also an early type of linen embroidery used for towels. Figs 101, 111, 114. See *Darning, Drawn threadwork, Pulled stitches.*

LINEN THREAD

Fibres of flax were widely used until recently, and were worked using a spindle and distaff, later a spinning wheel, and then mechanized. The thread, even when fine, is comparatively strong and good for laundering in embroidery and lace.

LOOP STITCH

Figs 94, 108, 185, 238, 278. See *Buttonhole stitch, Net.*

222 Initials in cross stitch on net on the right, worked en reservé – i.e. with background worked and motif in plain ground. A Join for double thread for outline or darning with a loop. B Pass thread through loop and draw up. C Join single thread with a small looped knot. On the right: two simple darned patterns.

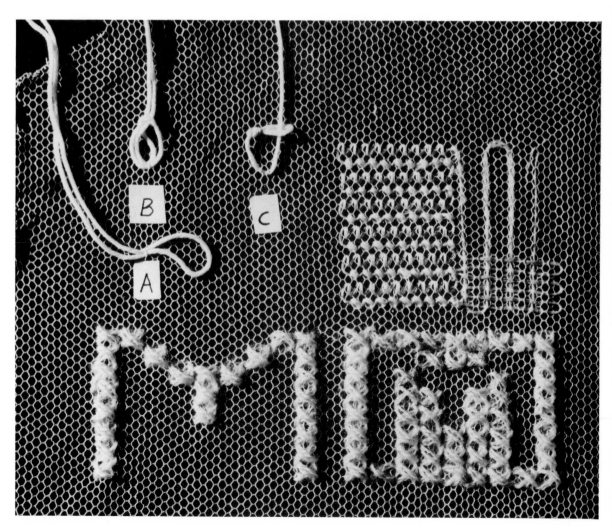

LÜNEBURG

A very famous and early centre in Germany for fine linen embroidery used for church purposes in the thirteenth century. The embroidery was figurative and illustrated biblical scenes in fine stitches such as stem stitch, usually in white, although colour is sometimes introduced.

MACHINE EMBROIDERY

As for other embroideries, there are many specialist and well-illustrated books on this subject, but as the invention of the embroidery machine made such profound changes in the production of white work, some aspects of machine work are particularly relevant, one being that it put many hand workers out of work and many workshops out of business.

However, the notion that lace and embroidery were a symbol of wealth and luxury was finally ended, because the machines produced almost unlimited quantities at a very reasonable price.

Following the inventions of mechanized spinning and weaving, the invention of the embroidery machine influenced both the background and the stitchery. The first experimental, but unreliable, sewing machine was made in the late eighteenth century, but later more successful inventions gave a more continuous performance, with the embroidery machine eventually developing from the lace machine and the sewing machine coming after the embroidery machine.

Over the previous centuries the commercial side of white work had been carried out entirely by hand for an exclusive clientele in highly organized and proficient workrooms. It was a considerable industry equal to that of other textiles such as weaving, and was purchased by affluent families.

As for the work of embroidery for pleasure, it represented time to spend on a luxurious art, and this indicated enough wealth to support an educated and civilized existence, as is confirmed by portraits of the time showing ladies at embroidery frames. Lady Leicester at a square frame and the sisters Waldegrave at a tambour are two examples.

The great influence on embroidery of the following inventors and machines is remarkable:

1809 – John Heathcoat invented a machine-made bobbin net (of two or three twists) which influenced hand embroidery on net, for appliqué, Carrickmacross, Limerick and also lace, by providing a new ground. Bobbins refer to disc-like carriers for the machine, and not the bobbins for hand lace.

1813 – John Leaver produced a machine-made lace, with the use of a pantograph which moves the warp or ground, and this invention, with the Jacquard system, was the basis for an embroidery machine later in the century.

1824 – Sewing machines with a fairly good performance were produced and were used to decorate machine-made lace and net with extra embellishment. Machines of this sort tended to be hired out for special items rather than being situated in a factory.

1828 – Josue Heilmann invented an embroidery machine at Mulhouse. Material was stretched vertically on an upright frame and moved slightly sideways or up and down by means of a pantograph, enabling a bank of needles to interpret repetitive, and usually floral, designs. This machine was a development of John Leaver's machine and the Jacquard weaving system. It embroidered 'accurately and expeditiously' and did the work of fifteen handworkers, but needed only one worker and two children to thread the needles to keep it working. A row of needles was pushed through the material and then released for the ground to move slightly (approximately the size of a stitch) and then, guided by a pantograph, the needles were pushed through to the surface again. These needles were pointed at both ends, with an eye in the middle, and produced a satin stitch. The material on a vertical frame and the pantograph were controlled by one operator, following a charted design.

1834 – The machine was shown at the Paris Exhibition, and Henry Houldsworth of Manchester bought the patents.

1840 – James Houldsworth produced sprigged dress material and furnishings decorated in this way.

1846 – A machine for lace curtains with a square mesh, similar to filet but not knotted, was developed and imitated net darning. A great vogue for this type of window drapery occurred. It did not prove very hardwearing, but fulfilled its purpose.

1851 – The embroidery machine increased in size but needed only three women operators and three children to thread needles. Satin stitch and a type of run stitch were produced. Fig. 223.

1851 – The machine was exhibited at the Great Exhibition at the Crystal Palace.

1860 – A reliable sewing machine was produced and came to be used in most homes, powered by a treadle or hand-turned handle.

1860 – Introduction of the Schiffli machine – a Swiss invention which eventually led to the production of vast quantities of white embroidery. The fame of Swiss embroidery now rests on the machine product. The work of the machine is immensely varied and of a high standard for dress wear, but handkerchiefs embroidered in floral designs for gifts are also synonymous with Swiss embroidery. Fig. 332.

The boat-shaped shuttle that holds the thread at the back inspired the name of the machine, as the Swiss-German name for a small boat is *schiffli* (skiff). The Schiffli machine has a bank of needles passing the thread simultaneously through the ground material, which hangs vertically. The threads are secured at the back by thread from shuttles, and the needles then withdraw to repeat the process. A continuous repetitive pattern is made by moving the ground material from side to side, or up and down, and not the needles. The movement of the material is controlled by a pantograph, which moves the material to interpret the design and requires only one person to operate it. At first the Schiffli machine was used on net, to become an embroidered net

223 A collection of machine embroidery made on the Schiffli machine. On the right: *a type of chemical lace often called guipure. Compare with gros point lace, just below.* Right of centre band: *needlerun net.* Centre band: *machine-made.* On the left: *a tatting border and a circular mat knitted by hand.*

called a 'needlerun net'. Fig. 223. This adds to the profusion of terms for net embroideries, but 'machine-embroidered net' gives the clearest definition.

Later the machine developed to work on all types of material and all processes of white embroidery, including satin stitch and broderie anglaise, stamping out the holes or eyelets and oversewing the edges. The mechanical precision is the means of identifying this work, as threads pass

224 A sample of machine embroidery. Note top; working thread carried across. 5 cm (2 in.) wide.

154

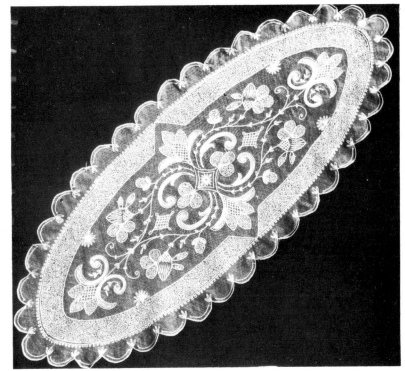

across the backs in precisely the same position throughout the embroidery. Figs 36, 116.

1865 – Cornely, a French engineer, invented a chain stitch machine. One needle is rotated by a handle; this allows involved work to be carried out, and typically decorates nets and bridal veils. Fig. 225.

1875 – The Cornely machine (US: Bornaz) was imported into Glasgow.

1880 – Cornely embroidery machines working at Macclesfield.

1883 – A worker called Wetter experimented in producing an imitation lace using the Schiffli embroidery machine, with a cotton thread on a silk ground. When the work was complete it was plunged into a bleach solution such as caustic soda or chlorine, and the silk rotted away leaving the closely worked cotton embroidery. A woven acetate rayon material is usually used today and it is dissolved away in acetone, so that the embroidery may be worked in nylon, wool or cotton. This imitation or chemical lace is often used in a design where the main motif is held together by bars and there is no background of any sort, which distinguishes it from the Leavers machine lace which has a net ground, and from hand-made lace

226 Detail of fig. 225.

which has form to the stitchery and a clear passage of the thread, whereas the machine shows a type of very close unclear or fuzzy oversewing or zig-zagging.

Power machines are used for all types of embroidery, such as:

- silk embroidery including satin stitch (fig. 223);
- metal threads;
- beading;
- stitching on net – needlerun net (fig. 223);
- satin stitch related to broderie anglaise on cotton with cotton thread;
- quantities of white eyelet embroidery including broderie anglaise on cotton;
- edgings – edging eyelets, similar to buttonhole;
- quilting;
- 'guipure', or chemical lace.

1885–1965 – In factories, machines powered by electricity, and known as power machines, expanded in versatility, for example:

1 The overlocking machine represented an important development, having three spools or bobbins, used for neatening edges and for picot edging in the early twentieth century.
2 The Irish machine, with a swing needle, produced satin stitch and run stitch while the material was held tight and horizontal in a frame.
3 The tufting machine, for a pile finish, gave many decorative opportunities.

(*Note*: hand-worked Ayrshire continued to about 1870, and cut work and broderie anglaise into the twentieth century, but many machines developed at such a rate that nearly every home had a domestic sewing machine for seams, dressmaking, household articles, sheets and curtains, using a treadle or hand-turned machine. Gradually the machines came to be powered by electricity and were improved and refined, and by 1960, with the use of a swing needle or zig-zag and a drop feed, enabled free embroidery to be carried out at home. Later, discs provided the means for rows of repetitive mechanical satin stitch patterns.)

Many refinements and intricacies in machines continued to be developed which almost defy description and explanation. The results even of early

227 *Machine-embroidered motif.*

machines in white work are incredibly successful and the famous test of viewing the working thread on the reverse is the only means of identification, while in other work a real appraisal has to be made. Many hand pieces are touched up with machine, and many machine pieces with hand work. Figs 36, 59–62, 116, 131, 132, 136, 139, 142, 143, 167, 182, 223, 230, 248, 250, 332.

Machine embroidery today has many aspects such as:

Commercial work

By the early part of the twentieth century nearly all white embroidery on sale was produced by machine and was on sale not only by the yard or metre but by the roll or bale, and in many styles of repetitive designs of broderie anglaise as borders and allover pattern. Most have a lively charm, some are very beautiful and some very crude, and nearly all are

inspired by the eighteenth or nineteenth century. A few echo Art Nouveau or Art Deco, and some show a fashionable foreign influence, such as Indian. All employ a varied use of different machines, such as Cornely and Schiffli.

Work at home

The machine is used for construction and decoration, and also for interesting experimental work exploiting the embroidery facilities of the machine, such as the drop feed and the swing or zig-zag needle, which gives an opportunity for artistic expression of creative flair and talent.

Early domestic machines of the following names are always a rewarding

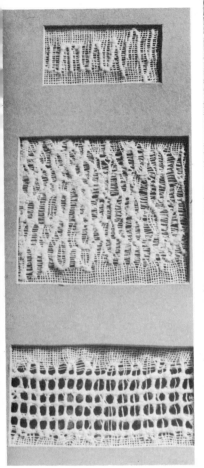

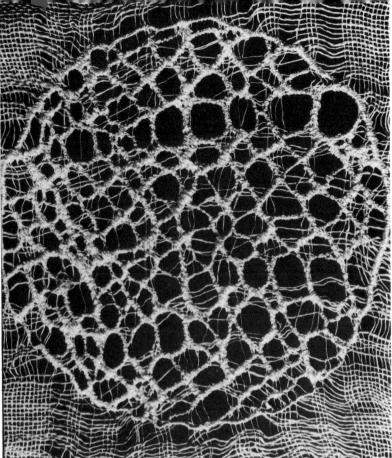

228 (Left)   Machine-embroidered
experiments on loosely woven linen.

229   Machine experiments with some
drawn threads.

find, not necessarily financial, but in interest:

Elias Howe, 1841 – highly thought
    of in the nineteenth century
Jones
Frister & Rossmann
Wheeler & Wilson's silent automa-
    tic tension machine
Wilcox & Gibbs' automatic
    machine
Grover & Barker
Thomas, the Florence and the
    Wanzer

Most of these were powered by treadle and worked by foot. Alternatively, a hand-turned handle made a
machine more portable.

230   A well worked out design
attributed to Rebecca Crompton, and
worked by Dorothy Benson, showing
many techniques of machine embroidery
in white thread on transparent material.
The vigorous design avoids the
lifelessness often associated with perfect
techniques. (On loan to the
Embroiderers' Guild by the Dorking
Branch).

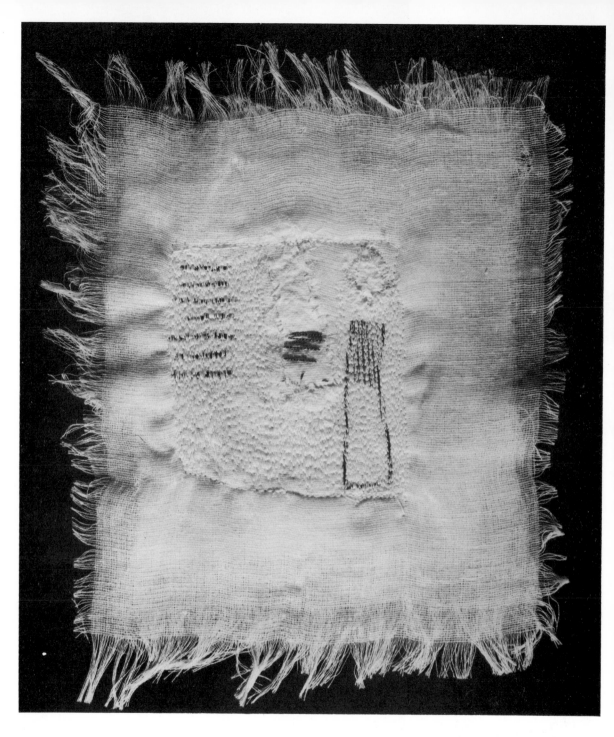

231　*Experiment in machine
embroidery, by Lynda Graham.*

Singer sewing machines, mainly
American made, held the lead in
popularity for the greater part of the

twentieth century. There are many
others from almost every country and
having special features, such as Necchi
from Italy and Bernina from Switzerland, to mention but two.

Artist–designer
The stitching of the machine, as of the
hand, on textiles, is used by many

trained artists for texture and is comparable with paint, canvas, wood,
plaster, plastics or other materials for
structures.

The speed of the machine gives a
spontaneity of expression and also
interprets restrained and calculated
designs which in white have great
impact and emphasize form. Fig. 183.
See *Lace, Net.*

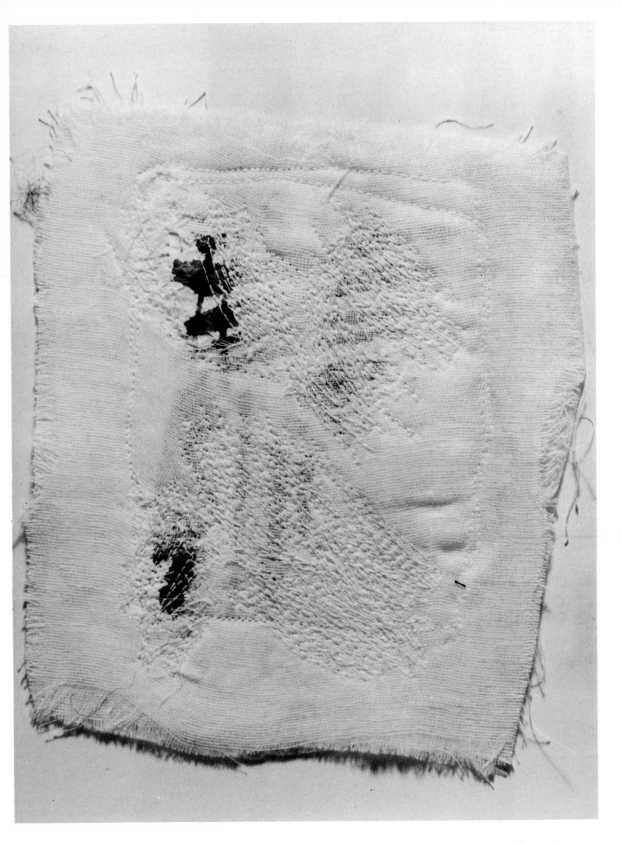

*232   An experiment showing inset
paper and paint, by Lynda Graham.*

MACRAMÉ

A decorative form of knotting, often in white or natural coloured string or twine. See also *Knotting*.

MADAGASCAR LACE

A lace produced using a gimp or cord twisted to form loops and scallops. Not considered of value in the nineteenth century but now probably the only such African product. It is unlike European work, but may be found in sales.

MADEIRA WORK

Nineteenth-century white embroidery on fine cotton, lawn or cambric, and rarely on linen. Similar to broderie anglaise and eyelet embroidery, and with Irish and Ayrshire influences. Made and taught by nuns to a high standard, it has buttonhole or overcast edges to openwork of eyelets, wheels or buttonhole-filled centres, satin stitch, seeding, small straight stitches. Designs of small flowers forming borders and sprays are used for blouses and children's clothes. It was eagerly sought after at the time it was made and is still in demand with tourists; it retains the same style of design and some of the same techniques today. Drawn thread work was also carried out in Madeira on cotton bedspreads, and copies of linen articles of Ireland and England. Introduced originally from Europe as a means of earning money after blighted wine crops.

MESH

Term applied to netting and to the tool made of boxwood, bone or ivory used in netting as a guide for the formation of even loops. A mesh is the size of the spaces in net: a large hole or space is a coarse mesh; a small hole or space is a fine mesh. Figs 111, 303–6, 312–15.

MOORISH LACE

A very early form of drawn thread work, brought in by Greek slaves captured by the Moors. It is Morocco-based with origins possibly as early as 2500 BC, and was another Victorian revival.

233 *Some examples typical of the variety of commercial machine embroidery in 1985. These white dress materials are easily available by the yard, and technically highly advanced, exploiting white texture and shadows. All are of polyester and produced in Austria. Left: a voile, of fine even weave (would originally have been of cotton), embroidered with simple flower forms in a variety of fillings. Note freely applied flower heads. Second left: background of organza (originally silk), applied with satin and worked in satin stitch, with repeating motif. Second right: heavy satin background richly and solidly embroidered in satin stitch. A sculptured hemline shows off the rose embroidery. Note the fall of light designed to give depth to the flowers. Right: a net extravagantly embroidered in imitation of Chantilly lace.*

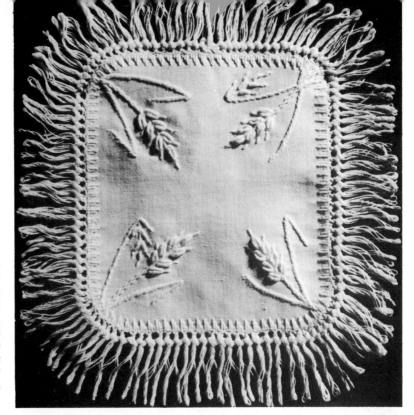

MOUNTMELLICK

Identification

There are no open areas in Mountmellick embroidery, but the stitchery is very heavy texturally, to display the design in relief. The plant form used in the design is noticeably textured, such as wheat ears and blackberries worked in bullion knots, which are sought-after features. Another feature peculiar to Mountmellick embroidery and which finishes some articles is a hand-knitted fringe. Figs 234–7.

History

Mountmellick is another type of embroidery which was set up to help overcome hardship in Ireland in the nineteenth century by selling to those more prosperous members of society who had a social conscience.

Items

Household articles and bags, purses and slippers.

Design

The design consists of naturalistically drawn flowers and leaves, especially with rough or broken surfaces or edges such as thorns and prickles, including brambles, thistles and moss roses as well as corn, wheat and passion flowers. Fig. 237.

The surface of the embroidery is raised by padding for satin stitch and by the use of knot stitches; the edge of the article is scalloped if not fringed. These features give the work a bold character of design and the use of a wide vocabulary of stitches provides interesting detail to a sculptural style.

Ground

Heavy, pliable and tough cotton satin, or a material known as white jean – a close, soft, fine twill more pliable than the jeans of today.

Technique

Framing-up – a square frame is preferable to keep the padding high on the right side.

Transfer of design – tack line or pale blue paint line. Fig. 335.

235 A pillow sham in Mountmellick embroidery with blackberries, bramble leaves, passion flowers and berries, a decorative buttonholed edge and a knitted fringe. 54 × 65 cm (21 × 25½ in.). Fringe 4.5 cm (1¾ in.). (Lise Mossery).

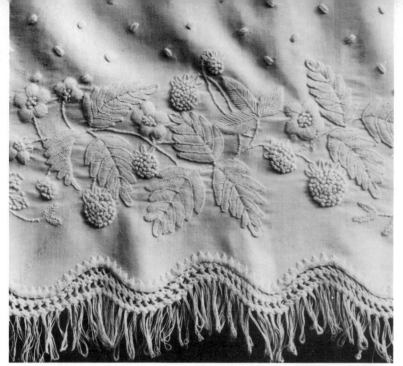

236 *Detail showing French knots for the blackberries, buttonhole stitch for the leaves and bullion knots used as a seeding for the centre of the mat. Note the exact and careful arrangement of the bullion knots.*

Needles – crewel.

Thread – preferably a matt or dull thread, as thick as can be comfortably drawn through the ground. A shiny thread tends to confuse the details of stitchery by catching the light and giving a spotty effect.

Join on/off – run stitch.

Process – stitches. A huge variety of stitches may be seen in Mountmellick embroidery: chain variations, twisted, knotted, threaded, detached, coral, zig-zag, cloud filling, vandyke, fern, Bokhara couching, fly, petal, scroll, raised stem, raised chain and French knots. See *Irish embroidery*.

NAINSOOK

Muslin plain and striped with the warp.

NEEDLEPOINT

All kinds of lace made with a needle rather than bobbins. (US: term for canvas work.) See *Lace*.

NEEDLEWEAVING

A form of darning over and under threads of the ground, either as spokes of bars in drawn thread work, or in a border pattern.

NEEDLEWORK

A term which now usually denotes dressmaking or embroidery. Previously referring to lingerie, i.e. underwear and sleepwear, blouses and children's clothes and housecoats.

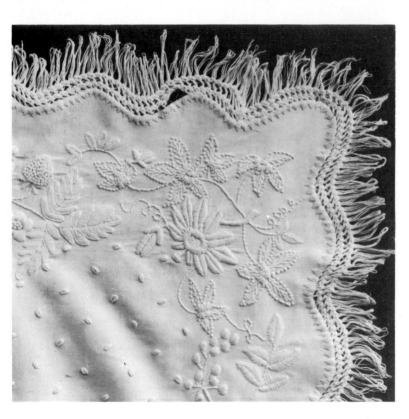

237 *Detail showing* (top right) *the completed edge before the fringe is attached. Note the outline of French knots in the embroidery to indicate a serrated edge to the leaves, and also the use of coral stitch for the stalks to* indicate thorns or for texture. Bullion knots also decorate the centre of the passion flower.

238 An example of a knotted net background showing cloth stitch darning and loop stitch with added stitchery in a thick thread. 34 × 50 cm (13$\frac{2}{5}$ × 19$\frac{1}{2}$ in.).

NET

Identification

Net is identified by threads crossing each other to form a mesh. The threads may be knotted or interwoven into a square mesh, or plaited or sewn into a hexagon, round, or diamond mesh.

The mesh may vary in size, from coarse heavy mesh 2 cm ($\frac{3}{4}$ in.) square to very fine and light, as found in lace. Designs on a square mesh are recognized by squared or angular edges. Net gives an extremely delicate background, and the embroidery appears to be close to lace. Figs 222, 238–54.

239 Net embroidery on a fine dress net. (Margaret Potts).

*240   A design showing typical
characteristics of net darning.*

Items

Embroidery on net in the form of
darning ranges from thick thread on
heavy net for furnishings, to very fine
thread on light dress net or tulle
worked in counted patterns.

Net may form the whole background for embroidered articles as
large as curtains, or be used as small
insertions on table linen or dress; it is
also used on upholstery, decorative
covers for pianos and mantel shelves,
and for purses, gloves, mittens, caps,
parasols and hammocks.

History

Net and netting have ancient origins,
and fishing nets are referred to in the
Bible. Although today nylon
machine-made net is in general use, it
is still made with a square knotted
mesh as before, and it is possible to see
fishermen mending their nets by the
shore.

However, some references to netting appear during the thirteenth century as a darned lace using linen floss,

for a heavy architectural type of decoration on net for churches in Europe.
It became known as Opus Filatorum
and Opus Araneum, Latin references
being one of the studies of the Victorians, and also the language of the
Church.

Finer nets gradually developed
with embroidery in darning, and
there are many examples of the seventeenth century catalogued as lacis in
museums, including the Victoria &
Albert Museum. An example of an
ecclesiastical hanging embroidered in
cloth stitch darning on an interlaced
square mesh (or buratto net) has beautiful detail and scale. It shows an
interesting arrangement of figures in
different sizes, all carrying candles in a
festival procession.

Darning on square net is bold and
easily recognizable compared with
the finer work of drawn thread and
lace of this time. Fig. 217.

Other very fine net is made by
twisting or plaiting, or with buttonhole stitch, originally as a background
(for réseau) or lace to replace buttonhole bars.

In the eighteenth century interest in
net embroidery, such as lacis and filet,

waned because cotton muslin became
the great new influence and fashion
obsession, but hand-made net was
produced for dress in large pieces. The
net was often of silk, very fragile,
exclusive and treasured.

In the nineteenth century a
machine was invented to make a fine
net, and although of completely different construction from square net, it
was readily available and interest
revived.

The first effort to manufacture net,
or lace, by machine methods was
made on the stocking frame in the
Midlands, the centre of the hosiery
industry, but it was unsuccessful
because of irregularities in the pattern
and a tendency to unravel when a
loop was broken.

A young man, John Heathcoat, son
of a Leicestershire farmer was apprenticed as a frame-setter in the textile
industry in Nottingham, and was
familiar with the making of the pillow lace in Leicestershire. He was
successful in reproducing mechanically the succession of twists and loops
to make a net.

The machine which he and a friend
named Lacey patented in 1809 solved
the problem of making a strong net
by a series of twists instead of 'stocking' loops. By embroidering with a
needle on such foundation nets, half
the manual labour of making lace was
saved.

In two years Heathcoat's machines
had become widely known and their
products were in great demand, but in
1811 the Luddites, an association of
displaced craftsmen, broke into his
factory and destroyed most of his
equipment. Heathcoat then moved to
Devon and in 1812 began many successful years of producing net. In
1823, when the patent expired, other
factories were set up in Nottingham
and soon the world markets were
being supplied from there.

Early machine-made net, embroidered in fine thread and nearly equal to
lace in interest, shows the Indian
influence on design by the rows of
chain stitch made with the tambour
hook, either in outline or in solidly
filled floral shapes. Sometimes a
glossy floss silk thread was used. Even
mosquito net was occasionally util-
ized for embroidery. In time the tambour embroidery spread to many
workrooms including those of
Middlesex and Essex, to become
known as Coggeshall lace.

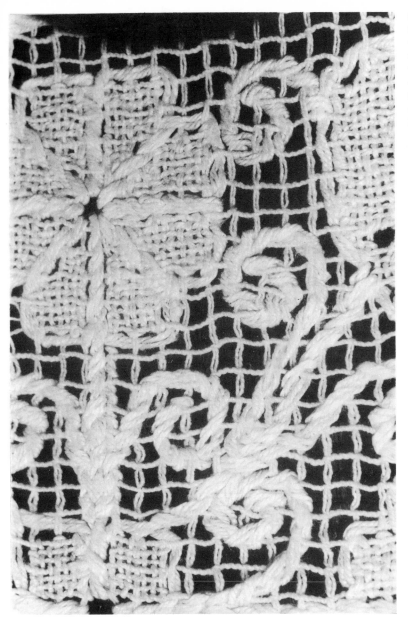

241 Detail of a machine-woven square net ground.

scale was generally coarse and the net machine-made, but the boldness of the work appealed to the prosperous, and especially to German states where the French term *filet* was often used to describe the work. All European needlewomen produced quantities of darned netting with additional embellishments of bullion knots, loop stitch and shiny thread outlines, and enjoyed using involved terms of description such as 'filet de Richelieu' and 'filet guipure'. The work was used for furnishings, dress and church linen.

Embroidered net known as needle-run net was produced on the Schiffli machine at this time in large quantities.

In some homes netting or net with a square mesh, i.e. filet, was made by hand as a studied return to authentic beginnings and as a reaction to the machine patterns of lace.

Crochet eventually took over in popularity from net embroidery, and many net or filet designs influenced those for working in crochet, so that care is needed to distinguish between the two types of work.

From 1945 onwards hand-embroidered net was hardly commercial, and was worked for couture dress or individual enjoyment, but about 1970 a somewhat studied revival of square netting and darning by enthusiasts and specialists occurred. Patterns on dress net are popular all over the world.

The terms and names used through the centuries show such confusing variety that 'embroidered net' or 'net darning', with a description of mesh and work, has come to be the only clear classification.

Designs

Designs for square net planned on square paper traditionally consist of geometric shapes or conventional flowers, leaves, vases and figures in the form of cherubs or angels, for table linen and furnishings.

Designs for church and ecclesiastical purposes, such as altar linen and white vestments, are particularly numerous, with grapes, chalices, saints and other figures and letters and symbols. Known as 'church lace', it is often large and coarse in order to be visible to the congregation.

All designs on square net have a bold flourish and are recognized by what is known as a characteristically

Darning and counted satin stitch patterns are also used to interpret designs on fine net; the patterns give different tones, or shades, of white, according to the closeness of the stitches, and are similar to the canvas patterns of Berlin woolwork. The net embroidery introduced to Ireland from England in the nineteenth century by nuns and teachers to set up an industry is now known as Limerick lace, and is used for dress, including bridal veils and evening stoles. Carrickmacross embroidery is also based on fine net, but with a fine muslin appliqué. Both districts suffered from poverty, and the work helped to provide an income.

In 1846 a machine known as a net curtain machine produced large quantities of machine-made net with a square mesh, and huge designs and patterns in imitation of darning were made very inexpensively in Nottingham, so that the windows of almost every house were hung with elaborate curtains.

Because of the interest in antique embroidery early in the twentieth century, there was a great revival of net embroidery on square mesh. The

242 *Detail of design made up of nineteenth-century square net embroidery, showing different types of square net, knotted and woven, hand- and machine-made.*

Italian style; on a small scale they have a quaint appearance.

The finer dress net gives a soft dewy lightness and the designs are freely flowing, with flowers, leaves, ribbons and arabesques for dress and fashions, such as mittens, gloves, caps, capes, veils, lappets and stoles.

Net grounds

Today net is available by the yard in square mesh from specialist suppliers

243 *Crochet bed cover in filet-style design. (Sheila Joss).*

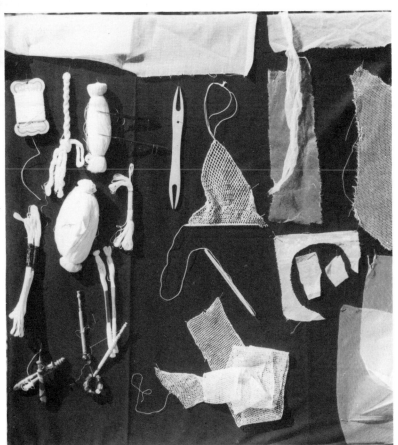

244 *Embroidery in floss silk on machine-made dress net, typical of twentieth-century work all over the world, and introduced to outlying places by magazines, schools and missions. This example is from the Philippines. See also fig. 180. (Constance Howard).*

and in hexagonal or round mesh of various sizes, as a dress net. For studying or collecting items consisting of or introducing net grounds, the following list includes the main differences.

1 A square mesh: (a) secured with knots, either with a mesh stick and shuttle and worked in rows, or on a metal frame with a needle and thread working diagonally across the frame. (b) Secured by interwoven threads, either on a frame by hand, or a loom as in early buratto. (c) Made by hand

245 *A sample of nets. Left centre: a netting shuttle and mesh bar. On the right: fine silk dress net, easily crumpled cotton net. Lower right: synthetic net. Lower centre: hand-made square net with knotting. Left: linen lace threads and lace bobbins.*

pass each other. This method, invented in 1809, is sometimes known as bobbin net and should not be confused with bobbin lace, which also produces a net background but in much smaller quantities. (c) Made by hand using buttonhole stitches, and also by plaiting threads found in hand-made lace. Figs 226, 239, 246.

3 Tulle: a silk net, very fine, light and soft, and easily crumpled. It is occasionally produced today, but is usually found in sales, having been popular early in the century. Fig. 246.

4 Synthetic or plastic net with various types of mesh. Figs 246, 248.

5 Diamond mesh: may be found as a variation of a square knotted net, not now produced but found at sales. Valenciennes bobbin lace has a diamond ground. (*Note:* spotted and sprigged net is usually machine-made, with a regularly spaced all-over arrangement of spots. Popular in the early nineteenth century.) Fig. 162.

6 A freely formed net may be individually made by the sewing machine stitching on vanishing muslin. The muslin is removed by a hot iron, leaving the lines of stitching as an open net. Other basic materials in place of the muslin are also available. Figs 249, 250.

Fibres of net ground: linen, cotton, silk, synthetic and some local or regional fibres.

Technique

Framing-up – useful for large articles. Wedding veils, for example, need a square frame. Motifs may be worked in a ring frame.

Transfer of design – design in ink on paper laid under net and tacked out.

Needles – tapestry, size according to the size of the mesh of the net. The blunt point slips smoothly through the mesh. Crewel for appliqué.

Thread – similar in size and quality to the net ground, such as fly silk, Drima, a machine cotton or single

247 Detail. A hank of lace thread, which is divided into as many smaller skeins as the size of the thread (in this case No. 14). All hanks are the same in size and weight, but the coarser size of thread has fewer skeins inside.

from the ground material, either by cut and drawn threads, or by pulled stitches on a loosely woven background. (d) Produced by machine manufacture and sold by the yard for curtains and other uses. (e) Produced by the net curtain machine in the past and not now available, but found at sales. Figs 238, 241, 303, 306, 242, 249.

2 A hexagonal mesh: (a) made by machine in various sizes, and when very fine may appear as a round mesh. Today made on the Raschel machine in a form of fine knitting in a nylon thread and having a slightly stretchy feel. It does not unravel or have interlocking threads. In the 1950s a net was stamped out of a thin layer of plastic in a huge tray by a finely perforated stencil. (b) Made by machine using a system of three sets of bobbins, one set hanging vertically, another working from left to right and the third from right to left, twisting together as they meet and

248 Synthetic or plastic net, embroidered by machine.

249 An example of a grid made of lines of thread attached with zig-zag machine stitching on a 'wash away' base. When the base is dissolved, the grid is interwoven with strips of different white textured material. This example is a practice piece for a wide shoulder cape. Worked by Margaret Gunston.

strand of stranded cotton, and also some mercerized threads. For coarse darning thick thread may be used, and finer thread for dress net.

Join on/off – to begin, see diagram. To join a working thread, use a weaver's knot. To finish, run end of thread into the back of previous work. Figs 2, 222.

Process – stitch.

Darning

Pass the working thread alternately over and under threads of the net. On square net the direction is easily seen; on dress net some practice is usually required to become familiar with the mesh. Darning may be worked horizontally, vertically, diagonally or as the design dictates. Figs 94, 99, 110, 222.

250 A freely formed net made of looped lines worked by the sewing machine on vanishing muslin, with appliqué by machine and added decoration of silver paper, cocktail sticks and a 'windmill'. Worked by Lindy Richardson.

169

stitch, and the stitch may also be used as a simple filling.

Other stitches may be added to the main work of darning, such as

Satin stitch– often used with counted patterns. Figs 222, 252, 296, 302.

Eyelets – Algerian and round. Figs 1, 51, 52, 244.

Bullion knots – added to a darned area or loop stitch. Figs 238, 240.

Tambour – chain stitch worked with a tambour hook.

Appliqué – muslin applied to net.

Buttonhole – used for eyelets and outer edges.

Couching – used for outlines and edges. Figs 5, 52, 235, 249.

Binding – an edging of solid material, such as satin or crêpe de Chine or a strip of white kid leather, and also flowers applied as a powdered motif to give a snowflake effect, which help the net to stand out and billow on the air for dress and veils. Fig. 254.

For collectors, specialists and students, the following list shows the wide and even confusing variety of terms used over the very long history of net embroidery. All the terms overlap, and they are often borrowed from lace, other countries and other embroidery; they also reflect the Victorian love of knowledge and desire to impress, and the names, which appear in instruction leaflets of the time, give a kind of romance evocative of comfort and leisure.

Everyone who could decorated the home with heavy net drapery, embroidered with darning in a coarse thread, with rich silk or glossy outlines to give a sumptuous feeling which the neat refinement and order of small lace did not have.

Not all the terms are professional, and the best way to describe net darning is as net darning, with any added details explained, e.g. loop stitch, outline in floss etc., and dates wherever possible.

Darned lace, Darned netting – terms for early square net darning.

Embroidered net – includes tambour, filet, lacis darning, counted satin stitch, run stitch, and appliqué.

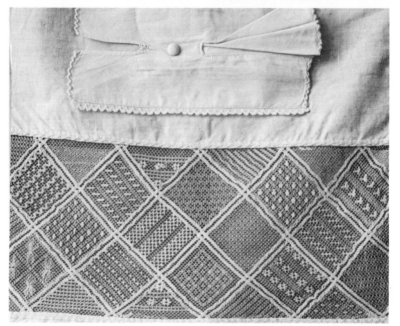

252   A sample showing counted patterns on net, from a sampler. Above: shirt gussets, in buttonhole stitch for strength. (Embroiderers' Guild).

Close darning
The working thread is passed alternately over and under the mesh. Figs 94, 99, 110, 222.

Cloth stitch or linen stitch
Worked on square net horizontally with sufficient space between threads to fit in another row vertically to form a darn or weave. May be worked horizontally or vertically. Figs 95, 238, 251.

Counted patterns
A large area of work in embroidery on net; the patterns require careful counting, but there is a wide almost limitless variety, and they are usually used on dress net, as in Limerick lace. Figs 222, 252, 292.

Loop stitch
Worked over four sides of a square, usually in fine thread as a change of texture. Also worked on a mesh of ground material.

Run stitch
Worked as an outline in thick thread round a darned area and sometimes used for emphasis. A design may be worked in outline only using run

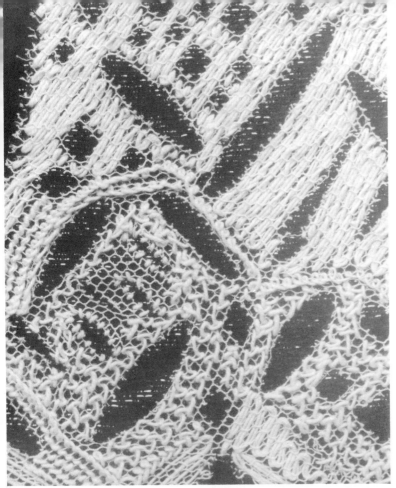

253 Patterns freely worked on cotton net in cotton threads, by Irene Ord.

Filet – darning on square net, the term used in the nineteenth century.

Filet brodé – French for embroidered net of the nineteenth century.

Filet Richelieu – term probably used at the time of the nineteenth-century revival; includes cloth stitch and shiny outlines.

Cluny filet, Cluny guipure, Filet guipure, Guipure d'art, Guipure filet, Richelieu guipure – all mean net darning, with detail.

Italian filet, Italian darned netting – possibly designate early work.

Lacis – darning on square net, the term used in the seventeenth century.

Net darning – used as a collective term for net embroidery and includes: (*a*) needlerun net on the Schiffli machine; (*b*) designs in outline only using run stitch by hand; (*c*) darning worked as a counted satin stitch on net.

Netting – refers to the making of a net ground, usually with a square mesh. See *Darning, Irish embroidery*.

OLD LACE

A romantic term for lace before the invention of machine-made lace, from before about 1810.

OPEN BACK STITCH

See *Punch stitches*

OPENWORK

A general term for any open areas in embroidery, such as cut, drawn or pulled.

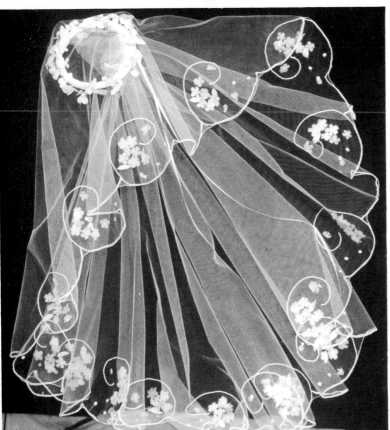

254 Veil on polyester net with flowers applied to give body to the hem. Headband of buttonhole stitched flowers and leaves. Worked by June Young.

OPUS

Opus is a Latin term for 'work' and is used in many embroidery books written before the nineteenth century to describe different techniques such as:

Opus araneum – netting.

Opus consutum – appliqué.

Opus filatorium – darned netting.

Opus pulvinarium – canvas.

Opus seissam – cut work.

Opus tagliatum – cut work for reticella, including drawn thread work of today.

Opus tiratum – pulled work (formerly drawn).

OVERCAST, OVERSEW

Oversew from right to left so that the left hand is able to hold and adjust the fold of material for two edges of a seam.

Overcast from left to right so that the thumb of the left hand controls the fall or lie of the stitch into parallel slanting angles, for neatening a seam or an edge.

Trailing or overcasting worked on a frame is usually described as left to right so that the right hand may pull the couched line firmly for a smooth line and does not then rub the work as it is completed.

However, it depends on which hand is used on the top of the frame and which hand is underneath, and is a personal preference nothing to do with right- or left-handedness.

If the left hand is on top of the frame and the right underneath, then the stitch is worked from right to left as the left hand does not rub up the finished stitch. Figs 96, 278 (C, D), 303.

P

PADDING

A method frequently used at the present time to exploit shadows and produce a work of self-colour, in white

or neutral textures, for hangings and panels. High stuffing is sometimes developed for effects of high relief. Fig. 282. See *Quilting, Satin stitch.*

PANES AND SLASHINGS

Cuts made in costume to display a material of contrasting texture or tone bursting or puffing through. This is a technique that might well be exploited to show qualities of shadow and strong texture in white textile work. Fig. 253.

PASSEMENT

A term which today has an antique air of mystery but which is a seventeenth-century French term for work connected with lace gimps and parchment for lacemaking. See also *Lace*

Passement à l'aiguille – needle-made lace, and *passementiers* – lacemakers, were terms used when *passement* denoted this type of trimming, including gold and silver. Huguenots excelled at craftsmanship.

PATCHWORK

Not a white work technique specifically, but one which displays the beauty of different textures of white materials. There are several very fine examples, both American and English. Figs 136, 218.

PEARL EDGE or EDGING

Refers to an edge neatened, strengthened or decorated with looped picots or with French knots, bullion knots or buttonholed picots to appear as a row of closely threaded beads, and also often seen as a woven-in edging to ribbons.

The term probably comes from gold and silver smelting where an edge decorated with small even granules or beads is also termed 'beading'.

PEARLIN, PEARLING

Romantic Scottish name for lace.

PERSIAN

Embroidery worked on fine white linen in heavy satin stitch but delicate design.

PICOT

This is a decoration to an edging or bar of buttonhole stitch or couching,

and is worked as a loop or knot, using a pin for a foundation. It is often found in broderie anglaise and cut work, lace and many embroideries.

Originally part of the highly decorative Venetian lace, which has an extra row of looped buttonhole added to the cordonnet and is collectively known as *fleurs volants* (wind flowers) to combine terms such as bobs, couronnes (crowns), spines, thorns and pinwork. Picots were added to the cordonnet to lighten outlines and to fill spaces of rose point and pointe de neige (snowflake) lace, and also as added decoration to the surface of padded areas.

The Victorians added this form of decoration to existing old lace, in a love of showiness and technical exactitude. Fig. 52, 83–6, 88, 105, 208, 209, 215–17. See *Lace (Venetian).*

PLAITINGS

Included as a term for plaiting string work carried on a frame as a type of weaving. Today it is a possible experimental method for nets based on bobbin lace and fillings formerly used in tape lace.

POINT(E)

The French word for 'stitch', now nearly obsolete in the English language. However, the term is sometimes used to describe types of lace, and a canvas stitch, i.e. petit point, which is a diagonal stitch worked over and up one thread of the background. Gros point is similar, but worked over and up two threads of background and sometimes over a trammed thread, i.e. a laid thread over several threads of background.

PUCKERING, IN EMBROIDERY

In some cases puckering or gathering can give a desirable uneven texture, working or manipulating the material for individual effects.

Puckering of the background round embroidery caused by too tight a tension on the working thread may be removed by stretching out and dampening the completed work. The first step is to pull out tightly the area with the most puckering. It is likely to be the area with the most embroidery. Measure horizontally and vertically. The measurement will probably be less than the outer edges of the background where there is no embroidery, but the work should be squared to the smaller measurement, which may result in easing to the outer edge.

To square the work, lay it out on the double thickness of an old cotton sheet and smooth the surface of the embroidery. Match the lower edge of the work exactly parallel with the edge of the stretching table, or a floor board, if the floor is used. Secure with nails for heavy linen, or with pins for lightweight work, on a soft board.

1 Begin at lower edge of the work and nail or pin in position at the right-hand corner. Pin the left-hand corner parallel to the edge of the table and at the measured horizontal distance along. Fix a pin at the centre of the edge between the two corners, spreading evenly any necessary ease, i.e. extra fullness. Fix pins halfway between the centre and each corner, then fix pins halfway between each space. Repeat until pins or nails are about 2.5 cm (1 in.) apart.

2 Repeat on the opposite or top edge. Check top edge measurement equals lower. Ensure that both side edges are at right angles to the top and lower edges and that both side measurements are the same.

3 Then pin one side edge, matching the centre and distributing the pins and ease evenly as before.

4 Do the same on the opposite edge.

Dampen the work thoroughly with a sponge and cold water. Soak up extra moisture and leave to dry for at least twenty-four hours. For light work, damp lightly.

The tightly worked areas will set stretched tight and the looser areas round the edge will shrink to size.

Synthetic fibres do not always respond to this treatment.

PULLED STITCHES

This type of work is sometimes known as 'linen embroidery', but it is frequently worked on material composed of other fibres and, in England, reached its height of popularity on cotton in the eighteenth century. There are also many other famous types of linen embroidery, such as drawn thread work and cut work. Frontispiece, figs 92, 255–71.

Identification

The identifying feature of pulled

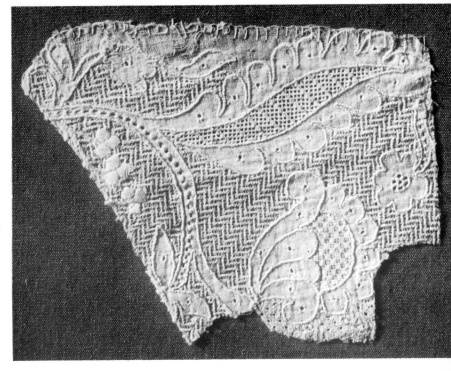

255 *Fragment of Dresden work showing pulled stitch pattern, couched outlines and open back stitch.* (Embroiderers' Guild).

stitches is the pulling together of threads of the background material with stitchery in the form of regularly counted-out patterns.

This makes small open or perforated holes, giving an effect of lace, with interest in the open patterns rather than in the stitchery. The background is usually an evenweave cotton muslin, linen or lightweight wool and occasionally silk, but recognizable in that the threads can be counted.

Pulled stitch embroidery is sometimes referred to as Dresden, Danish, Flemish or Saxony lace, and also as drawn fabric work, since the threads of the background fabric are drawn together. This last name, however, causes confusion with drawn thread work, where the threads of the background are cut and drawn out.

Pulled stitch embroidery, like much other white work, has been used throughout the centuries in ecclesiastical work, on vestments, fair linen or altar linen. It is also used for decorating household linen and personal clothing, and was especially fashionable for dress in the eighteenth and nineteenth centuries, when the

most abundant and the finest examples were produced before and alongside the work in Ayrshire.

The work is set off with a combination of other stitches for outline or texture, such as back stitch, double back stitch, French knots, satin stitch, stem stitch and eyelets. Double back stitch is worked on the wrong side of the material to raise the right side very slightly and give a faintly quilted surface texture in designs.

History

Early work from Arabic countries filtered through to the Mediterranean and North Africa to be absorbed by Spain and Italy, and examples of a European type of pulled stitch embroidery are recorded from the eleventh to fourteenth centuries. The work appears to be derived from stitches such as counted satin stitch or cross stitch tightly pulled together.

Other examples appear from about 1600, particularly of Italian origin on evenly woven grounds in the manner of cross stitches, tightly worked to make open holes, covering the background but leaving the design in unworked background material. Sometimes a coloured thread is used, such as dark red, blue or green. The design consists of figures, leaves, flowers, symbols, lettering or monograms.

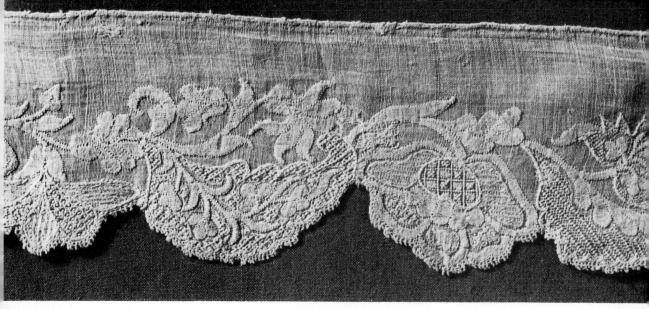

256 Dresden work with slightly raised flowers in double back stitch.

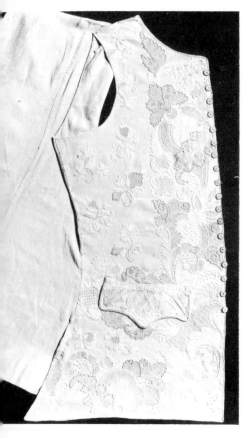

257 A waistcoat of the late seventeenth century worked in pulled stitches, showing the influence of Dresden work and the use of satin stitch. Note the Dorset buttons down the edge of the waistcoat. (Victoria & Albert Museum).

Church embroidery carried out in this method is often to be found on vestments such as albs, cottas and tunicles and also on fair linen.

Open pulled work on a fine cotton muslin is sometimes confused with the buttonhole fillings of Ayrshire, or with drawn thread work or punch stitches, as all were worked in Scotland. The style of design and a magnifying glass can help with correct identification.

Pulled stitches prospered, particularly in Denmark, the German states and the Netherlands, being named Danish, Saxony, Dresden or Flemish embroidery, according to the district. The Swiss also excelled at this type of embroidery. These countries and states did not have the enormously successful trading companies of England, Spain, France and Italy to bring in wealth to buy expensive laces. The pulled work became extremely fine, and this period was the heyday of a remarkably high standard of craftsmanship and design on very fine linen or cotton muslin, which gained a reputation for excellence and became a substitute for lace. Other embroidery stitches were used to give a marvellous display of texture which was quicker, cheaper and easier to produce than lace, and it also suited the more restrained character of the North better than the lace of the flamboyant South.

Famous historical examples are the embroidered muslin aprons, fichus, cuffs and caps of the eighteenth century, in intricate floral and rococo designs, which are often the work of embroiderers at home. Petticoats and waistcoats showed pulled stitches combined with quilting in elegant and elaborate floral compositions. The regency era used restrained pulled stitch borders with tambour motifs as dress decoration.

In the nineteenth and twentieth centuries pulled work continued to decorate church linen, household linen and some personal items such as collars and handkerchiefs.

In the 1950s Scandinavian countries produced refreshingly simple geometric designs, showing a refinement and a restrained use of stitch, thread and ground material, with delicate and accurate placing of the design for table linen and cushions.

Peasant/ethnic pulled work produced in rural and sometimes isolated communities shows a locally woven, coarse ground material, probably linen, with pulled work in robust designs.

A description of early historical examples of white linen embroidery is interesting because some stitches, which are still in use today, came to be combined with a pulled mesh background.

In the Cleveland Museum of Art, USA, there is a fine example of a white linen altar cloth, embroidered in white thread, and dated the second half of the thirteenth century (1250). It comes from Altenberg-a-d-Lahn, Germany, and the stitches used include satin, Florentine, square (presumably counted), stem, chain and surface buttonhole. (Frontispiece)

The design (and the pull of the

174

258 A pulled stitch mesh and variation, surrounded by satin stitch leaves on muslin. Probably nineteenth century, perhaps Ayrshire before buttonhole fillings, or possibly Indian in imitation of lace fillings.

background threads in the stitchery) is thrown up in silhouette, when hung against the light of the altar windows, and particularly so in apse windows. The tonal qualities are also enhanced.

This type of cloth, known as *hungertuch* or *fastentuch*, was used during Lent to hang between the nave and the chancel in order to screen or shroud the altar. The Lenten season mourns the death of Christ, and emblems to his memory are often draped.

The cloth is finished with a knotted fringe, an example of the probable forerunner of bobbin lace.

An idea of this embroidery may be viewed in a frame in the Study Collection at the Victoria & Albert Museum in London.

Other German linen embroidered altar cloths are of the same high standard and similar date. They come from the convent situated in the isolated moorland and although out of favour during the Lutheran Reforma-

tion, many embroideries have remained undisturbed, and were found much later to be carefully preserved.

Amongst these embroideries is one which has a ground of openwork mesh formed by wrapping or whipping round groups of threads of the warp and weft. It seems that the removed threads may be cut and withdrawn or pulled and the plain linen forms the design, which is outlined in chain stitch. It is rare to see such ancient and fine work so well preserved.

Other embroideries resembling examples of the fourteenth to fifteenth centuries in the Victoria & Albert Museum are a lectern cloth, and a panel illustrating the Chase of the Unicorn.

There are other historical examples in private collections and museums, such as remnants of farthingales of the early seventeenth century, and underskirts or petticoats of the eighteenth century. They come from Holland as well as England, and the embroidery from both countries is equally finely executed in design and technique. The varied use of embroidery, combined with pulled stitches, includes the

softly raised surface of quilting, the encrusted surface of French knots, backstitch and laid cords or couching.

In some instances, herringbone or double back stitch is also used to raise the surface. Punch stitch may be substituted for pulled, and satin stitch or long-and-short added.

The quilting served several purposes. It acted as a stiffening to the hem of garments, and raised the surface from behind to put parts of the design in relief, thus offsetting the delicate patterns of pulled work. In a practical sense, quilting added warmth to many items.

A backing is necessary when working quilting, and it seems there are two methods to be seen in this particular type of historical work. The backing, usually of a coarser and more loosely woven linen than the top surface of fine linen, gives support to the heavy stitchery such as french knots and cording. It also provides the double material for quilting in both the design and the hem.

The quilting is worked in white thread in rows of back stitch, about 1–2 cm ($\frac{1}{2}$ to 1 in) apart, and when the back stitch is complete, the padding of soft white cotton is inserted from the

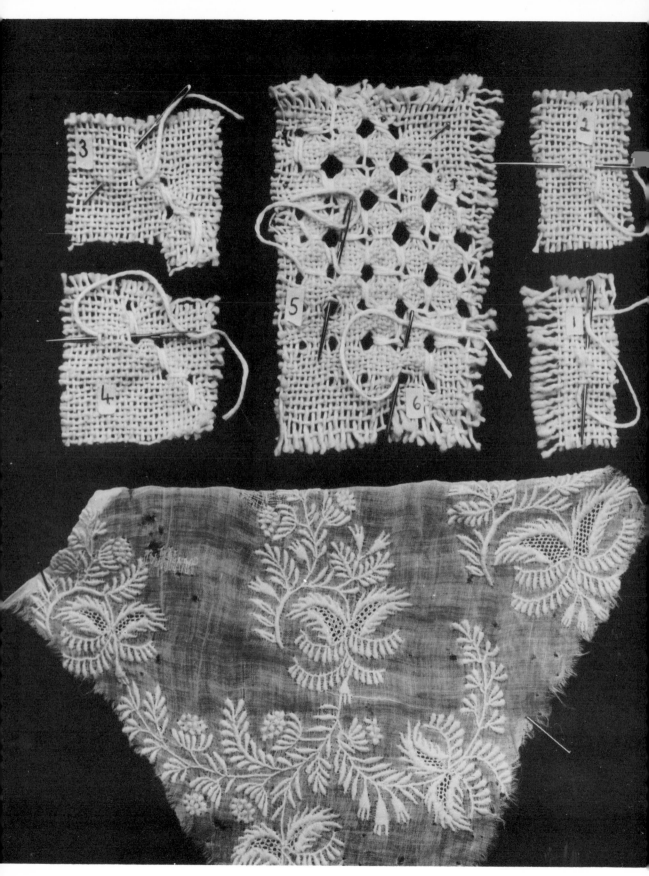

259 *The variation is seen in the centre shapes, and the basic pattern in the right-hand shapes. Like many other pulled stitches, such as Greek filling and Russian ground, it is important to find suitably woven material to form the patterns. As the variety of ground materials has become limited, many pulled stitches have fallen out of use. Nevertheless, it is often compelling to investigate past methods, and this variation of a basic pattern is easy and quick to teach. The very fine muslin allows discrepancies of one thread (6).*
1 Run in thread, to begin, and insert needle for a vertical stitch, as indicated. Six threads are taken up for a stitch. Work diagonally. The number of threads taken up depends on the scale of the weave of the background, and experiment may be necessary. 2 Insert needle for a horizontal stitch, taking up six threads. Draw stitch firmly together and repeat. Continue a diagonal row by working vertical and horizontal stitches alternately as at (1) and (2). 3 To work a return row, insert needle as at (3), down and across six threads. 4 Work a horizontal stitch as at (4), and then a vertical stitch over six threads, and into the same position of the first row. Repeat stitches to give a diagonal line of holes. 5 For the variation pattern, work the return row as at (3) and (4).
6 Continue by inserting needle, as at (5), into the stitch of the previous row, Draw up firmly and then work another stitch by the side but into the hole or position of the previous row, as at (6). Repeat (4), (5), and (6) to complete row. Work rows alternately.

back between the rows of stitching.

The coarse linen is then cut away from the back, cutting closely to the embroidery, and leaving the quilting in double material. On the remaining single layer of the top fine white linen, a design of pulled stitch patterns is carried out.

This method makes a flexible article capable of being drawn in to the waist, or gathered to form panniers.

Another development of the quilting is its incorporation in the main design with patterned fillings. The whole area to be embroidered is backed with a coarse soft linen as before, with the quilting in back stitch in white thread and the embroidery worked through two thicknesses.

The quilting is now of equal interest in the design, and french knots are

closely worked as a textured filling in white thread. The pulled stitch fillings which remain the real feature of the work, are also worked at this stage, sometimes through the double thickness, and this requires a strong blunt or rounded point to the needle. When the embroidery is completed the quilting is padded from the back with soft white cotton.

The finished effect of the openwork in the second method is not as soft and pliable as the first, but it is stronger and more hardwearing, and keeps its shape for use in jackets and coats. Some examples show that the backing may be cut away around the embroidery on the wrong side to give a suppleness for garments such as back between the rows of stitching.

Small eyelets are worked through the two thicknesses to allow tape to be threaded through the garment to help it fit to the body.

Waistcoats of the eighteenth century in white linen or cotton were produced in equally fine craftsmanship and with typical florid designs, and it is suggested that the waistcoats were worn in India, as the material would suit the climate and be more comfortable to wear than the floss silk embroidered silk waistcoats of the time. They were also washable. Acanthus leaves worked in long and short stitch, following the direction of growth and movement and worked in linen, gave a wonderful contrast to

the geometric pulled work. Fig. 257.

Design

The design of pulled work patterns is geometric, as they are controlled by the threads of the ground material but they are used in many characteristic styles.

As noted in the history of pulled stitches, the work has been adapted to designs of great variety, for interpretation in the style of nearly every century, and includes figures, foliage, geometric and rococo styles for religious and secular use. All incorporate pattern.

The patterns are set off with other techniques, such as line stitches and counted satin stitch of the 1300s, cording and quilting of the 1600s and 1700s, and experiments with the sewing machine today.

Another aspect of design is the distinctive worked background of a pulled mesh with a plain unworked design.

Pulled stitch embroidery has a very wide range but also a recognizable character which makes it a satisfying

260 *Sampler of various stitches and different patterns of counted satin stitch worked on synthetic linen. 1947.*
1 thread to 1 mm ($\frac{1}{25}$ in.), 10 threads to 1 cm ($\frac{2}{5}$ in.). 33 × 27 cm (13 × 10$\frac{1}{2}$ in.).

*261 Detail of fig. 260; a corner
showing single faggot stitch.*

technique in which to specialize, both
for working and collecting.

In the twentieth century a general
return to working restrained borders
has been made, particularly in Swe-

den, and with designs in simple shapes
and clear outlines to set off the embroidery. A coloured background has
also been introduced. Today personal
choices may be expressed in stitch and
threads integrated with the background to create a new textile, and
there is not usually a formal design.
One stitch worked in many different

ways, with changes of tension, of the
number of threads per stitch, and of
the size and texture of the working
thread, produces just as interesting
and harmonious a piece of work, if
not more so, than the introduction of
a lot of different stitches.

If a formal design is used, the selection of a stitch should be related to the

shapes of the design, for example a central square shape should be related to a stable symmetrical stitch, slanting stitches should work to or from the centre and balance with each other, and rounded shapes take round patterns, or follow the direction or shape of the article.

Early work in pulled stitches is often combined with some threads being cut and drawn out, but not in sufficient quantity to justify it being called drawn thread work.

Ground materials

The most important consideration in the choice of a background for pulled stitch embroidery is that the threads of the background can be reasonably easily counted and separated by a needle with a rounded point such as a tapestry needle.

An evenly woven linen is the ideal material for pulled stitch embroidery as the threads are firm, strong and smooth, making them clearly visible

262 Detail of fig. 260; showing steps in counted satin stitch.

263 Centre of sampler, showing plan of patterns.

encouraged embroidery. Pineapple cloth looks like a fine linen or muslin, but is crisp and has a cool, smooth feel when handled; it is an interesting addition to a textile collection.

Technique

Framing-up – when the work is framed up it is easier to count out the threads of the background material to make the patterns. It is considered best to frame up the work firmly, allowing enough tension or play to give the threads of the background the necessary movement for pulling.

Pulled stitch work is a technique that can be successfully worked in the hand, without framing-up. However, the finished work is more clearly defined when a frame is used, as continuous folding and creasing of the work puts wear on the fibres and displaces the stitches and, despite efficient stretching as a finish, more accurate detail is achieved by work in a frame. This must finally be a personal decision based on the style of design.

Transfer of design – The free creative designs of the present time are sometimes measured and counted out from centre tack lines directly on to the ground material. Use pins to mark the salient points and a tack line for more permanent lines. Large, spontaneous designs may require the ground to be divided into balanced areas.

To transfer a prepared design, the threads of the background must be square, i.e. at right-angles to each other; when in a frame this is easily checked. If a frame is not used the ground material should be pinned out on a drawing board with drawing pins. In both cases a tack line through the centre of the ground horizontally and vertically is a good guide to check right-angles.

The prepared design is drawn out with an ink line on firm white paper and is laid under the ground material. Match the right-angle lines of the design with threads of the ground material. The design can be seen through the ground.

The design is then transferred to the ground by painting out with a fine blue line or a tack line. A dark

264 A design showing the background work in pulled stitch and the motif in plain material. 1985. Worked by Sue Herbert.

for counting. Linen is a flexible fibre which allows the surface of the embroidery to lie smoothly when the threads are pulled together.

When linen is in short supply any mixture of fibres, natural or synthetic, may be used, providing there is an even weave to make a square grid. This means that the threads of the

weft should be the same size as the warp threads. Welsh flannel is a suitable example where the yarn is tightly spun before weaving, which makes the threads easy to separate.

Other materials may be found with an even weave, such as scrim. Cloth may be produced from yarns spun from suitable fibres in different countries. Pineapple cloth is an example from the eighteenth century and was produced in India and other eastern countries where the European influences of trade or government

265 Detail of Fig. 264 showing overcast stitch by hand in vermicelli pattern, counted satin stitch and french knots.

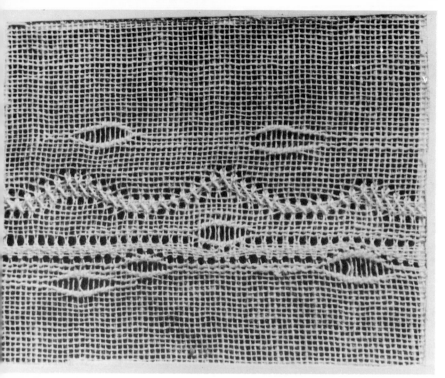

and avoids splitting when work is in progress. A crewel needle is useful for darning in the ends of the sewing thread when starting and finishing.

Thread – the working thread should be of the same thickness as the threads of the background, or finer, and of the same colour since this does not detract from the effect of the open patterns. A working or sewing thread of the same fibre as the ground is the usual choice, although a synthetic fibre such as polyester thread will suit most grounds.

In some examples, as in Norway, a coloured ground is used with a matching colour thread or a white thread, but these are a personal or regional choice. Self-colour thread gives most emphasis to the open patterns and is generally considered to give the most satisfactory result.

When a sewing thread untwists during work, the needle may be turned in the fingers to correct this by retwisting.

Start a stitch at the centre of the area to be covered so that a complete repeat of the pattern is registered rather than fragments round the edge.

To join on – run in the working thread on the outline or darn it into the background where it will be covered by the stitchery.

To finish – run in the thread on the outline or darn in where it will be worked over.

To join and finish – a back stitch may be used to help secure the working thread. A knot may also be used to help secure the thread when it is run in, but should be placed away from the design and cut off when the thread is secure. A series of knots remaining in the work makes visible irregularities in the pattern.

Process – stitch. It is worth remarking that one or two stitches in pulled work may be worked with such diversity that it is more intriguing to develop them as creatively as possible, exploiting the pattern, scale and thread, than to employ a large vocabulary of stitches.

Counted satin stitch is the simplest and most direct stitch for an introduc-

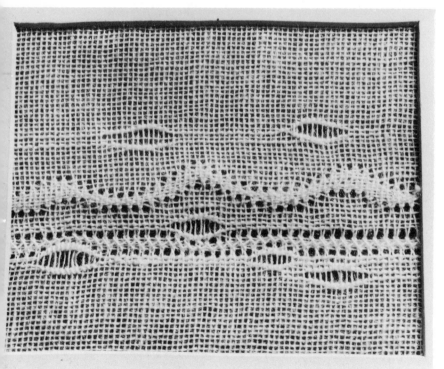

267 Reverse side of sampler in fig. 266.

line tends to be worked in permanently. If the ground is too solid for the design to be seen, the method of

pricking and pouncing should be used, or trace and tack. Figs 334–6.

Needles – tapestry needles, a crewel needle. A thick needle with a rounded point emphasizes the holes and the blunt point slips between the threads

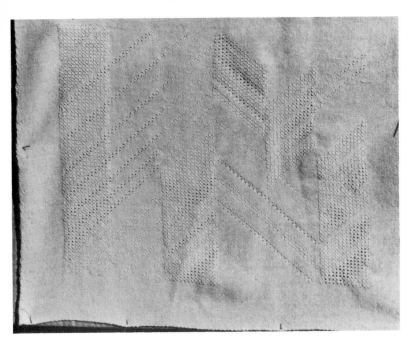

268 *A design using single faggot stitch only, but worked in different tensions on evenweave Welsh flannel. Size 45 × 28 cm (17¾ × 11 in.). 1980. Worked by Nicola Wright.*

tion. When worked at different tensions, in different sizes of thread and on different scales, it gives a great variation. Eyelets, Algerian eyelets, cross stitch and back stitch form a further basis for experiment. Single faggot and wave stitch and diagonal raised band are three adaptable pulled stitches. Rosette stitch and Indian drawn ground are more intricate stitches for individual experiment.

When one row of a pattern has been completed, turn the work for a return row. The outlines of a formal design are worked after the pulled

269 *Detail of fig. 268.*

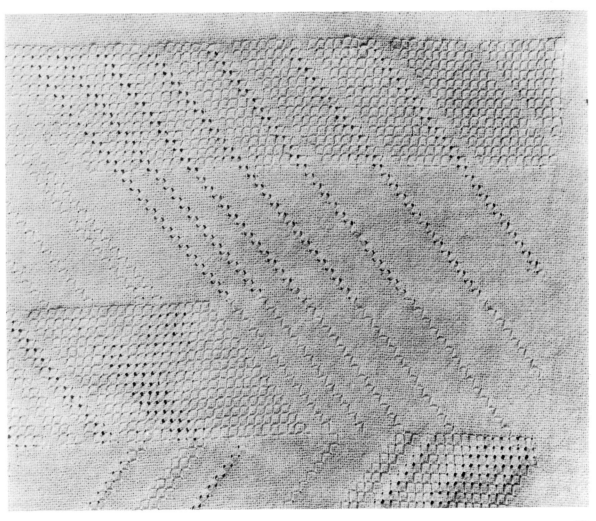

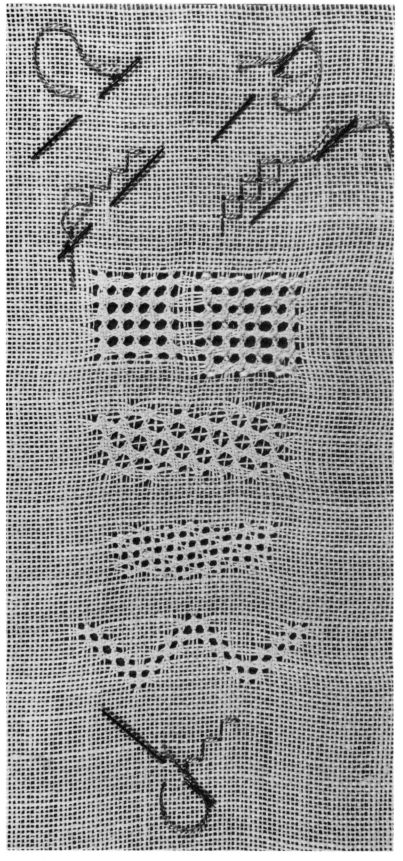

271 Simple pulled stitch. Start at top left to form diagonal row. Return as shown top right. Worked by Moyra McNeill.

work areas have been completed. This allows clear, well-formed outlines to be made. If outlines are completed first, the pulled work tends to distort them a little.

There are a myriad of different stitches for the specialist and enthusiast to explore, and many books giving details of the technique.

PUNCH STITCHES

So called because holes are punched into the ground with a large needle with a fine point and fine thread. It is usually worked on a fine closely woven ground such as silk crêpe or

270 Method of working single faggot stitch. Start at top left, work from top left to top right. Second row shows turning the needle for the second row. Worked by Moyra McNeill. (Goldsmiths' College Collection).

272 An example of punch stitches, eyelets and satin stitch on a figured silk ground typical of Chinese silk embroidery of the 1930s and often worked by embroiderers in England. The flowers show punch stitch used as a filling, probably pointe Turque, and pin stitch as a seam. (Margaret Walker).

274 Punch stitch. Work from A to E, pulling stitch firmly. Repeat from B. F(I) Completed row. F(II) Punch stitch used as for appliqué. See fig. 275.

273 Detail of the pin stitched seam and embroidery. Note use of stem stitch as a decorative gathering or type of smocking. Waistband 5 cm (2 in.) wide.

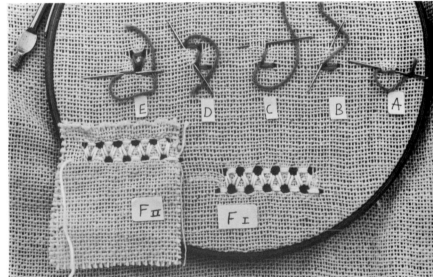

cotton or linen lawn, and is used for appliqué and seams. Punch stitches interchange with pulled stitches but are not counted out on the threads of the background.

A chenille needle is used, as this has a fine point to separate rather than break the fine background threads. The shaft and the eye are thick to keep the hole open while working the fine thread, which secures the hole to give the interest of a perforated line.

Punch stitch

Sometimes known as three-sided stitch, this has double width and is especially suitable for appliqué, as the material may be cut close to the stitch. Figs 274, 275, 291.

275 Punch stitch. F(I) Used as a filling. Note that the second row omits second stitch at (A) to make it even overall. Also the joining on and off thread runs in where it will be worked over. F(II) Applied material. B Edge of appliqué cut away.

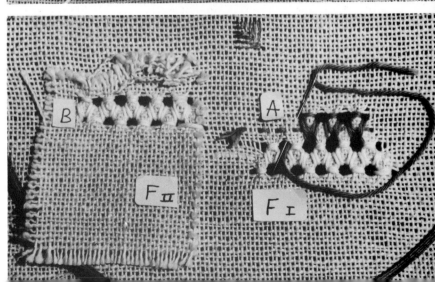

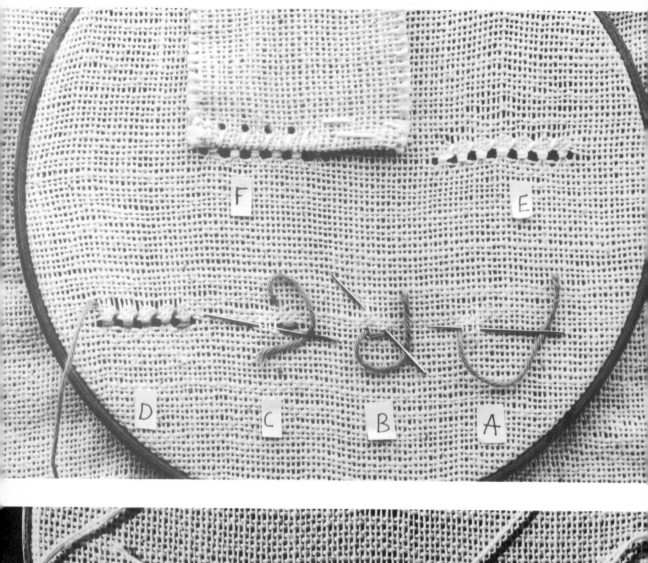

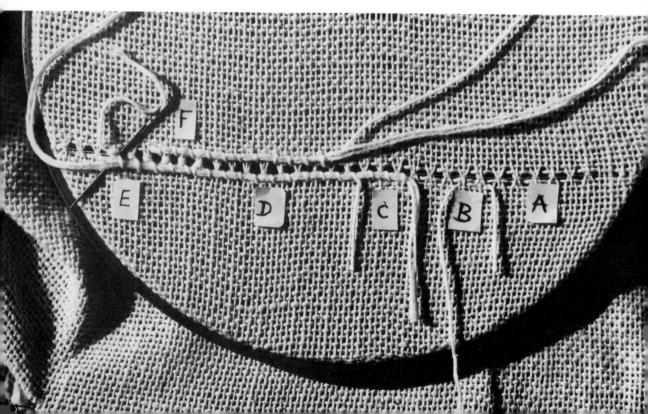

276 *Pin stitch. A Bring up the thread and insert chenille needle from right to left. Bring up the needle in exactly the first position. B Repeat, and bring out needle below the first stitch as indicated. Pull firmly. C Repeat (A), work into position of previous stitch. D Finished stitch. E Completed row of pin stitch. F Stitch used as for appliqué. Applied material tacked in place.*

Pin stitch

This serves a similar purpose to punch stitch but, although it is much smaller and less noticeable, it still makes a double line to hold appliqué securely. Pin stitch is often used on folded edges as a decorative hem. Figs 273, 276.

Open back stitch or ladder stitch

This is a traditional stitch in white work and is composed of back stitch or stem stitch worked with a very fine thread and a chenille needle. The thread is pulled up firmly to make a row of open holes. The edges of the row are then outlined with a fine couched thread, taking the sewing-down thread through the open holes already formed and also round between the holes. The stitch gives a light airy look to contrast with heavy satin stitch, for the veins of leaves, for example. Figs 277, 278.

See also *Italian hemstitch* as a punch stitch

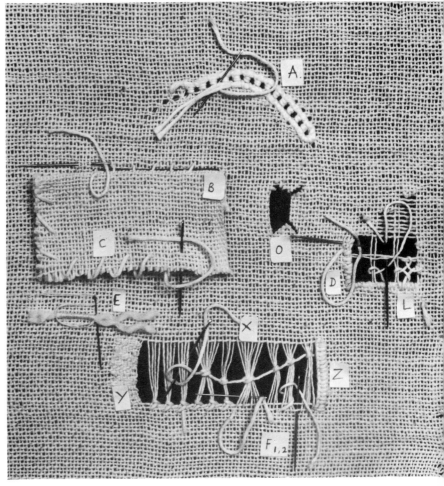

278 *A Ladder stitch completed, showing turn at top end with a stitch on either side and double stitches at tip. Ladder stitch may be worked as a curve, but hemstitch may not. B Slip hemming. Note position of thread and insertion of needle, opposite each other. C Overcasting stitch as a neatening. D Oversewing stitch. E Oversewing as trailing. F1 Hemstitch threads in groups.*

F2 Any uneven number should be hidden in a group before the final one, which should match the main work. See also Italian hemstitch (fig. 201). L Loop stitch. O A cut for broderie anglaise ladderwork. Y–Z Revision of drawn thread. Cut in centre and lift out thread. Reinforce edges either by darning in ends (Y), or buttonholing edge (Z), and cutting threads close to this.

277 *Ladder stitch. A Work back stitch or stem in very fine thread, Drima or machine embroidery thread and pull firmly as indicated. B Join on couching thread in one strand of stranded cotton. C Lay in couched thread (approximately two strands of stranded cotton). D Couch in place, inserting needle downwards into spaces of back stitch, and pass the thread once or twice round the threads between. E Complete stitch with the opposite side of back stitch, with simple couching and without wrapping the threads as on the first row.*

PUNTO

This is a Latin term for 'stitch' and is used in many early books before the nineteenth century. The most common occurrences are:

Punto in aria – 'stitches in the air', a type of needle lace.

Punto a groppo – knotted laces, macramé.

Punto a maglia – darned netting.

Punto a relievo – Venetian raised point, gros point.

Punto tagliato – early cut work or drawn thread; reticella.

Punto tirato – pulled work, formerly drawn.

Q

QUILTING

This technique is mentioned here because the raised areas which create light and shadow in a design are particularly well displayed in white material. The texture of changing lights on the fabric enables the design to be read in different ways, and can be sensitively employed in modern work. In the eighteenth century fine white embroidered linen waistcoats for men, waist petticoats for women and also caps for wearing in the home included quilting, which was often known as cord quilting because the

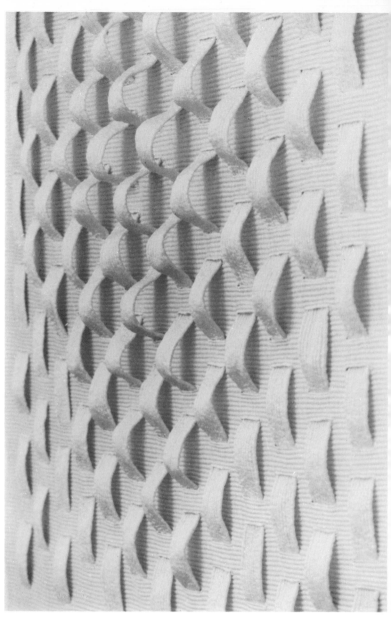

279 'Arches'. A wall hanging in quilting, with separate strips to form a pattern in relief. 1982. Worked by Phyllis Ross.

fine rows of stitching were padded with cords.

All types of quilting, such as trapunto, shadow, English and Italian, are attractive in white materials, from silk satin to textured cotton, in natural

280 Wall hanging in interwoven quilted strips, accenting the value of shadows. 1983. Worked by Phyllis Ross.

or synthetic fibres, and they can be used for dresses and interior decoration. See *Pulled stitches.*

QUILTS

Durham, Northumberland and Welsh quilts were made in all colours, but frequently in white cotton (whole-cloth quilts), and showed traditional motifs of feathers, shells and interlacing patterns. The quilts were often worked as communal efforts with many women sitting at one frame. The work was introduced into some areas to help raise money to relieve the poor conditions.

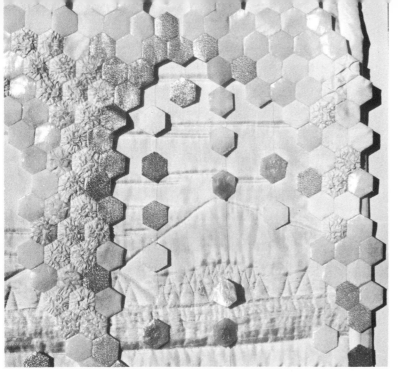

281 Detail of a patchwork hanging in various white textures, including silver lamé and ruched jap silk, which are used to suggest falling snow as a loose layer over a white quilted landscape design. 1985. Worked by June Linsley.

R

RACROC STITCH

An important lace stitch used in the finest Brussels lace to join invisible bands of vrai réseau (buttonhole background).

RAISED EMBROIDERY

Raised embroidery refers to padded satin stitch and possibly Mountmellick, and also to some Berlin wool where the contrast between a pile or tufting stitch (such as Turkey or Surrey), and tent stitch, is exploited in white and further enhanced by the use of different threads such as silk, wool and cotton. Raised chain band and similar stitches give character to work such as Castelguidi.

RETICELLA

Considered the first needlemade lace developing from cut and drawn thread work of the 1500s; gradually geometric designs evolved by darning or needleweaving a grid or mesh of the horizontal and vertical threads of the background. Diagonal lines were added to the pattern by being drawn out on a parchment support for working. Eventually the lines of the design on parchment were covered with laid threads held in place with

282 Quilting and stitches. Worked by Irene Ord.

189

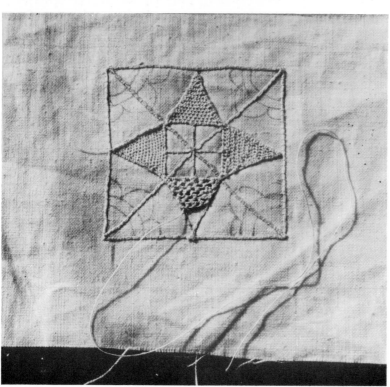

283 A cushion made of fragments of Italian linen embroidery dating from the sixteenth century. Note the join in the top section, right of centre. The four open borders in the reticella style of drawn thread work are repeated, and show the two quarter circles adjoining. This is a typical design motif of the much coarser work of the nineteenth century, known as Greek lace. Note the darned square grid foundation of background threads and the diagonal lines. The lower open border appears to be on a coarser and larger scale than the others; it is probably of a later date. (Hatfield House Textile Conservation Rooms).

couching stitches. On this foundation, buttonhole stitched bars and fillings were worked in figurative designs, or with curved lines and the additional decoration of picots and wheels or spiders. Fig. 207. When the design was complete the couching stitches at the back of the parchment were cut and the embroidery lifted off. Borders several inches wide and with a scalloped edge became known as punto in aria (stitches in the air), and examples can be seen in museums and in paint-

284 Couching used as a cordonnet, for a reticella-style design in buttonhole stitch, in a similar method to needle-made lace. The buttonhole stitches are worked from side to side of the triangle without passing through the linen. The triangle at the left shows one edge buttonholed for neatening. When the motif is complete, the couching stitches are cut from the back of the linen and the motif lifts off.

285 A nineteenth-century reticella or needle-made lace design, commercially produced for use at home as a kit.

286 Left: *a design marked out on card with the cordonnet or couched outline shown on the outer edge. Other lines of couching are worked over in buttonhole stitch following the reticella method. Worked by Sue Herbert.* Right: *a*

design in diagrammatic form.

287 *Reverse of fig. 286. On the left the couching stitches of the cordonnet. The couching stitches are cut to release the embroidery from the right side.*

ings, for instance in the exquisite ruffs of Elizabethan costume. The sparkling white work was a glorious foil to the silk and velvet costume of the sixteenth century and it was worn throughout Europe.

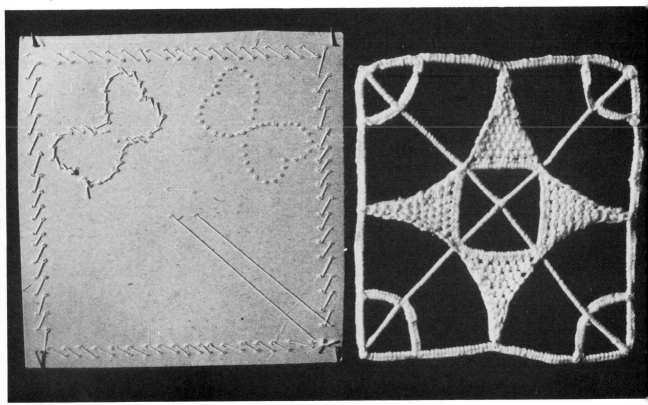

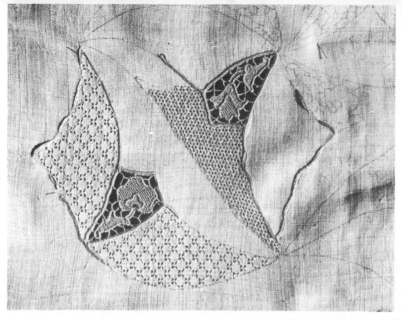

288 Buttonhole lace fillings in the form of reticella and pulled stitches, worked on hand-woven linen from the Lake District. Note the attractive irregularities in the weave. Similar grounds were used for canvas work until the mid-nineteenth century.

289 Detail of curved lines within square foundation threads. See drawn thread corners. (Hatfield House Textile Conservation Rooms).

290 A handsome cushion with finely worked motifs of reticella suggesting a two-headed eagle alternating with a cock or peacock, and interspersed with quarter-sized birds. The overcast or trailed motifs at the corners of the openwork suggest a date of about 1600. 51 × 38 cm (20 × 15 in.). Eagles 4.5 × 4 cm (1¾ × 1½ in.). (Hatfield House Textile Conservation Rooms).

291 Another cushion of finely worked fragments. Note the use of diagonal openwork in reticella, and darning edged with Italian hemstitch, punch stitch and counted satin stitch. On the lower edge of the centre panel is exquisitely fine needleweaving, some disintegrating, 7 mm (⅕ in.) wide. The four openwork borders in reticella drawn thread suggest a bird with a large tail, perhaps a cock or peacock. The counted satin stitch lightens up the centre pattern. Punch stitch is also used on a fine scale. Punto in aria edges at both ends are an early example of lace. The panels are typical of work recorded on samplers of the period. Cushion 38 × 30 cm (15 × 11⅘ in.). (Hatfield House Textile Conservation Rooms).

292 An illustration to compare the different scales of fine early work and later embroidery.

The work inspires experiments on other foundations of today, such as vanishing muslin and spun alginate and acetate dissolving fabrics. Figs 102, 106, 283–94, 298.. See *Lace*

RIBBON

White ribbon rosettes and streamers have often been used in white work embroidery, and were attached to bonnets for both christenings and fashion and to dresses as a festive decoration, especially as sashes for

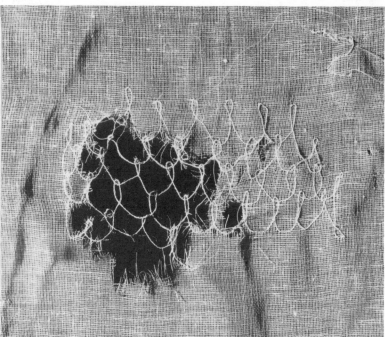

293 An example of free machine stitch on the domestic sewing machine using the embroidery adaptation. Worked on vanishing muslin in the form of buttonhole loops. When the vanishing muslin is pressed with a hot iron it dissolves away, leaving the stitchery for experiment.

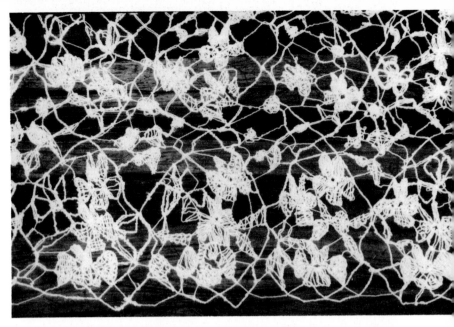

weddings and for evening dress. White satin favours were often worn by bridegrooms at country weddings.

Frills of white ribbon gathered together to decorate and outline the edges of cushions and bags, necklines, wrists and hems in dress are some of the many uses, as well as ribbon slotted through lace or embroidered insertions to give brightness. Figs 43, 295, 316.

RICE STITCH

This stitch is similar to seeding, but a little larger, with small straight stitches arranged to look like rice scattered closely on a table, usually with one stitch touching the end of the next.

In the nineteenth century this stitch was very popular in white embroidery, and predominantly in some designs which became known as rice embroidery. Satin stitch and stem stitch completed the floral designs. Also known as point de riz.

RICHELIEU

Cardinal Richelieu was an early-seventeenth-century French politician who deplored the expense of sumptuous dress, including the fashionable and elaborate lace. He wore simple, flat, square linen collars, which were sometimes edged with lace or embroidery.

When in the nineteenth century a popular study of past embroideries inspired a bold cut work with buttonhole edges and picots, the term 'richelieu' seems to have been borrowed to define the work.

However, this does not cover the many variations which evolved – the entry for *Cut work* explains most embroidery where the background is cut away and the design is characteristically formed of the ground material.

295 *A unique use of patterned ribbon in the frill of a baby's bonnet. This bonnet is fully authenticated as made for the birth of Lord Arthur Cecil in 1851. (Hatfield House Textile Conservation Rooms).*

The term 'richelieu' is also thought to describe a type of net darning, or filet, embroidery which is outlined with a coarse shiny thread.

Richelieu, like guipure, has acquired many interpretations over the years. See *Cutwork*.

ROPE STITCH

This is a variation of chain stitch, but is very closely worked to give a raised padded appearance similar to satin stitch. Rope stitch works well on curved lines and is particularly suitable for letters and stems. Care should be taken to avoid a long stitch, as this is easily misplaced and can destroy a smooth line. Fig. 201 (G1–2).

ROSETTE

An arrangement of ribbons gathered into a circle to decorate costume. White was used particularly for country wedding buttonholes or christening robes.

ROULEAU

A French term for piping used in faggoting. A bias strip folded in half and stitched to form a pliable piping. Fig. 122. See *Faggoting*.

RUCHE

A ruche, or ruching, is a decorative form of manipulating material, often adapted for present-day embroidery. It is basically a strip of material gathered on both edges and often applied to costume such as bonnets, bodices, skirts and sleeves. Ruching may be treated in different ways, such as feathered ruche with a frayed edge, a twisted or plaited ruche having strips cut on the straight or bias of the material, and a fluted ruche which is a box-pleated strip stitched approximately one inch from the edge so that the pleats flute out. Silk gauze and lightweight materials are suitable, as heavier materials tend to lie flat and require special laundering and ironing. All are displayed to advantage in white. Figs 29, 162, 296.

RUFF

A deep collar or frill gathered to surround the neck and made of white linen in varying widths, sometimes very wide and standing up behind the head, the edge being hemmed or bordered with lace. Ruffs were particu-

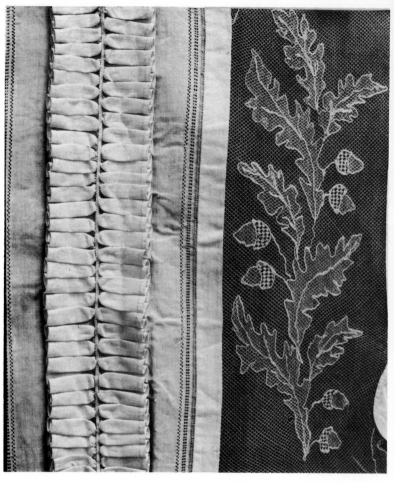

296   A fluted ruche with centre cord. Right: a design outlined on net with run stitch or darned patterns, in a simple form of Limerick embroidery. (Embroiderers' Guild).

larly fashionable in Elizabethan times, when they were highly decorated with reticella lace and also stiffened with wire. In the nineteenth century ruffs took the form of raised collars decorated with feathers and stiffened with boning.

RUFFLE

A frill at the wrist made of white linen, cotton, muslin or silk, frequently in fashion from Elizabethan times when they were depicted in many portraits by Holbein.

In the eighteenth century ruffles, falling from the elbow, were known as 'engageantes', and worn under velvet, silk, satin or brocade sleeves.

Ruffles are often decorated with embroidery or lace and regularly recur as a fashion accessory. Fig. 120.

RUN STITCH

A simple stitch where the needle is run in and out of the ground material, making the length of the stitch and the spaces between the same size.

Run stitch is used for joining on and off embroidery working threads by running in the thread where it will be worked over or into the back of previous work.

It may also be made decorative in white work by interlacing, or threading with a different texture, such as silk over wool, and by use on polythene or plastic, since the stitch makes

297   Run stitch in fine thread on satin used as a textural experiment. The edge is secured by scorching or melting synthetic fibres. Size 23 × 12.5 cm (9 × 5 in.). Worked by Caroline Robinson.

a pattern when seen showing through from the back of the work. It can also be used as an outline on net.

When run stitch is used to join two materials, as in a seam, the stitches should be made to appear the same size on both sides by adjusting the amount of material picked up as the needle passes through the double thickness.

Stab stitch is a version of run stitch, where the needle is brought up and inserted into the ground at right angles in order to make a reversible stitch. It is used to join stiff materials such as leather. Figs 296, 297.. See *Net*

Running

A term for run stitch used in embroidery for gathering, darning and texture, and for joining and finishing off threads by stitches into the ground. Running or run stitch is also used for construction, such as seams.

Running string

A tie of ribbon or tape carried through a fold of material by a bodkin for drawing in fullness. A normal method of fastening skirts, trousers, necklines and sleeves before the nineteenth-century invention of hooks and eyes and metal buttons, which were comparatively expensive. Figs 43, 71.

S

SAMPLERS

The famous white embroidered linen samplers of the sixteenth and seventeenth centuries are now mostly museum pieces, and are valuable and costly. They are records of stitchery and patterns made for future reference at a time when pattern books were few and far between.

The earliest dated white work sampler is of 1630 and shows typical drawn thread work, reticella, eyelets, buttonhole and counted satin stitch in borders approximately 5 cm (2 in.) wide, which are recognizably of the time. The samplers of this period are

298 *White work sampler c. 1580 showing drawn thread work and reticella patterns typical of the time. 8 × 100 cm (3 × 39⅓ in.) approximately. (Museum of London).*

long and narrow, averaging 56 × 15 cm (22 × 6 in.), and have rich arrangements of stitchery which contain hours of work and which, like so much white work, reward close study. Alphabets worked in these techniques are a forerunner of the later traditional and familiar sampler in coloured cross stitch.

Darning samplers in white silk on white gauze of the very early nineteenth century have charm, and although now sometimes discoloured, the texture is visible and sharp. The darning was worked as an exercise for possible future reference in the repair of valuable textiles at home, but now makes interesting abstract patterns. The samplers are sought after as collectors' items, especially when named and dated.

There is an early mention of a sampler in 1503 (see Kendrick, *English Needlework*, on the household accounts of Elizabeth of York), and other references of the 1500s onwards are made in wills, inventories and poems. John Skelton in 1523 wrote in *Garlande of Laurell*: 'the sampler to sew on, the lacis to embraid'. There are no earlier existing samplers, but many written references to white work embroidery throughout the centuries show it to have been an important part of daily life, either in the making or the wearing.

Passages from Jane Austen, approximately three hundred years later than

299 *Darning sampler dated 1809 and bearing the name Sarah Spark, with a white rose in long-and-short darning in silk on silk gauze. 34 cm (14½ in.) square approx.*

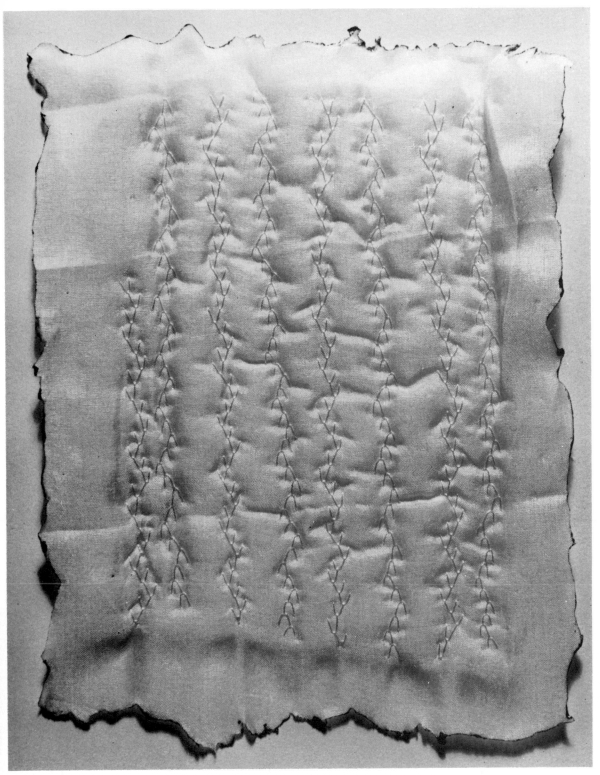

300 Feather stitch in fine thread on synthetic satin used as a textural experiment. Worked by Caroline Robinson. 23 × 12 cm (9 × 5 in.)

Skelton, also make fascinating reading, for example in *Northanger Abbey*, a novel published in 1818 but written in 1798, when the author was in her early twenties. 'I had entered my studies at Oxford while you were a good little girl working your sampler at home,' Henry Tilney tells Catherine in Chapter 14. Today samplers, or try-out pieces, have an extended meaning from the original purpose of records or exercises, and are now ex-

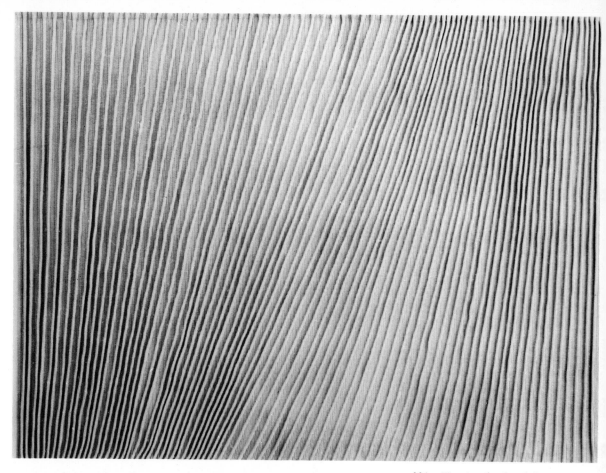

301 *Hanging developed from try-outs or samplers. Size 2.7 × 1.5 m (9 × 5 ft.). Worked by Phyllis Ross.*

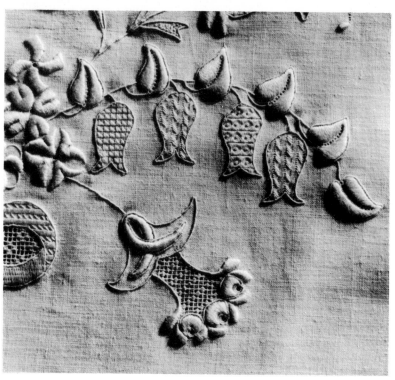

periments which show a valuable thought process and are successful in their own right. This type of sampler has become extremely important to the artist embroiderer and frequently shows the most original work at the present time. Figs 201, 217, 222, 249, 259, 274–8, 296–304.

SATIN STITCH

An important stitch in white work, giving a smooth shining texture. The length of the stitches should not be more than half an inch otherwise they become displaced and uneven.

302 *Detail of a sampler showing padded satin stitch leaves divided with ladder stitch and counted satin stitch patterns in the shapes below.*

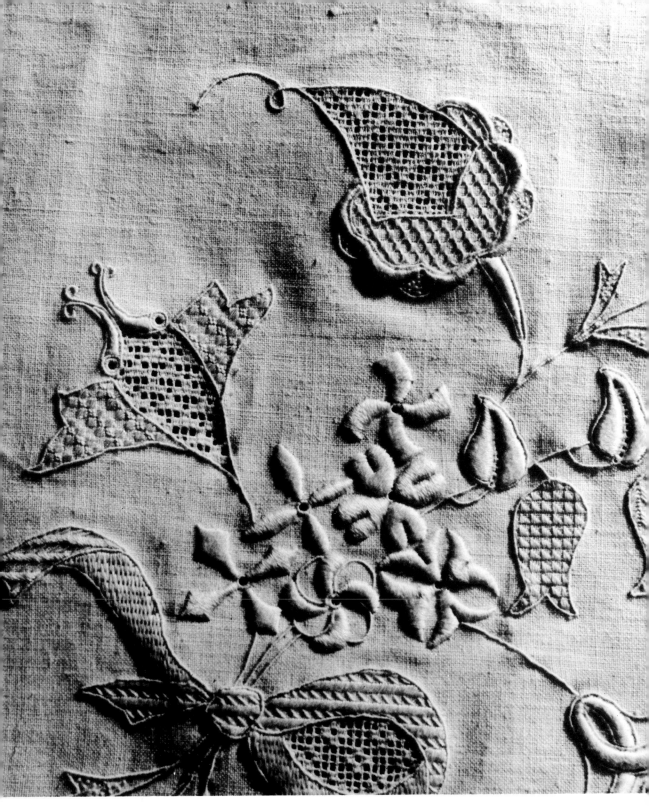

303 Satin stitch flowers. Left: *Morris darning in the ribbon. Also trailing or overcast stitch, darning patterns worked on open mesh, and counted satin patterns.*

The thread should be kept evenly twisted throughout the work, by turning the needle in the fingers when necessary, and short lengths of thread keep the work smooth and shining. It is a false economy to use a long length of thread in any embroidery, as it fluffs up in work and wears out. A very good reason in the past for the employment of children was that they

201

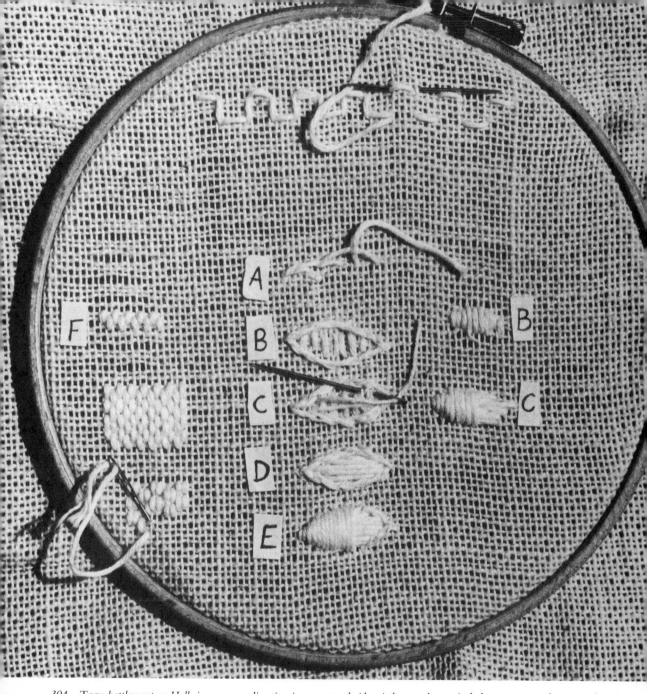

304 Top: *battlement or Holbein stitch. Begin at right and return from left as indicated. A Satin stitch padding. Outline shape in split stitch. B First layer of padding with laid stitches. On the right, satin stitch without split stitch foundation. C Second layer of padding with laid stitches. Note that needle comes up on the same edge as previous insertions. On the right, satin stitch with padding but no split stitch. D Keep top layer of padding in opposite direction to that of the satin stitch. E Satin stitch. Begin at the centre of a shape so that the*

direction is correct and side stitches work away either side evenly. F Morris darning. Top: one row worked over two threads. Centre: morris darning filling. Bottom: morris darning worked in pairs of stitches.

could have threaded needles at the ready.

The straight parallel stitches are arranged closely together to give the appearance of satin, and are worked at an angle to the shape to be filled. If the

stitch becomes too long or the space too narrow, the angle should be obliquely radiated or the shape divided.

Smooth, exactly even edges are required for a good finish, and it is noticeable that whenever the needle is inserted downwards a sharper and cleaner-cut incision is made than when the needle is brought upwards. The needle should be taken down against work already *in situ* and also in the centre of eyelets, as this causes less disturbance to stitches already worked. Avoid working into stitches

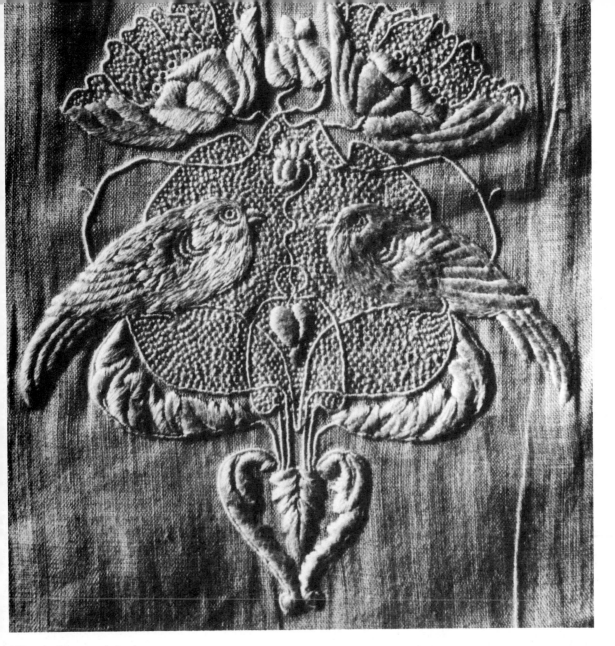

305 *Art Nouveau design in encroaching and slanting or oblique satin stitch with seeding background, trailing stems and birds in long and short stitch. 10 cm (4 in.) square. (Embroiderers' Guild).*

of previous work by slipping the needle beside them and into the same position.

A fine split stitch outline to the shape to be worked assists in forming a clear-cut edge and gives a light padding.

Light designs of satin stitch set off the open areas of drawn thread work and broderie anglaise. Figs 89, 302, 310.

Padding

Satin stitch may be padded in order to raise the surface and catch more light. It should be worked on a tight frame, otherwise half the padding recedes to the wrong side as in quilting and makes an uneven surface on the wrong side.

Padding usually consists of rows of split stitch, as this leaves most thread on the top surface. Laid threads are also suitable, arranged in layers in alternate directions, i.e. vertical and then horizontal. The final layer should be in contrast to the direction of the satin stitch. Figs 302, 304, 310, 312.

Counted satin stitch

Counted satin stitch, sometimes known as flat stitch, is frequently worked in borders of geometric patterns alongside drawn thread work borders and on an evenweave material. The two types of work are particularly harmonious together. Counted satin stitch is also used as a filling on linen and net.

This stitch needs careful counting of the background threads, and a working thread of similar thickness to the threads of the ground; a bold rich effect is easy to achieve. Back stitch also complements the bulk of counted satin stitch, with its fine line, and the

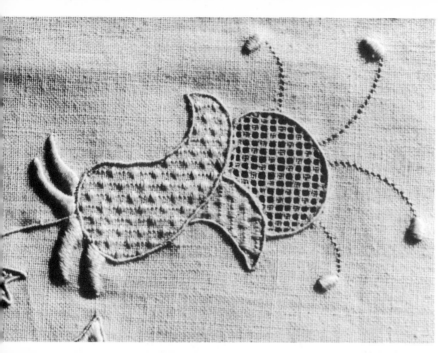

306 *Counted satin stitch pattern with back stitch, open mesh with loop stitch, open back stitch, trailing and padded satin stitch, make a related group of stitches.*

method of working is the same as for satin stitch in that the needle is put down against previous work (or that already in place) to give the best edge and definition.

Aim to finish with the needle working downwards on the outer edge, whenever possible, and to avoid splitting the thread of stitches previously worked by slipping the needle in the same position, as this settles them smoothly. Figs 89, 217, 222, 260, 291.

307 *Garden flowers, which seem to have inspired so much white embroidery, perhaps representing a wish to perpetuate summertime.*

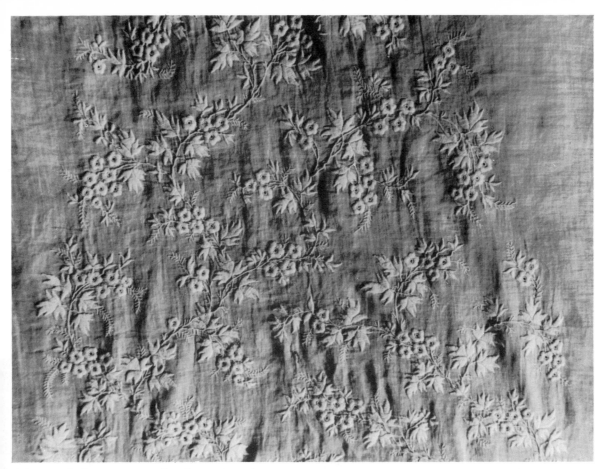

308 Sample showing satin stitch and fern stitch worked on muslin in unmercerized cotton, probably in Turkey for the English market. The floral designs are typical of the nineteenth century. From a skirt, length 150 × 80 cm (59 × 31½ in.). (Constance Howard).

309 *A design of the late nineteenth century using techniques of earlier years – i.e. open mesh fillings, divided satin stitch and fern stitch of a very high technical standard. Design of fruits, hops, pomegranates, fanciful leaves, flowers and seeds. (Joan Kendall).*

Dots

Dots of satin stitch are a popular decoration, made either by hand or machine, and they are often worked by machine singly or in groups as an all-over pattern or as an edging. In hand embroidery they may be introduced as a texture or as isolated details of decoration. Dots of satin stitch are more carefully formed than seeding, and are often padded and covered with a regulation number of stitches either side of a centre stitch. Dots are

Encroaching and voiding

Voiding shows rows of satin stitch worked decoratively with a small space between each row to show the background; the spaces form the design. In encroaching satin stitch, the stitches of the second row encroach between the stitches of the first row, which makes a shadowed line and is often seen in Chinese silk embroideries. Figs 54, 55, 305.

Machine

Machine satin stitch can be worked with a swing needle, either on the Irish machine or the zig-zag domestic machine, in somewhat restricted variety, although the skilled machinist can manipulate most shapes and designs.

SCHOOLS

There are many books on the teaching of white work, which probably

310 A chemisette of fine linen to be worn under a dress. Closely embroidered in satin stitch with flowers with Ayrshire buttonhole filling and surrounded with back stitch, eyelets in three styles, hemstitching at neckline and padded satin between the rows, to make a strong, impressive and unusual border. 20 cm (8 in.) square. (Clarice Blakey).

typical of English work. (*Note:* throughout the fashion for white embroidery businessmen arranged for embroidery to be worked cheaply abroad, for example in Turkey and India. Satin stitch is a typical import, and the designs are all European in style but have different influences, which is explained by their origin.)

Garden flowers, and roses in particular have always inspired embroiderers all over the world, and tend to acquire the characteristics of the country where they are worked. When one country produces work for another, the results usually show the foreign influence. Flowers, fruits and leaves were much portrayed in embroideries of the last century. Figs 182, 326, 330.

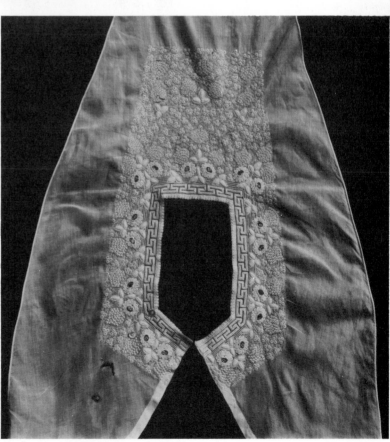

312 Corner of an exhibition piece of fine embroidery of the early twentieth century. The centre is very fine evenwoven cotton similar to organdie, edged with overcast stitch and satin stitched leaves. 55 cm (21½ in.) square. The wide border is of pulled stitch square mesh overcast, made of the ground from the centre. At the outer edge, a spotted pattern is added, plus leaf shapes in darning and flowers with a patterned filling. The extreme edge is in buttonhole. (Clarice Blakey).

has the earliest and most continuous history in embroidery. Although at one time thought to have been con-

fined to convents, it developed and became more widely used. As early as the middle of the sixteenth century schools were set up, often to give employment for the relief of poverty. A well-known founder was Barbara Ullman at Annaberg, Germany, where her school at first produced a coarse pillow lace. Over the years a more sophisticated standard evolved and led to the fine pulled stitch work of Dresden in the eighteenth century, but during the nineteenth century this declined to a coarse torchon type of lace.

It is reputed that thirty thousand workers came from her school's influence. These included seventeenth-century refugees from

Flanders, France and Spain, who were craftsmen and designers of high quality and also intelligent and outspoken, but unwanted by a nervous government and, therefore, forced to leave their homelands. The story of the Huguenot emigrés is well known. By the eighteenth century there were many schools of this type set up in Europe, and they became a valuable form of education.

However, apart from the convents, until the late seventeenth century instruction, learning and teaching were carried out in the form of apprenticeships in professional workrooms and also at home by expert needlewomen and designers, some of whom were visiting or itinerant

313 *The whole of the embroidery
shown in fig. 312. The rich border is of
satin stitch flowers with leaves of the
ground material. The satin stitch is
heavily padded and the outer petals are
softened with seeding. The work is so
regular that, at first glance, it seems to
be made by machine and appears
somewhat static. It is an incredible
display of tonal values from one material
and one thread. The work is folded in
the photograph, to indicate the fineness
of the ground and embroidery.* (Clarice
Blakey).

314 *Wrong side of the embroidery
from fig. 312, showing mesh formed
from the background, the actual
background in the leaves and the reverse
side of seeding and satin stitch in the
panels.* (Clarice Blakey).

teachers and designers in the manner
of journeymen artists. Books showing
white work patterns in drawn thread
work, buttonhole stitch and reticella
were highly sought after and very
precious. The patterns were much
copied and passed around between
families.

The information for books was
originally printed in Venice and an
example is the English edition of a
pattern book by Federigo di
Vincola, dated 1591: *New and Singular*

patternes and workes of Linen, serving for patternes to make all sorts of lace edgings and cut workes. This is at present on view at the Victoria & Albert Museum.

Other books followed, such as Shorleyker's *Schoolhouse for the Needle* in 1624 and 1632, which had 'certaine patternes of cut workes ... also sundry sorts of spots, as flowers, birds and fishes', spots probably meaning motifs.

John Taylor's *The Needle's Excellency* of 1634, another popular book, contained German patterns of 1597.

The cottage industry was another area of information often overlooked, since before the development of machinery quantities of embroidery were produced by hand, as were weaving, carpentry, shoes, tools, etc. Learning took place from childhood, probably by the hard way of trial and error, with children engaged in threading needles sometimes from the age of five.

Embroidery was an equal form of decoration with intricate weaves, and by about 1650 schools were being established to provide a wider range of information than the linen samplers.

Advertisements began to appear in England and other European towns and cities offering opportunities for instruction in the art of embroidery. The subjects included couching and raised work (quilting) on silk, linen, cotton and muslin, as well as cut work. Other subjects available to gentlewomen were arithmetic, writing, drawing and sewing. Sewing was usually at the top of the list.

The teachers could be men or women and probably had very good qualifications as artists or technicians. The reputation of their school would be dependent upon their success at teaching.

In the early eighteenth century schools developed to teach the form of white samplers for 'solace and sustenance', as mentioned in *American Needlework*, quoting 'The Diary of a Boston Schoolgirl' of 1773 by Anna Winslow, which also records instruction in Dresden work.

At a school in Bethlehem, Pennsylvania, during the eighteenth century, Moravian Sisters taught tambour and fine needlework in white, equal to that of Europe. This declined with the introduction of Berlin wool work in the nineteenth century.

In Scotland, at Edinburgh, Ruffini recommended his apprentices for training in design at the Edinburgh Art School, or Academy, to maintain a high standard of design for the embroidered muslin industry of Ayrshire. It was probably a model for art schools today where industrial design is taught, as at the Royal College of Art, South Kensington.

The nineteenth century began with the continuation of most workshops as from previous times, with hand weaving, embroidery and lace all achieving triumphs of craftsmanship as fashion dictated, but requiring years of apprenticeship.

Elaborate dress, which was associated with the French aristocracy and the guillotine, was decidedly shunned, and this showed in the startling change to very simple white muslin or cotton dresses, as an outward manifestation of a change of thought or philosophy.

The century had other changes on the way and one of the greatest was the Industrial Revolution, particularly powerful in Britain, which with the swift advance of machinery soon became the first industrial nation. The system of apprenticeships changed in many of the former hand trades and crafts.

Textiles and other goods were made so rapidly in many factories that they lacked the personal integrity in design of the small workshop. In an effort to improve the design of machine-made products, and in the hope of cultivating public tastes and extending trade, the government set up schools for this purpose, as did many other countries in Europe. In 1837 a School of Design was established in London, and other schools followed in Birmingham, Manchester, Glasgow and Paisley. By 1842 seventeen schools existed, more than in any other country, and were the foundations of state-aided art schools in England. A knowledge of the arts and principle of design was brought to the manufacturers and industrial designers.

The famous International Exhibition of 1851 in London at the Crystal Palace gave a boost to trade and to the prestige of British goods, including embroidery machines. In the following year, a museum was set up at Marlborough House to display goods bought by the government at the Exhibition and this became the first

museum of the type to be established in Europe.

A quotation from a government report of the Department of Practical Art reads: 'A collection of specimens illustrates progress and the highest excellence attained in manufacture, in material, workmanship and decoration ... indispensable to instruction. By proper arrangement a museum may be made in the highest degree instructional.'

In France in the same year the President of the French Republic was petitioned to establish a Museum of Fine Arts as applied to industry.

Within a few years the School of Design and the museum were moved to temporary buildings in South Kensington, and the profits from the 1851 Exhibition provided, at the recommendation of the Prince Consort, a new site for the museum, which became known as the Victoria & Albert Museum, and also for the School of Design, which became the Royal College of Art. Later the City and Guilds College and the Royal School of Needlework were on the same site, and all four establishments influenced the textiles and embroidery of the time.

In this way, incentives were given to improve the design, art and draughtsmanship taught in schools, and the increase in salary to qualified teachers and aid to students established the system of grant-aided education. There followed many schools of this type in England, Scotland, Ireland and Wales, and some in Europe, including France, Italy and Switzerland.

The greatest influence on design of the time came from William Morris, who was an undergraduate in 1853. His blue working smock became a symbol of all that was best in art, design and craftsmanship and it was adopted almost as a uniform for artists over the next hundred years.

As a student he reacted to the debased, repetitive design of machine-made products by creating rich patterns and holding a strong belief in hand-made articles. Textiles and embroidery were among his concerns in his design studio business.

By 1872 his daughter, May, was organizing the embroidery and founded a school for impoverished gentlewomen to carry out designs by artists such as Burne-Jones and Walter Crane. The school became in 1872 the

315　A typical example of serious
study of early lacis by one of the many
late nineteenth-century societies,
probably Fisherton de la Mere.
Compare the small circular motifs
surrounding the design with fig. 103's
motifs in the centre of wide borders.
Possibly a small cushion or glove sachet.
50 × 20 cm (19½ × 7⅘ in.). (Lise
Mossery).

Royal School of Needlework, and
flourished as a successful business until
the 1939–45 war, when it was reduced
in size. The training school, however,
continued to teach professional embroidery techniques, history and design, which in the hands of artists
could be widely applied, from original personal designs and official rega-
lia to peasant embroideries. Changed
conditions led to the closure of the
training school in 1961, leaving workshops, salerooms and embroidery
teaching centre. The City and Guilds
and Royal College expanded.

In America, white embroidery,
which had been popular in the eighteenth and early nineteenth centuries,
revived again at the end of the nineteenth century after the Civil War.
An exhibition sent to Philadelphia
from England led to the formation in
New York of the Society of Decorative Art, which spread throughout the
United States and employed English
teachers. After the middle of the
twentieth century the American
influence was very strong in England
for a few years, but has gradually
waned and influences now come from
other countries such as Italy, Poland
and Japan.

In England, from before the beginning of the twentieth century, the
enthusiasm for all crafts, including
embroidery and white work, was the
foundation for a spate of societies for
the exhibition of work and the interchange of ideas. Examples were the
Lakeland Guild of Linen and a group
at Fisherton de la Mere, both having a
thoughtful design (Figs 312–15). The
Arts and Crafts Society, now the
Society of Designer Craftsmen, and
the Embroiderers' Guild are well-
known organizations today. The
Crafts Council and the British Crafts
Centre are foundations of the later
twentieth century; both foster craftsmen designers and are supported by
government grants.

Early in the present century, the
impetus of design moved to many
different and famous schools of art,
such as Glasgow and later, in England
in 1950, to Bromley, now Ravens-
bourne, and to Goldsmiths' College
Art School, where in the 1960s embroidery was established as an art
form with a course of study leading to
a BA Honours Degree in Embroidery. The degree provides a status
equivalent to other degrees and gives
a basis for future artistic activity in
textiles.

Many talented teachers, whose
work in schools continues to give a
high standard of variety and interest,
and many students attending summer
schools and short courses, ensure the
survival of embroidery and experiments in white textures. There is an
interesting change in the time and
purpose spent on embroidery today
by comparison with the past. The
present purpose is mainly as a creative
form of original expression, with a
discipline of craft. Both elements are
equally important for individuals
with different talents.

SEEDING

Seeding is a popular texture widely
used in white embroidery, composed
of small detached back stitches
worked at random over the ground,
representing scattered seeds. The
stitches may be single or double (one
on top of the other) for a greater
emphasis. Figs 148, 181, 219.

SEME

A medieval French term meaning to powder, sow, sprinkle, spot or strew with irregular and haphazard pattern, including detached sprays or a design motif, on to a background. The term derives from heraldry and the decoration of the field of a shield.

SHADOW WORK

Identification

The background of shadow work is always semi-transparent and the design is shown up as a shadow by the embroidery, which is typically in herringbone. Appliqué is sometimes used and additional light stitchery may be added as supporting texture. Figs 317–21.

Items

Lightweight blouses, dresses, lingerie or underwear, children's clothes, some household articles such as sachets, cushions, tea cosies, tray cloths, tea cloths and napkins.

History

Shadow work developed during the craze for fine cotton muslin in the mid-eighteenth century, inspired by the muslin goods imported from India, some of which had decorative

316   Fastening for a cushion, authentic to early times of c. 1600, when a fine cord or hand-made button would probably be used, rather than ribbon.

317   Shadow work in herringbone and appliqué, on organdie.

motifs, either woven or embroidered.

Simple stitching in herringbone, or similar stitchery, gave a very quick and easy result which at first glance suggested the character of the popular Dresden embroidery.

Other surface stitchery was added, such as eyelets, french knots, knotted line stitchery and sometimes shadow appliqué, and in the early twentieth century pale colours were introduced.

The work is often mounted on bright coloured satin or similar showy material, which sets off the embroidery with an attractive gleam. Other names or types of shadow work are:

Indian shadow work – stitches do not cross but are worked as a running stitch picking up a very small amount of material on the right side, to form a back stitch outline on the right side.

Shadow appliqué. Figs 3, 4.

Shadow darning – darning on thin material.

Shadow quilting

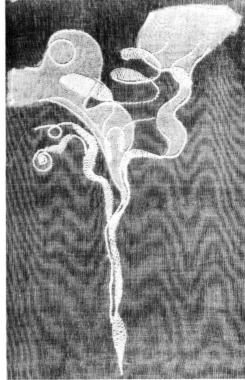

Design

Floral designs are usual, although some Art Deco designs were interpreted in this method. The shapes require a simple outline when ap-

318 Shadow work in heavy cotton thread on thin material, worked in a variation of double back stitch. (Goldsmiths' College Collection).

pliqué is used and, when in stitchery, areas need to be divided to accommodate lines of herringbone or double back stitch variations. Flowing lines such as ribbons or stems of narrow-shaped leaves like willow are a typical feature, as well as monograms and initials.

Ground

Fine cotton such as muslin, silk ninon or crêpe de Chine, fine linen or synthetic fibre – all lightweight semi-transparent materials are suitable. In the 1930s organdie, a very crisp, stiffened, thin and loosely woven cotton, was used for this technique, especially for children's clothes, in spite of the fact that the edges of the garments rubbed the skin of the young wearer and the surface of the material retained the marks of creases even after pressing.

Technique

Framing-up – optional; a ring or square frame may be used.

Transfer of design – by the use of a hard pencil, light blue line of paint or a tack line, to draw a design laid under

319 Wrong side of embroidery in fig. 318.

the muslin backing of the quilting.

Needles – crewel 7–8.

Threads – slightly thicker than the ground threads, but easily drawn through to give a dense appearance to the stitches. One strand of stranded cotton is frequently used.

320 *A design worked in fine silk on organdie, using the same method.*

Join on/off – a run stitch in line of design.

Process – stitch. Herringbone or a variation, as in some Indian work. Knots for texture and similarly punch stitch, satin and stem stitches or those suited to the design.

SHETLAND POINT LACE (*trina de lana*)

An unusual use of wool, during the last century, when lace motifs in fine wool were outlined in chain stitch and held together with bars. Like the lacy knitting for which fine Shetland wool is traditionally used, it can be found in infants' shawls and similar items.

SHIFT

See *Shirt*

SHIRRED or SHIRRING

A nineteenth-century American term, derived from the German *schirren*, to

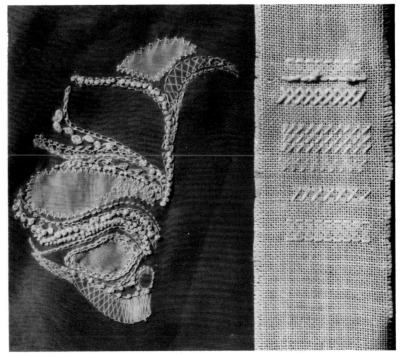

321 *A sample showing appliqué and herringbone with knot stitches for texture. On the right: shows the* position of herringbone stitches. Top right: *considered correct. Worked by Margaret Hall.*

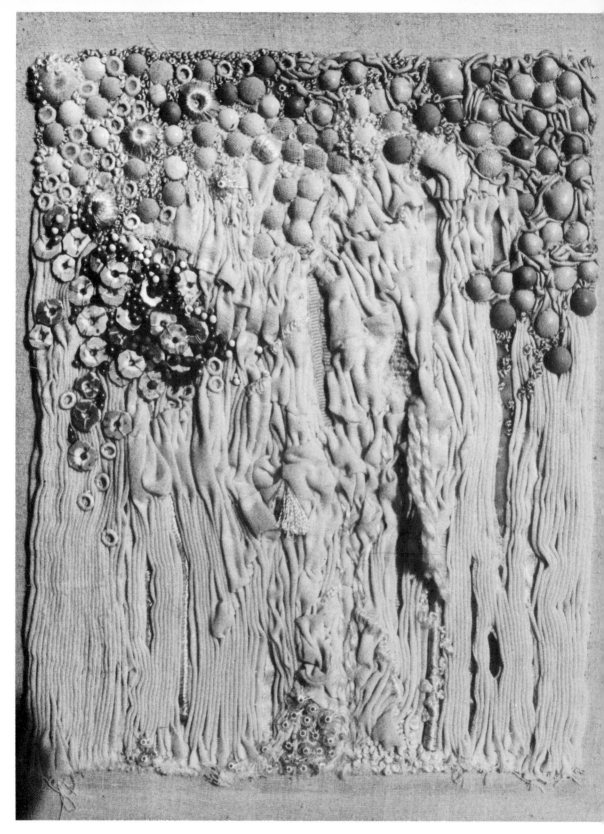

322   *Design worked on the shirring machine with added texture of beads,*   *padded circles in leather and other textures, to show different densities of*   *white with some added colour. Worked by Sue Herbert.*

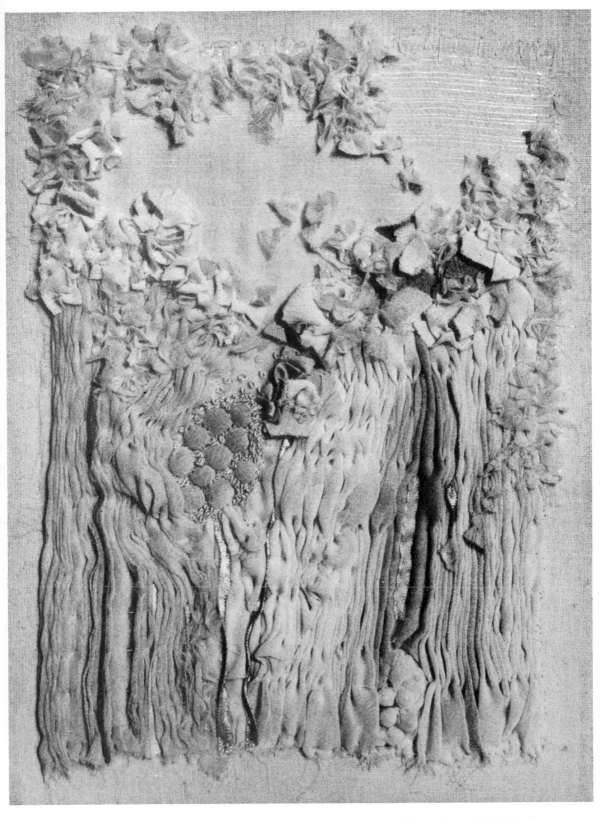

*323   A design with shirring lurex
threads, cut material for texture, padding
and French knots. Worked by Sue Herbert.*

324 *Detail of fig. 323.*

leaving only the lightweight muslin. The braid is sewn down on each side over the cut edges of cambric. Buttonhole finishes the edge of the work with picots.

SMOCK

Old English name for a working garment or overall of natural or bleached white linen for farm workers. By the nineteenth century this was already coming to be considered rustic and unrefined, although it was still worn by agricultural workers into the present century. In the early twentieth century the smock was seized upon as 'artistic' and there was a good deal of interest in the smocking and additional embroidery, traditionally feather stitch, thought to denote the wearer's trade or craft, for example trees for a woodman. Nowadays the smock is studied as a true ethnic garment, but its history is in fact somewhat romanticized.

Smocking
Smocking is decorative stitchery added to the surface of gathering and originally used for holding the fullness of smocks into a yoke. Smocking is now mainly used for children's clothes and for 'peasant-style' blouses, frequently in bright colours, but also in white when texture is displayed. Fig. 325.

SORRENTO EDGE

An example of the Victorian love of giving a name to every pattern. This name refers to a buttonhole edge with stitches of alternate length and to a buttonhole filling in which two stitches of one row are worked leaving a space of four and in the next row four stitches are worked leaving a space of two; these are repeated alternately. Fig. 201 (B).

SPANISH LACE, IMITATION

Worked on linen or muslin, the ground of the design is sewn first as an open buttonhole filling, covering the surface of the background material but not working into it. After working to the edge of the motifs, the design is outlined in cord, which is covered with buttonhole stitch to neaten and strengthen the edge. The background is then cut away from the wrong side, leaving the open button-

denote irregular gauging or lines of gathering. Shirring was often used as a decorative insertion, incorporating elastic, for garters and even braces, and became popular in the 1930s for skirts in peasant style with a shirred waist. Figs 150, 322, 324.

Shirring machine
Now in use in many schools and colleges for creative experimental work, as well as for its usual function.

SHIRT or SHIFT

A full-length linen undergarment worn from the earliest times by both sexes, but later becoming shorter as a shirt for men. It was also made of calico, and later a finer white or natu-

ral cotton or even silk for those who could afford it. The Norman nobles wore embroidered examples, but embroidery was forbidden in England under sumptuary laws and worn only by knights and lords. A shirt or shift was used for casual wear, with court or formal dress added as separate garments over the shift, and pinned in place with brooches or pins or tied with tapes. Such garments included sleeves, bodice and skirts.

SICILIAN EMBROIDERY

A nineteenth-century term for embroidery on muslin, similar, in some ways, to shadow appliqué. Muslin and cambric are tacked over the design, which is marked out on stiff paper or architect's linen. Braid is tacked down over the outline of the design. The solid areas of the design are left as double material and the ground has the cambric cut away

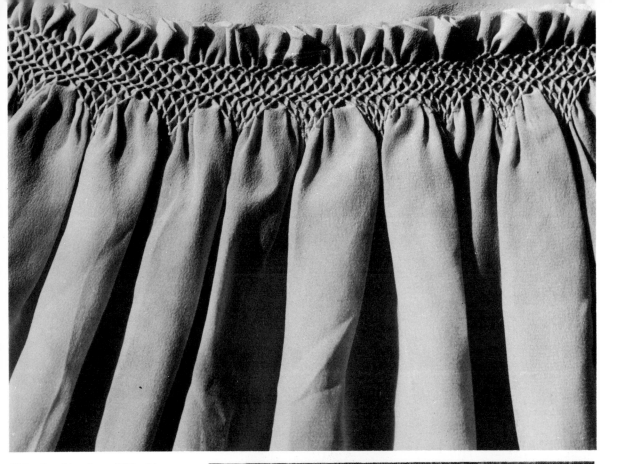

325 *Smocking for a child's skirt.*

hole as the ground and the motif in plain linen. This type of work is also considered typical of the Portuguese.

SPIDER STITCH

See *Wheels*

SPINES

Small bullion knots worked to decorate cordonnet or the padded surface of satin stitch or lace. See *Picot*.

SPLIT STITCH

Split stitch makes a fine line composed of one thread which is split to give a faint appearance of chain. It is useful for outlines and as a support and padding for satin stitch. Split stitch gives form to shapes when the direction of working is planned, as for faces. Fig. 304.

SPOTTED NET

A machine-made net with spots regularly planned over the surface. Used for caps, usually cotton, sometimes

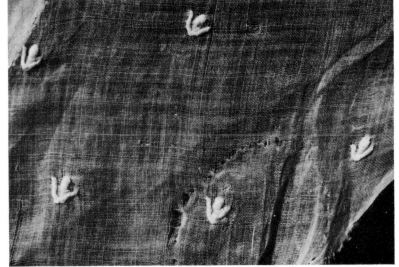

silk, sometimes with chenille spots, and sometimes with beads, in the early nineteenth century, when machine-made net was first introduced and fashionable. Figs 326, 330.

SPRIGS

Detached motifs of lace before being joined by réseau or applied to net, as

326 *Examples of sprigging or dotting on muslin, possibly the work of eight-year-old apprentices. c. 1840.*

in Honiton or Brussels. Also nineteenth-century sprigged muslin, typical of hand embroidery in Scotland

327 Satin stitch and overcast in soft unmercerized cotton thread. 2.5 × 2 cm (1 × ¾ in.). c. 1850.

328 Eyelets, ladder stitch and satin stitch. 2 × 1.5 cm (¾ × ½ in.). c. 1860.

and later produced by machine. Jane Austen refers to the fashion for such fabrics in *Northanger Abbey* (1798): 'I wanted you not to buy that sprigged muslin but you would,' Mrs Allen tells Catherine (Chapter 13). Figs 326–331.

STEM STITCH

Stem stitch is a simple and attractive stitch with a smooth surface for outlines, curved lines or for rows as a filling. As it follows curves it catches the light and changes from dark to light tones. Many ways are found of working the stitch, and the one shown in fig. 109 is most frequently found in white work, as it is reversible and therefore suitable for working on single material such as dress fabric, handkerchieves and table linen, although not identical to the right side, as the underside forms a back stitch. It is neat, strong and practical for frequent laundering. Stem stitch sometimes has the appearance of rope stitch.

Insert the needle in the same position as the end of the previous stitch, forming a back stitch on·the wrong side. Alway keep the thread to the same side of the needle.

A seond method is to work a row of stem and whip over (overcast) the right side with another thread. Join on and off into the back stitch or on the working line. Figs 10, 54, 219.

STILETTO

During the seventeenth century the term 'stiletto' referred to a dagger or surgical instrument. From about 1828, however, it denoted a sharply pointed metal instrument, about 10–15 cm (4–6 in.) in length, like a large needle without an eye, with an ivory or bone handle. Stilettos made of bone, steel or ivory were used for making eyelets in dresses or corsets, for embroidery or tailoring, and to take a tape for tying on skirts, trousers and shirt necks, since there was little else in the way of fastenings. Stilettos became a more efficient tool for the purpose than bodkins. See also *Bodkin*.

STRAWS

Needles used for millinery or straw hat making and sometimes nowadays for beadwork; they are very long with a small round eye.

329   Back view of a wedding dress designed for Lady Rose Cecil by Lindka Cierach. The dotting or sprigging of three pearls over the folds of the bow and the sleeves relates to the bodice.

SWEDISH LACE

Originally cut and drawn thread and also darned netting worked by nuns from an early date, but later examples are of a coarse bobbin-made torchon-type lace.

SWISS CAMBRIC

Switzerland has a long-established industry in linen textiles, and also produced cotton long before its production in Britain.

The name 'cambric' originally referred to linen from Chambray, France, but was also used to describe a fine cotton of comparable weight to the linen. This distinguished it from the coarse cotton that was generally produced before the nineteenth cen-

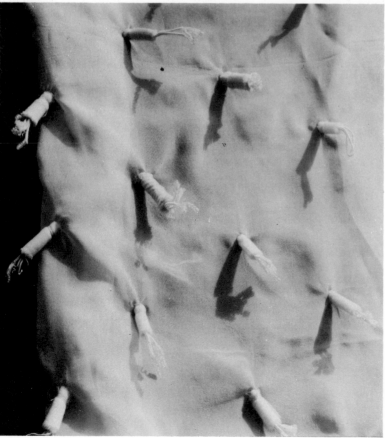

330 *Sprigging on spotted muslin, typical of hand work, but in this case probably machine. Midland Counties hand lace edge.*

331 *Modern sprigging. Decorative hand-made three-dimensional motif freely applied to ninon. Worked by Lindy Richardson.*

tury. Cotton or linen lawn has a similar derivation. 'Lawn' is thought to be a derivation of the word 'linen', and cotton produced in a fine quality took the name 'lawn' to indicate that it was not of the usual calico or muslin quality. It therefore appears a suitable procedure to state cotton or linen cambric, as it is to state cotton satin, silk satin or nylon satin, when describing materials.

Swiss cotton textiles were an important import from Zurich and St Gallen to England for dress and embroidery before the establishment of the Lancashire cotton trade and the Scottish muslin industry. In the early nineteenth century, Lancashire developed the machine inventions for spinning and weaving which the Swiss later adopted. Fig. 332.. See *Fibres (cotton, linen).*

332 *A collection of handkerchiefs typical of work for tourists from countries all over the world. Top row: (centre) labelled 'warranted all pure linen. Hand embroidery'. Second row: (left) pin stitched hem and hemstitching design. (centre) labelled 'Fine embroidery. Made in Northern Ireland' – in fact machine embroidery motif applied to cotton. (on right) shadow appliqué and hemstitching. (far right) shadow work. Third row: (left) elaborate embroidery from China or the East, including satin, punch, overcast and buttonhole stitches. (centre) silk handkerchief with silk lace in the form of Maltese. (right) small edging of hand-made lace, typically English, with the top from a box of Swiss embroidered handkerchiefs. Bottom row: handkerchiefs from Brittany, France, 1937, showing tape lace edging, insertions of hand faggoting, buttonhole fillings and wheels or spiders' net machine-embroidered motifs.*

SWISS EMBROIDERY

Similar to broderie anglaise, Irish, Madeira, and Ayrshire work, this is on fine cotton muslin with satin and stem stitches, eyelets, open fillings, seeding and knots.

In the first part of the nineteenth century local villagers worked it by hand, but this died out with the machine embroidery in imitation of hand work which soon gained a world-wide reputation. Fig. 332.

SWISS LACE

Early records at Zurich show interesting lace examples, mainly narrow with some cut work and darned netting. Refugees from religious persecution took their knowledge to Switzerland, but in the nineteenth century the advanced standard of machine work soon outmoded hand work, and the term now denotes a machine lace, also known as imitation lace. Fig. 332. See also *Imitation lace.*

T

TABLE LINEN

Tablecloths, tea cloths, dinner cloths, table mats, dinner napkins, afternoon tea napkins and small napkins for finger bowls all carry white embroidery, often with heraldic devices, monograms or other personal emblems. Fig. 33.

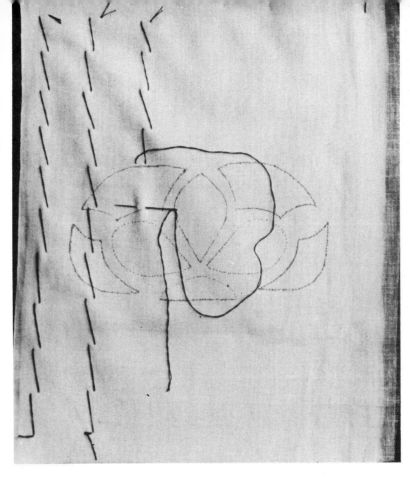

Upright tacking for joining a backing. Ensure that the top and side edges are cut straight on the grain by drawing a thread. Secure at top with pins or drawing pins and check that left-hand edges are parallel. The material is prepared for quilting with the right side face down and the mull backing, with design drawn out, right side up. Begin upright tacking at the top of the left-hand edge and work to the base. Insert the needle horizontally. The embroiderer's left hand is able to check that the left-hand edges are kept parallel, while working the rows of tacking approximately 3 cm (1⅕ in.) apart. Tacked in this way, all fullness is eased out to the right hand and to the base, to make the two materials as one.

335 Shows material secured with upright tacking over a design inked out on stiff paper. On the left, the design outline is marked out with straight tacking, making stitches at the points of design. Alternatively, the design inked out on greaseproof paper may be laid over the background, and secured with upright tacking as in fig. 334. Tack out design with straight tacking. The upright tacking is removed, and the greaseproof is torn away, leaving the tack line of the design. Upright tacking keeps distracting knots out of the design. On the right, the design is couched out through the two materials as for Carrickmacross. Note thread run in on outline to join.

TACKING (BASTING)

Figures 334–6 show how tacking, or basting, can be used to transfer designs for white work embroidery. For the purpose of the illustrations, the tacking is in a dark thread, but in working it should be light-coloured or white. (Old workroom saws dictated:

Tack in black you get your work back.
Tack in green should never be seen.
Tack in red – you're dead.)

Black and dark threads mark and stain material. Green is a strident colour and 'grins through'. Red is also obvious and tends to run when damp-pressed.

A pale blue, neutral or white tack is most satisfactory, as if left in the work it is unobtrusive. See also fig. 74.

333 A heraldic device worked in satin stitch and seeding for a table napkin, for use with a finger bowl. Edwardian or early twentieth century. Approximately 3.5 cm (1⅓ in.) high. (Embroiderers' Guild).

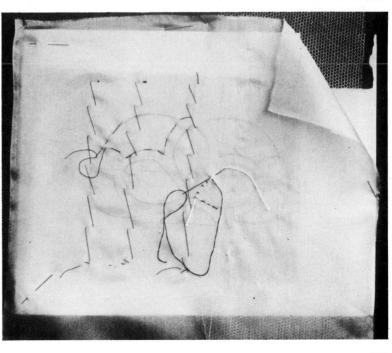

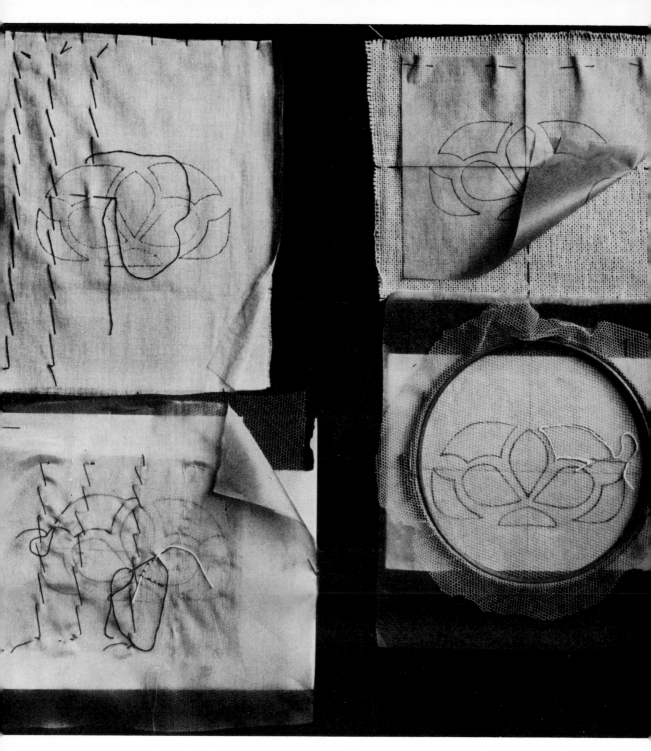

336 Top: *the vertical and horizontal threads of the ground are tacked out to match those of the design. Secure with upright tacking (fig. 334) and then tack out with straight stitches (fig. 335).* Below: *a design drawn out in ink on* firm paper. Net is laid over the design and run stitch is then worked over the outlines, into the net only, for net darning or Limerick lace. Note use of ring frame for small designs instead of pinning out a large area.

TAMBOUR WORK

Tambour was known in China, Persia, India and Turkey, where chain stitch was a characteristic of the embroidery long before European tambour work. About the mid-eighteenth century tambour was introduced into Switzerland and Germany, where it was worked in white thread on white linen and decorated caps, blouses, dresses, curtains and other furnishings. This work reached the usual high standard expected of the Swiss, and was exported back to the East.

Tambour work is named after the circular frame in which the material is framed up as tight as a drum (tambour being French for drum). In England it was carried out to provide work in Middlesex, Essex, Nottingham and Ireland.

In *Northanger Abbey* (written 1798),

a book full of detail on fashionable dress, Jane Austen describes how Catherine 'lay awake ten minutes on Wednesday night debating between her spotted and her tamboured muslin' (Chapter 10). Eventually the Cornely machine overtook the hand tambour work, which then declined, and fashions also changed. In any case, hand chain stitch eventually revived for decorative embroidery, as this did not require a frame and was more practical and mobile. Bed covers and cushions of the 1920s to 1940s show Cornely chain stitch on a shiny rayon ground. Today, tambour embroidery is used in dress decoration mainly for beadwork, which is very effective in white on white.

Tambour needles

Similar to a crochet hook, with a handle of ivory, wood, bone or steel, which is often hollow to hold a sup-

337   Tambour work on fine muslin, sometimes described as 'Evening Dew'. c. 1790. (Joan Kendall).

ply of other hooks or needles screwed into the handle.

Tambour lace

A term for tambour on net or a very fine ground, sometimes confused with Limerick lace. Made at Islington, Coggeshall, Middlesex and Nottingham, sometimes in silk thread. It flourished on machine-made net, but the Cornely chain stitch machine took over the work.

Tamboured muslin

Embroidered muslin worked in a circular frame, called a tambour, which

338 *Part of a canopy for a cradle in an Italianate-style design in tambour on fine muslin that might be described as 'Flowing Water'. c. 1800. (Hatfield House Textile Conservation Rooms).*

derived its name from a drum or a tambourine since the muslin, stretched in the frame, resembled a tambourine. The designs are familiar: spots, sprigs in groups, worked in rows of chain stitch. Late eighteenth- and early nineteenth-century tamboured dress lengths were made. See *Chain stitch.*

339 *Detail of fig. 338. Tambour on muslin in a tightly twisted thread. Note the attractive raised points as the thread makes acute turns. A bobble fringe of later date edges the work.*

TAPE LACE

Originally an early bobbin-made lace of the sixteenth and seventeenth centuries in Italy, Spain and Flanders. It was revived in the nineteenth century and known as modern point lace; it was often well worked and, using machine-made tapes or braids for the design, was joined by needlemade buttonhole bars, with buttonhole fillings introduced to the enclosed areas. It was produced mainly by women in the home and not to the professional standard of work by nuns or workshops.

Tape is tacked on the lines of the design, which is on firm paper, and held in place by worked bars and wheels, with some fillings in suitably enclosed areas. The tacks are removed to free the completed work.

'Renaissance braid' and 'lacet' are alternative names, and braids, being slightly heavier than tape, were sometimes used for heavy bold church embroideries or for mantel covers. Cucumber braid, a series of oval shapes joined together, is typical of the machine-made tapes used in this work, and may still be found in sales.

Tapes may also be worked as an outline design on net, with counted patterns used as fillings. Fig. 340.

Tape work

Nineteenth-century designs or patterns interpreted by working tape into rosettes or chevron lines or similar shapes and sewing together to make a cloth or textile.

TASSELS

An effective decorative addition of recurring popularity. Figs 30, 125, 199, 341, 342.

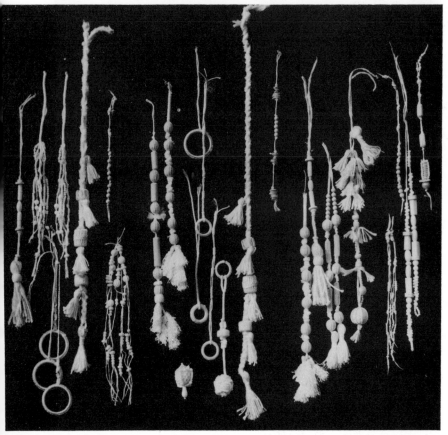

340   Sample of tape lace showing buttonhole fillings and faggoting stitches.

341   Sample of tassels. Worked by Gwenda Fairburn.

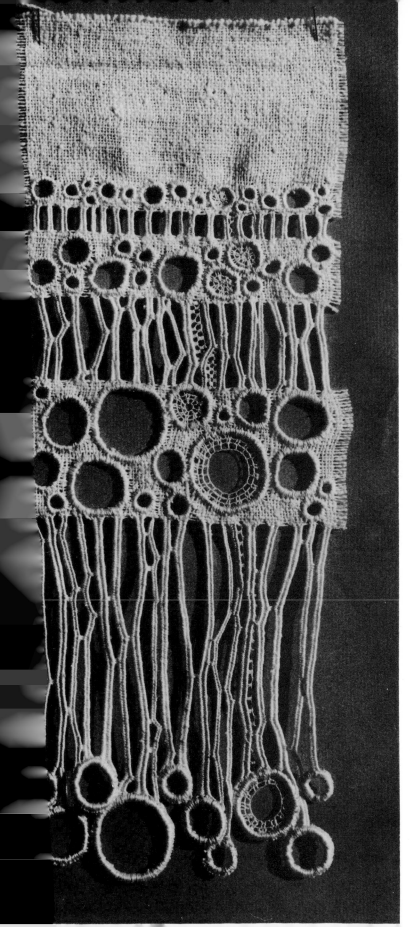

342 *Experimental sampler showing tassels, overcast stitch and buttonhole fillings with darned threads or needleweaving. 20 × 10 cm (8 × 4 in.). Worked by Margaret Potts.*

TATTING

An early knotted type of lace braid, also known as ragusa gimp lace and knotted work. A whole area of study similar to crochet and knitting but of more limited application, it has occasional revivals of interest. It is a useful addition to a collection and it is interesting to identify it used as an edging or as a complete small mat or doyley.

Tatting is a form of knotting worked with a shuttle; it does not involve any embroidery stitches apart from the stitchery which applies it as a decorative edge. Fig. 223.

TENERIFE WORK

Tenerife work is produced on a circular scaffold of pins, on to which threads are worked and then interwoven to make circular motifs. (For a fuller explanation of the method, see Nenia Lovesey's *Technique of Needlepoint Lace*.). Figs 85, 216, 343.

TOWELLING EMBROIDERY

A late nineteenth- and early twentieth-century decorative darning worked into the pattern of the weave of a smooth linen towel, such as huckaback (rather than a looped terry tow-

elling). Heavy drawn thread work borders were also made, and fringed edges were popular, especially as borders for guest towels. Sometimes Holbein stitch in white was an addition. Figs 79, 216.

TRAILING

Trailing is a form of couching, with the couching stitches laid so closely together that the laid thread is invisible and appears as a fine satin line. The number of laid threads is a matter of choice. The stitch is most successfully worked in a frame, with the laid thread pulled firmly as the work pro-

343   A modern application of the techniques of Tenerife work (detail of sampler in fig. 85), by Sue Herbert.

344 (Opposite page)   A panel showing composite techniques, trailing (as outline to satin stitch border), eyelets, bullion and french knots, seeding, ladder stitch, punch stitch and net darning. Note that the lower left and upper right patterns are identical but worked in a different angle of the mesh. 1949. 10 cm (4 in.) diameter. Worked by Barbara Dawson, 1949.

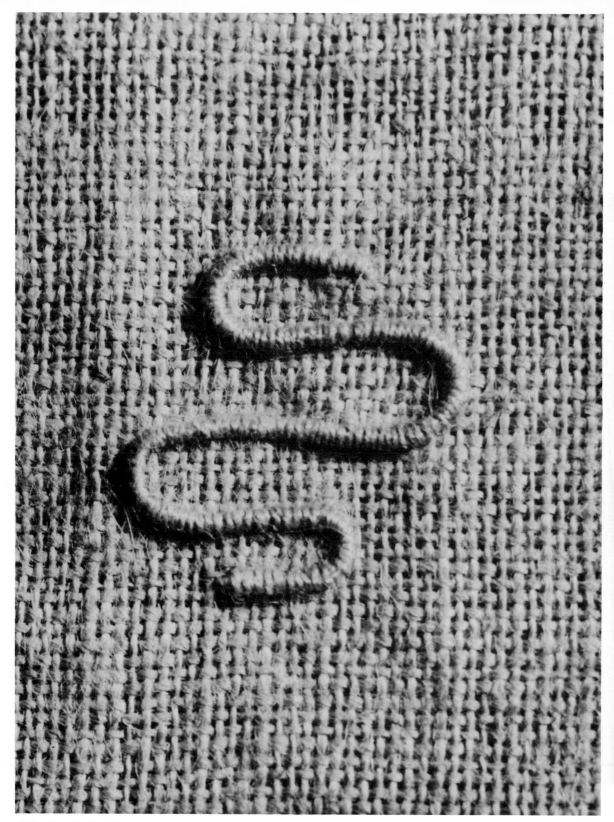

345   *Sample of trailing or overcast
stitch.*

ceeds; this makes a smooth line and prevents it shifting and becoming irregular. The tying-down stitches should come up and down almost in the same position so that the laid thread is rounded and not flattened. Trailing is particularly suitable for curving lines and outlining the edge of fine work.

The stitch is sometimes known as overcast stitch, but overcast stitch has a much heavier, coarser appearance. Figs 105, 205, 265, 290, 344, 345.

TRANSFERRING DESIGNS

See *Tacking*

TUCKS

A process which, when worked in white material, is displayed to great advantage, as the double fabric shows solid in lightweight material, and it also acts as a decorative stiffening for frills, as well as a method for decoratively controlling fullness. Tucks become a basis for fabric manipulation, with variations such as shell tucks for additional decoration. Figs 59–61, 346.

346   Sample of tucks. Worked by Jane Poulton.

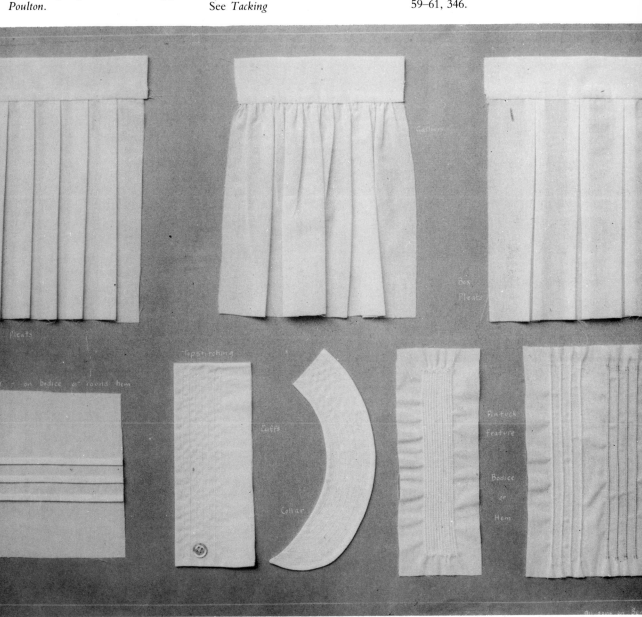

TUFTING

A decorative tufted texture seen on surfaces from velvet to canvas work, and also a machine stitch variation known as candlewick, often used for bedspreads. Figs 201, 347, 348.

347 Tufted cloth (typical of bed covers) used as a background for a personal design, with hand seeding, run stitch, blanket stitch, Cornely chain and applied velvet and papers. Black stitching appears as an open stitch. Worked by Lindy Richardson.

348 Sample showing Turkey rug stitch, with uncut loops below, cut tufts above. See also sampler in fig. 201.

VANDYKE

A pointed border or pattern composed of a zig-zag line. Much used as a dress trimming in the early nineteenth-century Regency period. Worked in contrasting textures of white, such as white satin edging to white wool. Crenelle, battlement and festoon are similar finishes. Figs 51, 197 (F).

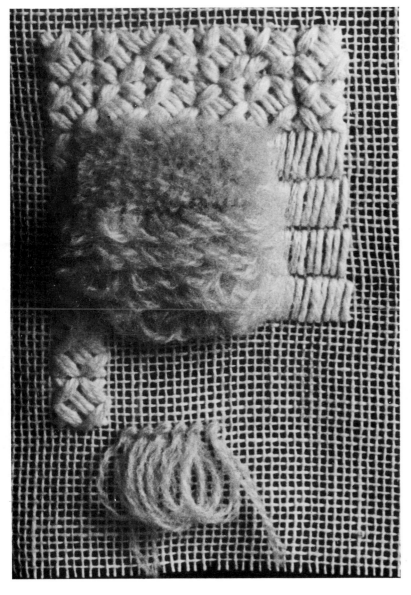

VRAI RÉSEAU

A prestigious and well-known term for the famous, fine and beautiful net worked in bands 2.5 cm (1 in.) wide, since it was so delicate, for the ground of the highest quality Flanders lace. The introduction of machine-made net led to its decline. Another term is Fond and Droschel.

WEAVER'S KNOT

Used to join a thread for darning or weaving. Fig. 2.

WEDDING DRESSES

There are innumerable examples of wedding dresses displaying every type of white embroidery: net, embroidered silk satin, cotton broderie anglaise, lace, in linen, and mixtures of them all, including man-made, for frills and tucking. The wedding dress is often a very breathtaking and flattering display of the art of white textures. Figs 329, 350.

WHEELS

Wheels, back stitched, wrapped or whipped, buttonholed, woven or interlaced, are used in many forms of white embroidery, including broderie anglaise, cut work, lace and also in button making, to fill and strengthen an open space and connect areas of openwork.

Alternative names are 'Catherine wheel' and 'spider'.

WHIPPING

A term used until recently for wrapping threads, and also for drawing up material as a type of gathering over a rolled edge and as a decorative rolled hem. Figs 5, 118.

WHITE

The deep-seated awe of white is symbolic of innocence, sparkling life, pur-

ity and a spirit of peace, surrender and non-aggression. White is apparently easy and soothing to live with.

The display of form is shown to effect successfully in white sculpture as well as white embroidery, since shadows are given the greatest emphasis. Figs 155–7, 349, 350.

WRAPPING

See *Whipping*.

WRISTBANDS

An important item of dress embroidery. In the eighteenth century they were embroidered in very fine and elaborate pulled stitches, becoming full and deep to fall from the elbow, and known as 'engageants'. Wristbands were boldly designed in the nineteenth century, often of cut work, and known as undersleeves, and in the twentieth century they were characteristically neat and machine embroidered. Wristbands are a recurring fashion, and tend to reflect the fashion influences of the time. Figs 120, 121.

Z

ZANTE LACE

Early Greek Island lace, and a type of reticella. This is of historical interest and typical of the Ionian Isles, coming from the area of very early civilization and the working of embroidery and textiles.

349   *Three standing forms composed of gathered heavy cotton with paint. 1985. Worked by Beverley Clark. Figs 159, 184.*

350 An appreciation of costume is shown in the wedding dress designed for Lady Rose Cecil by Lindka Cierach (February 1985). The textures of a tinted satin are enhanced for a great occasion by the sensitive use of groups of pearls resting in the puffed ruching of the sleeves, and in the folds and drapes of the back. The smooth satin contrasts with the crystals outlining the waist scallops, and the scooped neckline.

Mother-of-pearl spangles cover the centre front and back panels of the bodice, and the side panels are more delicately adorned with fine gold thread and pearls. The muted softness of white fur is inspired for a winter wedding dress which is so discriminatingly and beautifully crafted together. (Hatfield House Textile Conservation Rooms).

Bibliography

Books with asterisks give details of most white work techniques.

ALMQUIST, Jane Houston, *Mountmellick Work*, Dryad Press

BAINES, Patricia, *Spinning Wheels, Spinners, and Spinning*, Batsford

BATH, Virginia Churchill, *Needlework in America*, Mills & Boon

BEANEY, Jan, *Stitches: New Approaches*, Batsford

BENSON, Dorothy, *Singer Instructions for Art and Lace Work*, Singer Sewing Machine Co.

BIRD, Gail, *Russian Punchneedle Embroidery*, Dover Publications

BRIDGEMAN, H., and DRURY, E., *Needlwork: An Illustrated History*, Paddington Press

BURKETT, M. E., *The Art of the Feltmaker*, Abbot Hall Art Gallery, Kendal

BURTON, Anthony, *King Cotton*, BBC Publications

BUTLER, Anne, *Batsford Encyclopaedia of Embroidery Stitches*, Batsford

CAULFIELD, S. F. A., and SAWARD, B. C., *The Dictionary of Needlework*, Hamlyn (A. W. Cowan 1882)

CAVE, Oenone, *Cut-Work Embroidery*, Dover Publications

COOK, Bridget M., and STOTT, Geraldine, *Book of Bobbin Lace Stitches*, Batsford

CHRISTIE, Mrs Archibald, **Samplers and Stitches*, Batsford

DE DILLMONT, Thérèse, **Complete Guide to Needlework*, DMC

———, **Encyclopaedia of Needlework*, DMC

DEAN, Beryl, *Church Needlework*, Batsford

———, *Embroidery in Religion and Ceremonial*, Batsford

EARNSHAW, Pat, *The Indentification of Lace*, Shire Publications

———, *Lace Machines and Machine Laces*, Batsford

FANGEL, WINCKLER and MADSEN, *Danish Pulled Thread Embroidery*, Dover Publications

Fibrearts Magazine, *The Fibrearts Design Book*, Fibrearts

———, *The Fibrearts Design Book II*, Lark Books

FINCH, Karen, and PUTNAM, Greta, *The Care and Preservation of Textiles*, Batsford

GRAY, Jennifer, *Machine Embroidery*, Batsford

HOWARD, Constance, *Constance Howard's Book of Stitches*, Batsford

———, *Twentieth Century Embroidery in Great Britain* (4 vols), Batsford

JOHNSON, Beryl, *Advanced Embroidery Techniques*, Batsford

KENDRICK, A. F., *English Needlework*, A. & C. Black

KROOS, Renata, *Niedersachsische Bildstickerein des Mittelalters*, Deutschen Verlag für Kunstwissenschaft

LADBURY, Ann, *Fabrics*, Sidgwick & Jackson

LANDI, Sheila, *Textile Conservator's Manual*, Butterworth

LEVEY, Santina, *Discovering Embroidery of the Nineteenth Century*, Shire Publications

———, *Lace, A History*, Victoria & Albert Museum (Maney)

LOVESEY, Nenia, *The Technique of Needlepoint Lace*, Batsford

LOWE, David, and RICHARDS, Jack, *The City of Lace*, Nottingham Lace Centre Ltd

MCNEILL, Moyra, *Machine Embroidery: Lace and See-Through Techniques*, Batsford

———, *Pulled Thread*, Bell & Hyman

PRICKETT, Elizabeth, *Ruskin Lace and Linen Work*, Batsford

PULS, Herta, *The Art of Cutwork and Appliqué*, Batsford

RISLEY, Christine, *Machine Embroidery*, Studio Vista

RUSSELL, Pat, *Lettering for Embroidery*, Batsford

SHUETTE, Marie, and CHRISTENSEN, Sigrid Muller, *The Art of Embroidery*, Thames & Hudson

SNOOK, Barbara, *Embroidery Stitches*, Dryad Press

SWAIN, Margaret, *The Flowerers: The Story of Ayrshire White Needlework*, W. & R. Chambers

———, *Scottish Embroidery, Medieval to Modern*, Batsford

———, *White Work*, Shire Publications

SWIFT, Gay, **The Batsford Encyclopaedia of Embroidery Techniques*, Batsford

SYMONDS, M., and PREECE, *Needlework through the Ages*

THOMAS, Mary, *Mary Thomas's Dictionary of Embroidery Stitches*, Hodder & Stoughton

———, **Mary Thomas's Embroidery Book*, Hodder & Stoughton

YUSAI Fukuyama, *Tambour Embroidery*, Yusai International

Museums

It is worth contacting all museums, including local and county town museums, for an appointment to view white work embroidery. The collection may be very large or specialized and therefore carefully stored. This also applies to country houses.

UK

England

Bucks County Museum, Aylesbury
Castle Howard, Yorkshire
Castle Museum, York
Cecil Higgins Art Gallery, Bedford
The Embroiderers' Guild Collection, Hampton Court, Surrey
The Royal Albert Museum, Exeter
Fitzwilliam Museum, Cambridge
Gawthorpe Hall, Padiham, Lancs
Gallery of English Costume, Platt Hall, Manchester
Guildford House Museum
Honiton Museum, Devon

Industrial Museum, Wollaton Park, Nottingham
Killerton House, Devon
The Lace Centre, Castle Road, Nottingham
Merseyside County Museum, Liverpool
Museum of Costume, Bath
Museum of London
Royal School of Needlework, London SW7
The Silk Museum, Macclesfield, Cheshire
Tunbridge Wells Museum
Victoria & Albert Museum, London SW7
Waddesdon Manor, Bucks
Whitworth Art Gallery, University of Manchester

Scotland

Blair Castle, Blair Atholl, Perthshire
The Burrell Collection, Glasgow
Glasgow Art Gallery
Royal Museum of Scotland, Edinburgh

Ireland

Ulster Folk and Transport Museum, County Down

USA

American Institute of Textile Arts, Boston, Massachusetts
Brooklyn Museum, New York
Chicago Art Institute, Illinois
Cleveland Museum of Art, Ohio
Detroit Institute of Arts, Michigan
Houston Museum of Fine Arts, Texas
Indianapolis Museum of Art
Metropolitan Museum of Art, New York
Minneapolis Institute of Art, Minnesota
Philadelphia Museum of Art
Smithsonian Institute, Washington
Texas Technical University Museum, Lubbock, Texas

Slides held by the Crafts Council of Great Britain record contemporary embroidery, and new work in white can often be seen at embroidery exhibitions.

Conservators

UK

Textile Conservation Centre, Hampton Court Palace, East Molesey, Surrey
Royal School of Needlework, 25 Princes Gate, London SW7
The Textile Restoration Studio, 5 Oxford Road, Altrincham, Cheshire
Kysnia Marko, Textile Conservation Studio, Unit 39, Limehouse Cut, Morris Road, London E14

USA

Mary Ballard, Detroit Institute of Arts, 5200 Woodward Avenue, Detroit, Michigan 4802
Pat Collins, Textile Conservation Centre Inc., Houston, Texas
Marguerite Morgan, Studio 1, 6 Highland Cross, New Jersey 07070
Helen von Rosenstiel, Restorations, 382 Eleventh Street, Brooklyn, New York 11215
Thérèse Schoenholzer, 501 West 43rd Street, New York 10036

Suppliers

UK
*Mail order service

General embroidery requirements
Beldale Crafts, 121 Raby Road, Hartlepool, Cleveland TS24 8DT (Cold water soluble fabric)

de Denne, 159–161 Kenton Road, Harrow, Middlesex HA3 0EV

Irish Linen Depot, 39 Bond Street, Ealing W5 5AS

Leven Crafts, 23 Chaloner Street, Guisborough, Cleveland TS14 6QD

*MacCulloch and Wallis, 25–26 Dering Street, London W1R 0BH (Vanishing muslin)

*Mace and Nairn, 69 Crane Street, Salisbury, Wiltshire (Evenweave and lawn)

Model and Craft Centre, 260 Dewsbury Road, Wakefield WF2 9BY

The Nimble Thimble, 26 The Green, Bilton, Rugby, Warwickshire (leather)

Pongees, 184 Old Street, London EC1 (Silk specialists)

Christine Riley, 53 Barclay Street, Stonehaven, Kincardineshire AB3 2AR

Royal School of Needlework, 25 Princes Gate, London SW7 1QE

Arthur Sells, 49 Pedley Lane, Clifton, Shefford, Bedfordshire (Tambour needles and acetate film)

Spinning Jenny, Bradley, Keighley, West Yorkshire BD20 9DD

*Whaleys·(Bradford), Harris Court, Great Horton, Bradford, West Yorks BD7 4EQ

Welsh Flannel, Rural Industries, Wimbledon Common, London (Dress and furnishing fabrics and braids)

The Embroiderers' Guild journal *Embroidery* gives up-to-date names and addresses for many stockists

Grounds
In addition to the suppliers named above, interesting ground materials such as satin, voile, velvet, openweave, felts, nets and textured fabrics may be obtained from larger department stores.

Beads
Ellis & Farrier Ltd, 5 Princes Street, London SW1

Fleece
May Eve, Three Ply House, 57a Lant Street, London SE1 1QN

Handweavers Studio, 29 Haroldstone Road, London E17 7AN

Wingham Wool Work, The Building Yard, Wentworth, South Yorkshire S62 7TL

Handmade paper
Falkiners, 111 Long Acre, London WC2

Leather
Alma Leather Co, 17 Wakeley Street EC1

The Embroiderers' Guild journal *Embroidery* gives up-to-date names and addresses for many stockists.

USA
American Thread Corporation, 90 Park Avenue, New York

Bucky King, Box 371, King Bros., 3 Ranch Buffalo Star, Sheridan, Wyoming 82801

Frederick J. Fawcett Inc., 320 Derby Street, Salem, Massachusetts 01970

Robin and Russ Hand Weavers, 533 N. Adams Street, McMinnville, Oregon 97128

Threadbenders, 2260 Como Avenue, St Paul, Minnesota 55108

The Thread Shop, 307 Freeport Road, Pittsburgh, Pennsylvania